PERSPECTIVES

4

Amanda **JEFFRIES**

Lewis **LANSFORD**

Daniel **BARBER**

NATIONAL GEOGRAPHIC
LEARNING

Australia · Brazil · Mexico · Singapore · United Kingdom · United States

NATIONAL GEOGRAPHIC
L E A R N I N G

Perspectives 4b Combo Split
Amanda Jeffries, Lewis Lansford,
Daniel Barber

Publisher: Sherrise Roehr

Executive Editor: Sarah Kenney

Publishing Consultant: Karen Spiller

Senior Development Editor: Brenden Layte

Senior Development Editor: Lewis Thompson

Editorial Assistant: Gabe Feldstein

Director of Global Marketing: Ian Martin

Product Marketing Manager: Anders Bylund

Director of Content and Media Production:
Michael Burggren

Production Manager: Daisy Sosa

Media Researcher: Leila Hishmeh

Manufacturing Customer Account Manager:
Mary Beth Hennebury

Art Director: Brenda Carmichael

Production Management and Composition:
Lumina Datamatics, Inc.

Cover Image: © Alexander Remnev / Aurora
Photos

For product information and technology assistance, contact us at
Cengage Learning Customer & Sales Support, cengage.com/contact
For permission to use material from this text or product,
submit all requests online at **cengage.com/permissions**
Further permissions questions can be emailed to
permissionrequest@cengage.com

Student Edition: Level 4 Combo Split B
ISBN: 978-1-337-29745-5

National Geographic Learning
20 Channel Center Street
Boston, MA 02210
USA

National Geographic Learning, a Cengage Learning Company, has a mission to
bring the world to the classroom and the classroom to life. With our English
language programs, students learn about their world by experiencing it. Through
our partnerships with National Geographic and TED Talks, they develop the
language and skills they need to be successful global citizens and leaders.

Locate your local office at **international.cengage.com/region**

Visit National Geographic Learning online at **NGL.Cengage.com/ELT**
Visit our corporate website at **www.cengage.com**

Photography Credits **4** (tl1) © Will Stauffer-Norris, (tl2) © Shao Feng, (cl) CB2/ZOB/Breef/Newscom, (bl1) © Devlin Gandy, (bl2) Blaine Harrington III/Corbis Documentary/Getty Images, **5** (tl1) © Ryan Lash/TED, (tl2) © James Duncan Davidson/TED, (cl) © Ryan Lash/TED, (bl1) © James Duncan Davidson/TED, (bl2) © Bret Hartman/TED, **6** (tl1) © Nigel Dickinson, (tl2) Ton Koene/Alamy Stock Photo, (cl) © Tyrone Bradley, (bl1) © Karolis Janulis/Offset, (bl2) © Marla Aufmuth/TED, **7** (tl1) © Marla Aufmuth/TED, (tl2) © TED, (cl) © James Duncan Davidson/TED, (bl1)) © Ryan Lash/TED, (bl2) © TED, **8-9** (spread) © Will Stauffer-Norris, **10-11** (spread) Anadolu Agency/Getty Images, **13** Chayanee Jongthai/EyeEm/Getty Images, **14** Carsten Peter/National Geographic Creative, **15** David Grossman/Alamy Stock Photo, **16-17** (spread) © Ryan Lash/TED, **18-19** (spread) Joe Morahan/NewSport/Zumapress.com/Newscom, **20-21** (spread) © Shao Feng, **22-23** (spread) Natthawat/Moment Open/Getty Images, **25** (bgd) Matthieu Paley/National Geographic Creative, (tc) © 1983 by Harcourt, Inc. Book design by Lizzie Scott, (tr) © Northwestern Universoty Press, 2002, **26** Stefano Politi Markovina/Alamy Stock Photo, **27** PA Images/Alamy Stock Photo, **28-29** (spread) © James Duncan Davidson/TED, **30-31** (spread) Panoramic Images/National Geographic Creative, **32-33** (spread) CB2/ZOB/Breef/Newscom, **34-35** (spread) © Enric Sala, **37** (t) (ct) (cr) (bl) (bc) Steve Boyes/National Geographic Creative, **38** Ralph Lee Hopkins/National Geographic Creative, **39** Michael Nolan/robertharding/Getty Images, **40-41** (spread) © Ryan Lash/TED, **42-43** Rich Carey/Shutterstock.com, **44-45** © Devlin Gandy, **46-47** NASA/JPL-Caltech/MSSS, **49** Robert Clark/National Geographic Creative, **50** Erik Simonsen/Getty Images, **51** Merydolla/iStock/Getty Images, **52-53** © James Duncan Davidson/TED, **54-55** John Mccarhty/EyeEm/Getty Images, **56-57** (spread) Blaine Harrington III/Corbis Documentary/Getty Images, **58-59** (spread) © Joao Pina/Redux, **61** Blend Images/AlamyStock Photo, **62** Zuma Press, Inc./Alamy Stock Photo, **63** © Purnima Sriram Iyer, **64-65** (spread) © Bret Hartman/TED, **66-67** (spread) Patti McConville/Getty Images, **68-69** (spread) © Nigel Dickinson, **70-71** (spread) Jan Riephoff/laif/Redux, **73** Christian Kober/robertharding/Getty Images, **74** Jonas Gratzer/LightRocket/Getty Images, **75** Abir Abdullah/European Pressphoto Agency/Dhaka/Bangladesh/Newscom, **76-77** © Marla Aufmuth/TED, **78-79** (spread) China Daily/Reuters, **80-81** Ton Koene/Alamy Stock Photo, **82-83** (spread) Nigel Hicks/National Geographic Creative, **85** Robert Clark/National Geographic Creative, **86** Ricardo Ribas/Alamy Stock Photo, **87** © Pim Hendriksen, **88-89** (spread) © TED, **90-91** (spread) Xinhua News Agency/eyevine/Redux, **92-93** (spread) © Tyrone Bradley, **94** (bl) Jodi Cobb/National Geographic Creative, (br) Lucas Vallecillos/Redux, **95** (bl) Dan Kitwood/Getty Images News/Getty Images, (br) Bloomberg/Getty Images, **97** Alberto E. Rodriguez/Getty Images Entertainment/Getty Images, **98** Glow Asia/Alamy Stock Photo, **99** redsnapper/Alamy Stock Photo, **100-101** (spread) © James Duncan Davidson/TED, **102-103** (spread) © Juan Pablo Velasco, **104-105** (spread) © Karolis Janulis/Offset, **106-107** (spread) NurPhoto/Getty Images, **109** Gianluca Colla/National Geographic Creative, **110** ivstiv/E+/Getty Images, **111** SolStock/E+/Getty Images, **112-113** © Ryan Lash/TED, **114-115** (spread) Adrian Sherratt/Alamy Stock Photo, **116-117** (spread) © Marla Aufmuth/TED, **118-119** (spread) Top Photo Corporation/Alamy Stock Photo, **118** (cl) National Geographic Learning, **121** NASA, **122** General Photographic Agency/Hulton Archive/Getty Images, **123** JOSÉ LUIS SALMERÓN/NOTIMEX/Newscom, **124-125** © TED, **126-127** (spread) Kevin Winter/WireImage/Getty Images.

Text Credit **25** (tl) From "An African in Greenland" by Togolese writer Tete-Michel Kpomassie, 1981 published by the New York review of Books,Inc (24 April 2003) ISBN-10: 0940322889 ISBN-13:978-0940322882, (tr) From "House of Day, House of Night" by Olga Tokarczuk, 2003.

Printed in China
Print Number: 01 Print Year: 2018

ACKNOWLEDGMENTS

Paulo Rogerio Rodrigues
Escola Móbile, São Paulo, Brazil

Claudia Colla de Amorim
Escola Móbile, São Paulo, Brazil

Antonio Oliveira
Escola Móbile, São Paulo, Brazil

Rory Ruddock
Atlantic International Language Center, Hanoi, Vietnam

Carmen Virginia Pérez Cervantes
La Salle, Mexico City, Mexico

Rossana Patricia Zuleta
CIPRODE, Guatemala City, Guatemala

Gloria Stella Quintero Riveros
Universidad Católica de Colombia, Bogotá, Colombia

Mónica Rodriguez Salvo
MAR English Services, Buenos Aires, Argentina

Itana de Almeida Lins
Grupo Educacional Anchieta, Salvador, Brazil

Alma Loya
Colegio de Chihuahua, Chihuahua, Mexico

María Trapero Dávila
Colegio Teresiano, Ciudad Obregon, Mexico

Silvia Kosaruk
Modern School, Lanús, Argentina

Florencia Adami
Dámaso Centeno, Caba, Argentina

Natan Galed Gomez Cartagena
Global English Teaching, Rionegro, Colombia

James Ubriaco
Colégio Santo Agostinho, Belo Horizonte, Brazil

Ryan Manley
The Chinese University of Hong Kong, Shenzhen, China

Silvia Teles
Colégio Cândido Portinari, Salvador, Brazil

María Camila Azuero Gutiérrez
Fundación Centro Electrónico de Idiomas, Bogotá, Colombia

Martha Ramirez
Colegio San Mateo Apostol, Bogotá, Colombia

Beata Polit
XXIII LO Warszawa, Poland

Beata Tomaszewska
V LO Toruń, Poland

Michał Szkudlarek
I LO Brzeg, Poland

Anna Buchowska
I LO Białystok, Poland

Natalia Maćkowiak
one2one, Kosakowo, Poland

Agnieszka Dończyk
one2one, Kosakowo, Poland

The author and publishers would like to thank
the following for their help: Dr. Emily Grossman; Ms. Li.

Perspectives teaches learners to think critically and to develop the language skills they need to find their own voice in English. The carefully-guided language lessons, real-world stories, and TED Talks motivate learners to think creatively and communicate effectively.

In *Perspectives*, learners develop:

● AN OPEN MIND

Every unit explores one idea from different perspectives, giving learners opportunities for practicing language as they look at the world in new ways.

● A CRITICAL EYE

Students learn the critical thinking skills and strategies they need to evaluate
new information and develop their own opinions and ideas to share.

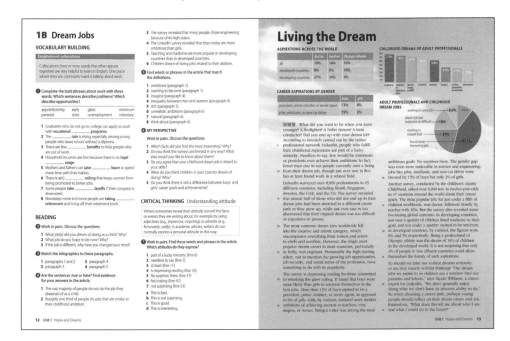

● A CLEAR VOICE

Students respond to the unit theme and express their own ideas confidently in English.

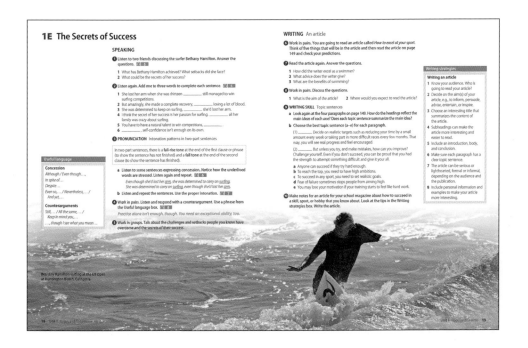

CONTENTS

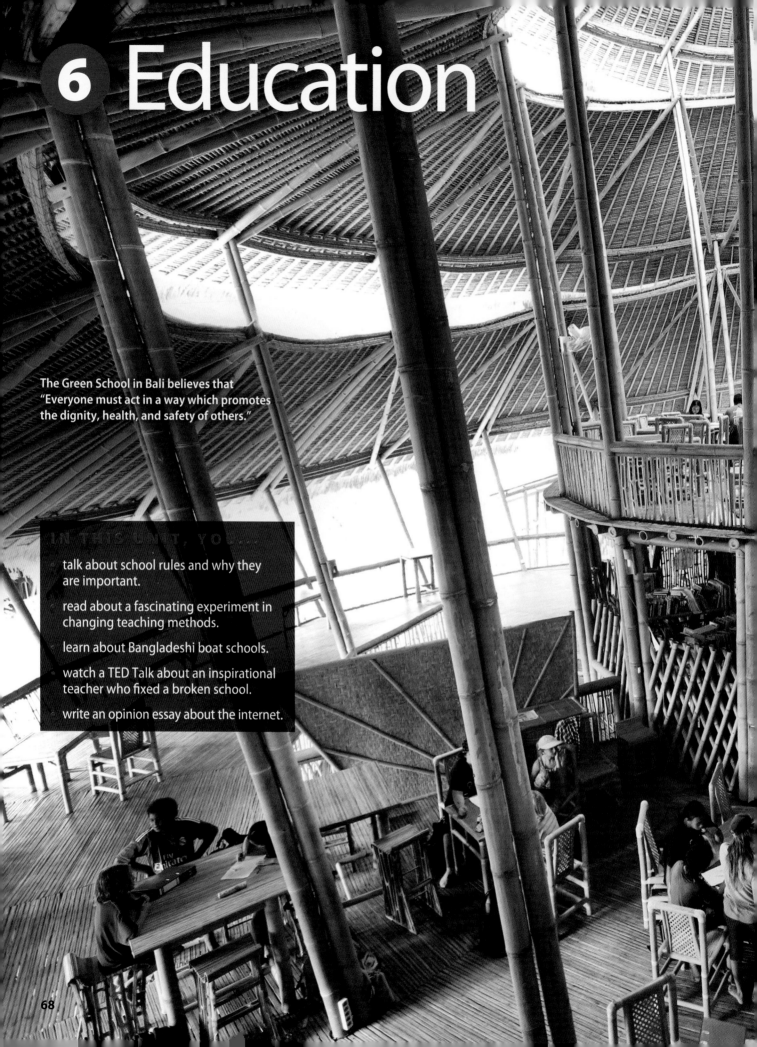

6 Education

The Green School in Bali believes that "Everyone must act in a way which promotes the dignity, health, and safety of others."

- talk about school rules and why they are important.
- read about a fascinating experiment in changing teaching methods.
- learn about Bangladeshi boat schools.
- watch a TED Talk about an inspirational teacher who fixed a broken school.
- write an opinion essay about the internet.

6A Play by the Rules

VOCABULARY School rules

1 Work in pairs. Look at the photo and read the caption. Give three examples of how you think students would be expected to act at the Green School. Do you agree with the quote?

2 Work in pairs. Discuss the questions.

1 Why do schools have rules or codes of conduct?
2 How are they set up? Should students have any say in what the rules are?

3 Match the excerpts from the Green School's Code of Conduct about expected behavior (1–5) with the rules below (a–e).

1 Students are expected to respect the rights, needs, and feelings of others. In return, they can expect such consideration to be shown to them.
2 It is everyone's right to have a safe, clean, and comfortable place to work.
3 Courtesy is an important part of our daily lives. It costs nothing but shows our respect for each other and makes life more pleasant for everyone.
4 Absence of even one day will cause students to miss lessons and lose out on essential teaching.
5 Students are responsible for their personal appearance and are expected to take pride in it.

a No **inappropriate** clothing. _____
b No **vandalism**. _____
c Don't **bully** other students and don't **show disrespect** to anyone. _____
d No **offensive** language or **disruptive** behavior in class. _____
e Don't **skip class**, and **be punctual**. _____

4 Read the consequences of not following a code of conduct. Are they fair? How can they help students improve their behavior?

The school will **give** a range of **punishments** if students misbehave. Students who are not punctual will **be given a warning**. With regard to truancy, students who skip classes will **be given a detention** after school, where they will do extra homework so they don't fall behind with schoolwork. If the student's conduct does not improve, the school may **take away some privileges**; for example, they will not be allowed to leave the school at lunchtime. In cases of more severe **misbehavior**, different punishments will be applied. If students bully or disrespect staff or other students, we take a **mediation approach** in which students and staff discuss the effects of their behavior on other people. If their behavior does not improve, they will be **suspended** from school, either temporarily or permanently. With everyone's cooperation, the rules will not need **enforcing**, but they will ensure that we can all live and work happily together.

5 Work in pairs. Explain the difference between the options in bold.

1 The school promotes caring and positive relationships. We will **suspend** / **take a mediation approach with** students who **bully** / **show disrespect**.
2 Students learn best in a calm, friendly environment. It is disruptive to the class if students make **offensive** / **inappropriate** comments.
3 You need to be in class in order to learn. Students who **are not on time** / **skip class** are given a **detention** / **warning**.

LISTENING

6 Work in groups. Discuss the questions.

1 What type of behavior is expected at your school?
2 What punishments are given if students misbehave? Which are the most effective / appropriate? Why?

7 Listen to a podcast about school rules around the world. Note the punishments you hear. 🎧 **37**

8 Listen again. Choose the correct options to complete the sentences. 🎧 **37**

1 In the school in Mexico, phones can *sometimes / never* be used in class.
2 In the school in Thailand, *students got away with / punishments were given for* lateness.
3 In the school in South Korea, punishments were *very serious / relatively lenient*.
4 In the school in Brazil, students may be suspended for *serious / minor* misbehavior.
5 The Japanese high school had a *strict / lenient* attitude toward students' appearance.
6 In the school in Colorado, US, the students' behavior *improved / got worse*.
7 In the Argentinian school, the students *were punished for / got away with* speaking Spanish.

9 Listen again. Which of the students (1–7) mention the following? 🎧 **37**

a a punishment that benefits the school
b different rules for elementary and high schools
c a regret about the past
d people discussing problems together
e a public punishment
f a popular punishment
g an unnecessary worry

10 MY PERSPECTIVE

Work in pairs. Discuss the questions.

1 Which of the schools is most similar to your school?
2 Which one would you most like to attend?

GRAMMAR Modals of permission and obligation

11 Work in pairs. Look at the extracts from the podcast in the Grammar box. Which other ways can you think of to express the words in bold in each context?

Modals of permission and obligation

a *In some schools in Mexico you **'re allowed to** use phones… in class.*
b *But in my school, you **can't** use them at all, except for emergencies.*
c *We**'re supposed to** leave them in our lockers.*
d *… shouting "I **must** be punctual" or "I **must not** be late."*
e *… students who break the rules **have to** do jobs like cleaning the classrooms.*
f *At Japanese elementary schools, children usually **don't have to** wear a uniform.*

12 Complete these sentences from the podcast with the past forms of the modals and expressions in parentheses. Then listen and check your answers. 🎧 **38**

1 … students who arrived late _____ (must / run) around the school several times…

2 We _____ (not be allowed / wear) make-up…

3 … and the boys _____ (not can / have) long hair…

4 … we _____ (be supposed / answer) them in English, but nobody did.

13 Work in pairs. Look at sentences *a* and *b* in each pair. Is there a difference in meaning? Discuss the difference if there is one.

1 a We **must not use** our phones at all during school hours.
 b We **couldn't use** our phones at all during school hours.

2 a The girls **couldn't wear** pants to school.
 b The girls **didn't have to wear** pants to school.

3 a You **didn't have to write** a 2,000-word essay this time.
 b You **weren't supposed to write** a 2,000-word essay this time.

4 a If we're late three times in a row, we **have to see** the principal.
 b If we're late three times in a row, we **must see** the principal.

5 a We **aren't supposed to bring** any phones into the class.
 b We **shouldn't bring** any phones into the class.

Check your answers on page 138. Do Activities 1–3.

14 Read the paragraphs from a college guidebook for students. Identify parts where a modal verb or expression from Activities 12–13 can be used. Rewrite the paragraphs from the students' point of view.

Assignments

You are expected to turn in your assignments on time and with a high standard of legibility. Typed assignments are preferable; handwritten is acceptable in certain situations, but it is necessary to request your professor's approval. It is also necessary to request an extension from your professor if you are unable to turn in a piece of work on time. If you disagree with any grade given to you, it is necessary to discuss it with your professor.

We have to turn in our assignments on time and…

Exams

You are forbidden to take books, mobile devices, or other aids into the exam. Students who arrive more than five minutes late may not be allowed to take the exam. Students are obligated to remain in the exam room for the first half hour, after which time they are allowed to hand in their exam and leave.

15 Work in groups. Discuss the rules relating to these areas at your school. Do you think they are fair? Rewrite some of the rules to make them more fair in your opinion. Justify your new rules.

bullying	electronic devices
food and drink	homework
other areas	punctuality
speaking in class	truancy
uniform and appearance	

Students in school uniforms in Havana, Cuba

6B Culture Shock!

VOCABULARY BUILDING

Nouns and prepositions

Some nouns, as well as some verbs and adjectives, are normally followed by the same preposition (e.g., *have admiration for someone, have a talent for something, have a reason for doing something*). When you learn new vocabulary, make a note of the prepositions it is used with.

1 Match each group of nouns with a preposition that the words are all commonly used with.

between	for	in	on	to

a approach   attitude   challenge   damage   threat
b need   punishment   respect   responsibility   talent
c advice   ban   focus   influence   impact
d change   decrease   improvement   increase   rise
e clash   comparison   conflict   difference   gap

2 Complete the sentences with nouns from Activity 1. There may be more than one possible answer.

1 Although teachers have a significant _____ on how well students learn, in the end students should take _____ for their own learning.
2 The huge _____ in the use of computers in recent years presents a significant _____ to older people.
3 There is a _____ for a radical _____ in teaching methods for certain subjects.
4 There is sometimes a _____ between students' abilities and their parents' expectations.
5 If schools establish a _____ on smartphone use, it could lead to an _____ in concentration.

3 MY PERSPECTIVE

Work in pairs. Do you agree with the statements in Activity 2? Why?

READING

4 Read a review of a television show called *Are our kids tough enough? Chinese School*. Answer the questions.

1 Who are the kids referred to in the title of the TV show? Why do they need to be "tough"?
2 What exactly was the experiment, and what was the reason for it?
3 What is the reviewer's opinion of the show?

5 Work in pairs. Find differences between the British and Chinese educational systems in these areas that are mentioned or suggested in the review.

1 talking in class
2 the teacher's authority
3 educational achievement in math and science
4 the length of the school day
5 class size
6 attitudes toward competition
7 hobbies and extracurricular activities
8 concentration and paying attention
9 teaching methods

6 Choose the best meaning for these words and phrases in the text.

1 talk back (line 9)
  a argue   **b** reply
2 insights into (line 11)
  a new understandings of   **b** descriptions of
3 counterparts (line 24)
  a rivals   **b** people in a similar situation
4 let off steam (line 35)
  a release tension   **b** be allowed to play
5 a far cry from (line 52)
  a very different from   **b** separate from
6 thrive (line 58)
  a succeed and be happy   **b** compete

7 Work in pairs. How do you think the experiment ended? Why?

CRITICAL THINKING   Evaluating an experiment

8 Read about the results of the Chinese school experiment. Compare them with your ideas in Activity 7.

After four weeks, the two groups were tested in science, math, and Mandarin, and the group taught by the Chinese method had higher scores in all subjects.

9 Read some comments* about the experiment. Do you think they are true? How could the experiment be improved to get a better result?

1 Of course the students using the Chinese method got better scores. They had many more hours of teaching.
2 I wonder what was in the tests. Did they test knowledge or understanding?
3 They probably got higher scores because they were on television. They wanted to show off in front of their friends.

*The comments were created for this activity.

Schoolchildren exercising before class in Beijing, China

Are our kids tough enough? Chinese School

🎧 **39** "This is why you learn less than Chinese students. You slow the teachers down. We have to wait until you stop talking." Miss Yang's class of British teenagers stares at her with a mixture of bewilderment and amusement. "You can't
5 say that. That's so rude," retorts 13-year-old Sophie. "Please be quiet," says Miss Yang. Such a challenge to a teacher's authority would be unthinkable back in China, where respect for the teacher is absolute, students do as they are told, and it would not occur to students to talk back.

10 The first episode of the BBC's *Are our kids tough enough? Chinese School* was full of such entertaining insights into the clash between two very distinct educational cultures. Part innovative educational experiment, part reality TV*, the four-part series will follow the progress of a class of relatively
15 well-behaved 13- to 14-year-olds in a successful British comprehensive school* who are to be taught math, science, and Mandarin by highly-experienced and qualified Chinese teachers using traditional Chinese teaching methods. At the end of the four-week period, the students will have been
20 exposed to very different teaching styles than their peers, who they will be tested against. This is in the context of an increasingly competitive employment market in which British schoolchildren are three years behind their Chinese counterparts in math and science. Will it be possible for their
25 academic performance to be improved by a drastic change in teaching methods and educational principles?

There were some shocks in store for the British children. Not only did they have to attend classes for twelve hours a day, almost double the length of their normal school day, but they
30 were also taught in a class with fifty students, as opposed to the normal UK maximum class size of thirty. The day started at 7:00 a.m. with a two-hour mandatory PE session which entailed running several laps around the sports field, and which turned out to be the most popular class—a chance to
35 let off steam and have fun. But there was also a competitive element, with students being timed, tested, and ranked.

This proved disheartening to Joe, who excelled academically but finished last. It was also a contrast from the system they were used to, in which they competed not
40 against each other, but against themselves.

This was followed by ten grueling hours of classes until seven p.m., when the students were allowed to go home for two hours of mandatory homework to review what they had learned. Unlike British schoolchildren, Chinese students
45 do not normally have time for hobbies or extracurricular activities*; their focus is often on achieving the high test scores, which allows them to get a place at a top university. This also instills in them the ability to concentrate and pay attention, a skill that the British children evidently lacked.
50 British children yawned their way through hours of lessons in which the teacher taught from the board at a fast pace, expecting them to absorb information. This was a far cry from the discovery-style learning the class is used to, which involves figuring things out for themselves, questioning
55 what they are taught, and learning from their mistakes.

The show raised as many questions as it answered. Is there such a thing as an ideal teaching method? Can students thrive in an educational system from a country whose assumptions and norms differ so radically from
60 their own? Having been exposed to a different way of learning, would the students prefer to be taught using the new teaching methods? How would the Chinese teachers cope with extremely disrespectful students? And would the experiment work the other way around, with Chinese
65 students taught by British teachers? It will be fascinating to see the results after four weeks.

reality TV *a TV show about the real lives of ordinary people*
comprehensive school *a UK school that does not pick students based on their ability*
extracurricular activities *activities held at school after classes finish*

Students sit in the classroom of a solar-powered boat school in Bangladesh.

6C Education Initiatives

GRAMMAR Passive *-ing* forms and infinitives

1 Work in pairs. List four things you can remember about the Chinese school experiment.

Passive *-ing* forms and infinitives

1 *... a class of relatively well-behaved 13- to 14-year-olds... who are* **to be taught** *math, science, and Mandarin by highly-experienced and qualified Chinese teachers...*

2 *At the end of the four-week period, the students will* **have been exposed** *to very different teaching styles than their peers, who they will* **be tested** *against.*

3 *Will it be possible for their academic performance* **to be improved** *by a drastic change in teaching methods and educational principles?*

4 *But there was also a competitive element, with students* **being timed, tested, and ranked***.*

5 **Having been exposed** *to a different way of learning, would the students prefer* **to be taught** *using the new teaching methods?*

6 *And would the experiment work the other way around, with Chinese students* **taught** *by British teachers?*

2 Look at the examples in the Grammar box from the review on page 73. Circle examples of the passive gerund (*-ing* form). Underline examples of the passive infinitive.

3 Work in pairs. Look at the examples in the Grammar box again. Answer the questions.

1 Look at the sentences containing an infinitive. Why is the infinitive without *to* (base form) used? Why is the infinitive with *to* used?
2 How do you express the passive infinitive in the past?
3 Look at the examples of the passive *-ing* form. Why is the *-ing* form used?
4 The verb *be* is missing from sentence 6. Rewrite the sentence with the full passive form.
5 Why does the writer use the passive in each sentence?
6 Which sentences include the agent of the passive verb? Why?

Check your answers on page 138. Do Activities 4 and 5.

4 Read about a school in China. Put the verbs in the correct passive or active form.

A private school in China is taking its students back to traditional ways of learning, which involve (1) _____ (learn) the ancient art of calligraphy, or decorative handwriting, and (2) _____ (study) ancient Chinese texts rather than (3) _____ (teach) math or science. After (4) _____ (show) how to form the Chinese characters used in calligraphy, the students are then expected (5) _____ (memorize) long passages from Chinese philosophy. The teachers believe that (6) _____ (educate) in such traditional ways enables the students (7) _____ (develop) better concentration skills. Despite these methods (8) _____ (consider) old-fashioned by many, students appear to enjoy (9) _____ (challenge) in this way. The teachers hope their ideas will (10) _____ (adopt) by mainstream schools in the future.

5 Work in pairs. What do you think of the idea of the school in Activity 4? Could something similar work in your country? Why?

6 Choose the correct options to complete the article about a different type of school.

The Boat Schools of Bangladesh

Every day during the rainy season, Anna Akter, a nine-year-old student in Bangladesh's remote Natore district, waits by the river to (1) *being picked / be picked* up by the boat that has become her school for the duration of the annual monsoon floods. Then, (2) *having been picked up / being picked up* from different riverside stops, Anna and the other children are taught their usual material before (3) *being dropped / to be dropped* off at the end of the day. These "floating schools" mean that, instead of (4) *be prevented / being prevented* from going to class because the roads have been flooded with water, Anna and hundreds of children like her can (5) *be educated / to be educated* on the boat, without their education (6) *being interrupted / be interrupted*.

Up to two thirds of rural Bangladesh is hit by annual flooding, a situation that may (7) *have been made / having been made* worse by the effects of climate change. In 2007, for example, it was estimated that around 1.5 million people were affected by floods. As a result, every year many of the country's schools have (8) *to be closed / be closed* temporarily. The founder of the Boat Schools, Mohammed Rezwan, was lucky enough (9) *being taken / to be taken* to school in his family's boat as a child, but he remembers many of his classmates (10) *having been forced / have been forced* to stay at home. As a result, he launched the Floating Schools initiative with his own money in 2002. It was the first such program (11) *to be launched / having been launched*, but its success has led to floating schools (12) *being introduced / to be introduced* in other flood-prone countries, including Cambodia, Nigeria, the Philippines, Vietnam, and Zambia.

7 Work in pairs. Read the article again. How do Floating Schools improve children's education?

8 MY PERSPECTIVE

Work in groups. Discuss the three educational initiatives you have read about: a Chinese school in the UK, traditional learning, and floating schools. Which did you find most interesting? Why?

9 Make brief notes to answer each question. Then discuss your answers in groups.

1 Which subjects should students be encouraged to study these days?
2 What can you remember being told when you first started learning English?
3 Is there anything you regret not learning when you were younger? What?
4 When your parents, or other older members of the family, buy a new phone, do they need to be taught how to use it? What do you do to help them?
5 Do you like being challenged? By what?

10 CHOOSE

Choose one of the following activities.

- Think of your favorite lesson from last week. Work in pairs. Explain why you liked it and what you learned.

- Work in pairs. Think of another interesting type of school—either one you know or one you research on the internet. Write a short essay about it. Then share the essays in class and vote on the most interesting one.

- Research teaching methods used when your parents and / or grandparents went to school. Report back to the class in a later lesson.

A teacher leads the class in a well-equipped classroom in a Bangladeshi boat school.

6D How to Fix a Broken School? Lead Fearlessly, Love Hard

" We have to make sure that every school that serves children in poverty is a real school. "

LINDA CLIATT-WAYMAN

Read about Linda Cliatt-Wayman and get ready to watch her TED Talk. ▶ **6.0**

AUTHENTIC LISTENING SKILLS

Deducing the meaning of unknown words

It is often possible to guess the meaning of new words that you hear, especially when someone is speaking slowly. You can do this by using the context and your knowledge of other words and word-building. Often you can guess the spelling, too, even if you have never heard the word before. You can then look the word up in a dictionary.

1 Look at the Authentic Listening Skills box. Then listen to two extracts from the TED Talk. Complete what Linda says with one word in each space. 🎧 **40**

1 I graduated from Philadelphia public schools, and I went on to teach special education for 20 years in a low-income, low-performing school in North Philadelphia, where crime is _____ and deep poverty is among the highest in the nation.

2 After things were quickly under control, I immediately called a meeting in the school's _____ to introduce myself as the school's new principal.

2 Work in pairs. Compare the words you wrote, and see if you can figure out their meanings. Use a dictionary to check your ideas.

3 Listen to two more excerpts. Write down any words that you do not recognize. 🎧 **41**

4 Work in pairs. Compare the words you wrote down and see if you can figure out their meanings. Use a dictionary if you need to.

WATCH

5 Work in pairs. Discuss the questions.

1 Which of these might you expect to find in a "broken school"? Use your dictionary if you need to. Can you think of other things?

affluence assaults	bullying	creativity
high exam scores	high morale	illiteracy
juvenile delinquency	truancy	vandalism

2 If you were in charge of a "broken school," which of these areas would be your top priority to fix? Why? Would you choose any other areas to tackle?

behavior	morale	school environment	test scores

3 Imagine it is your first day in charge of a "broken school." How would you spend it? Why?

6 Watch Part 1 of the talk. Are the statements *true* or *false*? ▶ **6.1**

1 Linda had never been to Philadelphia before becoming principal.

2 She spoke to the school on her first day as principal.

3 She was not used to working in schools with social problems.

4 Ashley interrupted Linda's lecture to challenge her.

5 Ashley's words helped Linda understand her own school days.

6 She met Ashley again at Strawberry Mansion School.

TEDTALKS

7 Watch Part 2 of the talk. Number Linda's actions in the order she describes them. ▶ 6.2

a throw away unwanted equipment
b appoint an excellent team
c redecorate and clean the school
d give students safe lockers

8 Watch Part 3 of the talk. What problems among the students does Linda mention? How did Linda and her team improve the students' performance? ▶ 6.3

1 poor attendance
2 bullying
3 poverty
4 difficult home life
5 violence
6 problems with learning
7 vandalism
8 poor academic achievement

9 Watch Part 4 of the talk. Match the sentence beginnings with the endings. ▶ 6.4

1 Linda holds regular "town hall" meetings at school so that _____
2 She is strict about discipline so that _____
3 It is important to give students a "real school" so that _____
4 Teachers should remember students are sometimes scared so that _____

a her students respect her and they can work together better.
b communication can be improved.
c they can provide them with hope for the future.
d they can do well in life after school.

10 **VOCABULARY IN CONTEXT**

a Watch the clips from the TED Talk. Choose the correct meaning of the words and phrases. ▶ 6.5

b Complete the sentences in your own words. Then compare in pairs.
  1 I hope that one day I'll be able to _____ , but I still have *a very long way to go*.
  2 *Fast forwarding* to _____ (time / date), I'll probably be _____ .
  3 Something that's often *on my mind* lately is _____ .

11 Work in pairs. Discuss the questions.

1 Which of these words describe Linda's leadership style?

approachable	authoritarian	compassionate
democratic	empathic	imaginative
inspirational	tough	

2 Linda described the improvements made at her school. What do you think were the three most important factors in achieving these?
3 Would you like to have a principal like Linda? Would her approach work in your school? Why?

12 Which of the ideas you discussed in Activity 5 were mentioned in the talk? Have you changed your mind about any of your ideas as a result of watching the talk?

CHALLENGE

Work in pairs. Can you remember Linda's three slogans? If you could create three slogans for your school, what would they be? Why did you choose them?

6E Testing Times

Useful language

Partially agreeing

I know what you mean, but…
I hear what you're saying, but…
I see your point, but…
I agree somewhat, but…
That's partly true, but…

Challenging an argument

Yes, but don't you think… ?
Are you really saying that… ?
I'm not so sure about that.
I don't think I agree.

Settling an argument

Maybe we'd better agree to disagree (on that).
It's a complex issue. / It's not black and white.
There are no easy answers.
Maybe we should change the subject.

SPEAKING

1 Work in pairs. Discuss the questions.

1 What do you think the difference is between tests and continuous assessment?
2 Which do you prefer?
3 Can you think of other types of testing?

2 Listen to two students discussing tests and continuous assessment. Complete the table. 🎧 42

	in favor of tests	against tests	arguments used
Mateo			
Sofía			

3 Listen again. Which expressions from the Useful language box do you hear? 🎧 42

4 Listen again. Write down the expressions for agreeing and disagreeing that you hear. What others do you know? 🎧 42

5 PRONUNCIATION Rise-fall-rise intonation

a Look at the expressions for partially agreeing in the Useful language box. Then listen and underline the word(s) with the main stress. Notice the rise-fall-rise intonation at the end. 🎧 43
b Listen again and repeat the intonation. 🎧 43

6 Work in groups. Discuss two or three of these opinions.

1 In my opinion, schools should do more to develop children's creativity.
2 Frankly, I think that studying literature is a waste of time.
3 I don't think people should have to wear a school uniform.
4 I personally feel that it should be mandatory to study computer skills starting at the age of five.
5 My view is that speaking English fluently is more important than learning grammar rules.

Students take their examination in an exam hall at Dongguan University of Technology in south China's Guangdong province.

WRITING An opinion essay

7 Work in pairs. Read the essay question. Discuss your opinions.

Some people believe that the main goal of schools is to prepare students for work. Others say that personal development is a more important focus. What is your opinion? Support your ideas with arguments and examples from your own experience.

8 Read the essay on page 151. Answer the questions.

1 In the writer's view, what is the key goal of schools?
2 Does the writer mention your ideas?
3 What other ideas are mentioned?

9 Work in pairs. Answer the questions.

1 In paragraph 1, which two opposing views are introduced? What background information is given?
2 In paragraph 2, what two arguments are mentioned for seeing education as preparation for work?
3 In paragraph 3, what other purposes of education are mentioned?
4 In paragraph 4, what is the writer's personal view and what justification is mentioned?

10 **WRITING SKILL** Avoiding repetition

a Work in pairs. Read the essay on page 151 again. Find at least two different words and phrases which have a similar meaning to the words below.

a aim	**c** get a job	**e** be a good citizen
b most important	**d** enable	**f** do well at school

b Read two opinions about the internet. Which one do you agree with more? Why?

Some people <u>think</u> that the internet <u>enhances</u> people's lives because they can <u>get</u> all the information <u>they need</u> for their lives and studies. Others <u>maintain</u> we have <u>far too much</u> information nowadays.

c Match the underlined words and phrases with those with a similar meaning (a–f).

a access	**c** improves	**e** necessary
b an excessive amount of	**d** say	**f** consider

d Which alternatives are more formal, and which more informal? Can you think of other alternatives?

11 You are going to write an essay discussing the opinions in Activity 10b. Make notes for a four-paragraph essay. Support your ideas with arguments and examples from your own experience.

12 Write your essay. Use phrases from the Useful language box. Avoid repetition.

Moving Forward

- talk about ways of commuting to school.

- read about innovative designs inspired by nature.

- learn about sustainable cities.

- watch a TED Talk about transportation systems of the future.

- write a report.

Subway trains in Tokyo, Japan, get so crowded that people are hired as "pushers" to make sure everyone fits.

7A Getting There

VOCABULARY Everyday commutes

1 Look at the photo. Is public transportation busy where you live? Could a scene like this happen?

2 Complete the text about getting to school with these words and phrases.

breakdowns	carpool	commute	commuters	commuting
congested	congestion	connection	drop them off	exhaust
shuttle service	smog	stuck	subway	

Some trips to school can be as simple as walking ten minutes down the road, but, increasingly in our urbanized world, the daily (1) _____ is taking longer and uses several methods of transportation, making it more complicated.

In Tokyo, Japan, students regularly take the train, bus, or (2) _____ to get to school, and (3) _____ can be as young as six. Their journeys can easily be an hour or more and can include several types of transportation. Although public transportation in Japan is reliable, (4) _____ can happen, so the youngest kids have yellow flaps on their backpacks so that adults know to look out for them if they miss a (5) _____ or appear lost.

In UK towns and cities, the trip to school is usually by school buses or public transportation (i.e., trains, buses, and the Tube in London), though a lot of parents take younger kids by car and (6) _____ at school. This adds to the volume of rush-hour traffic and can result in vehicles getting (7) _____ in gridlock. One way of helping the problem may be to (8) _____—several people traveling to school in a single car. Another may be encouraging students to bike or walk to school. While that may ease the (9) _____ , students will then be among the cars and therefore breathing in (10) _____ .

If you live in Istanbul, Turkey, (11) _____ to school can involve changing continents! Crossing the Bosporus, a waterway in the city, means going from Asia to Europe or vice versa. In a city known to be badly (12) _____ , the ferry (13) _____ is the most pleasant means of avoiding the (14) _____ that can occur in parts of the city, and it has connections to the city's bus and subway services.

3 Work in pairs. Answer the questions.

  1 Find the three forms of *commute*. What parts of speech are they?
  2 Look at these groups of words from the text. Do the words in each group have the same meaning? If not, what is the difference?
    a commute (n), crossing (n), trip (n)   **d** congestion, gridlock, rush hour
    b transportation, vehicles   **e** subway, Tube
    c exhaust (n), smog

4 MY PERSPECTIVE

Work in groups. Discuss the questions about your commute to school.

  1 How do you commute to school? Is it expensive? Is it tiring?
  2 How far do you travel and how long does it take you?
  3 What are the advantages and disadvantages of your commute?

LISTENING

5 Listen to a radio show about commuting in cities. Identify the problems mentioned for each city. 🎧 **44**

	Mexico City	Istanbul
air pollution		
the city's location		
shortage of public transportation		
the number of traffic lanes		
congestion at rush hour		
lack of incentive to use public transportation		
overcrowded public transportation		

6 Listen again. Complete the sentences. 🎧 **44**

1 There is air pollution in Mexico City because the smog _____ .
2 Gloria's father commutes from his home _____ to the business district.
3 He regularly spends _____ a day commuting.
4 The population of Mexico City is more than _____ .
5 Mexico City has experimented with _____ .
6 Mexico City may soon have a new _____ system.
7 Many streets in Istanbul are too _____ for cars.
8 People need to use bridges to get from _____ .
9 In heavy traffic, motorists often _____ lanes and _____ their horns.
10 Istanbul has a large new _____ and will soon have more _____ .

7 Work in pairs. Do you think these solutions relate to Mexico City, Istanbul, or both?

1 They're planning to introduce more ferries to ease the congestion.
2 They've improved emissions testing for vehicles.
3 They've increased the number of bus lanes.
4 They're looking into building a fourth bridge.
5 They're introducing a bike-sharing program.

GRAMMAR Ellipsis and substitution

8 Work in pairs. Look at the sentences from the radio show in the Grammar box. Answer the questions about the words in bold.

1 In sentences a–e, which words are omitted?
2 In sentences f–j, which words do the underlined words replace?

Ellipsis and substitution

a *It's infuriating.* **Yes, it must be.**
b *Could you move closer to the center?* **We'd really like to.**
c *You can imagine how heavy the traffic gets during rush hour.* **I definitely can.**
d *Hasn't the government widened the roads?* **Well, maybe they could have,** *but no.*
e *Has the government come up with any solutions?* **They have, but we need more.**
f *Why not use public transportation instead?* **He's tried** <u>doing that</u>.
g *Are things any better where you are?* **I'm afraid** <u>not</u>.
h *We have a similar problem to* **the** <u>one</u> *Gloria talked about.*
i *Do you get to school by car?* **I** <u>don't</u>**, but lots of my friends** <u>do</u>.
j *I hope that'll help.* **I hope** <u>so</u>**, too.**

Check your answers on page 140. Do Activities 1–3.

9 Choose the best answer in each response to the questions below.

1 What is public transportation like where you live?
  a It's better than it used to.
  b It's better than it used to be.

2 Do towns and cities have enough bike lanes?
  a Well, there are some, but not enough.
  b Well, there are some ones, but not enough.

3 Are towns and cities likely to introduce bike-sharing programs?
  a I don't know, but I definitely hope to.
  b I don't know, but I definitely hope so.

4 Do drivers usually obey the rules of the road?
  a Well, most drivers do obey, but some don't obey.
  b Well, most drivers do, but some don't.

5 Does the government need to build more sidewalks in rural areas?
  a Walking in the country can be dangerous… so yes, they really need to.
  b Walking in the country can be dangerous… so yes, they really need.

6 Has your country introduced strict regulations for private drivers and taxis?
  a They must, but I don't know the details.
  b They must have, but I don't know the details.

10 MY PERSPECTIVE

Work in pairs. Discuss the questions in Activity 9.

11 Rewrite the underlined phrases to use ellipsis or substitution.

Dad's a civil engineer, and he travels a lot for his job. His company had been saying they would send him abroad, and last year they (1) finally sent him abroad—to Thailand. I'd always wanted to visit Bangkok, so at last I was finally able (2) to visit Bangkok. I'd heard that public transportation in Bangkok could be really busy, and (3) it was really busy! *Tuk-tuks* (three-wheeled taxis) are great. They're disappearing, but I got a ride in (4) a tuk-tuk once; but they're too dangerous for the school commute. I would have loved to commute on the Skytrain—an elevated railway—but that's mainly for the business districts, so (5) I couldn't use it.

12 Work in pairs. Write questions for these answers. Then ask another pair your questions. Answer using ellipsis and/or substitution.

1 Can you ride a bike?

1 No, I wish I could.
2 I might, some day.
3 No, never, but I'd like to.
4 No, but I will be very soon.
5 I don't, but I have a friend who does.
6 Because I was told to.
7 I wouldn't have if I'd known.
8 I definitely am!
9 I should have, but I didn't have time.

Ferries at Eminonu with the Topkapi Palace in the background in Istanbul, Turkey

7B Nature's Algorithms

VOCABULARY BUILDING

Verb suffixes

Many verbs in English have the suffixes -ize, -ify, -ate, or -en.
Examples: *civilize, minimize; clarify, identify; estimate, operate; harden, weaken.*

1 Complete the words with -ize, -ify, or -ate.

circul_____	collabor_____	communic_____
imit_____	innov_____	just_____
maxim_____	memor_____	priorit_____
pur_____	regul_____	replic_____
subsid_____	un_____	util_____

2 Add the suffixes -ize, -ify, -ate, or -en to these words to form verbs. You may need to change the part of speech.

electric	formula	long	origin
simple	stable	strong	urban

3 Complete the sentences with a verb from Activities 1 or 2 in the correct form. There may be more than one possible answer.

1 There are many ways in which we design technology to _____ the natural world in some way.
2 The doctors needed to _____ the patient's heart rate in order to do the operation.
3 Many species of insects _____ in groups to work more effectively.
4 Increasing online crime has _____ efforts from IT experts everywhere to improve online security.
5 Sometimes new transportation ideas are too complex and need to be _____ .

READING

4 Work in pairs. You are going to read an article about biomimicry. Can you think of any connections between these pairs?

a bullet train—a kingfisher's beak
a car windshield—a butterfly's wing
a drone—a moth
a sailboat—a shark
traffic—a swarm of ants

5 Read the article and check your answers. What other examples of biomimicry are mentioned?

6 Work in pairs. Read the article again. Choose the best subtitle for each paragraph and say why it is best. There is one subtitle you do not need.

a A field of study uniting experts
b A smart way to save money and electricity
c An improvement inspired by a hobby
d Designing new roads for the future
e Flying machines designed to copy nature
f Working together to prevent gridlock

7 Underline the evidence in the article for these statements.

1 Natural systems and organisms have evolved over a long period of time.
2 The designer of the bullet train decided to rethink the shape of the engine.
3 Modern flying machines cannot completely avoid risks in the natural environment.
4 Smart energy grids copy the way bees communicate with each other.
5 Smart traffic solutions require drivers to have a new mindset.

CRITICAL THINKING Understanding connotation

Writers can create a positive or negative impression with the words they use. Some words (e.g., *relaxed, young*) have **positive connotations** (they suggest positive ideas), while others (e.g., *lazy, immature*) have **negative connotations**.

8 Work in pairs. Answer the questions.

1 Find words and phrases with positive or negative connotations in paragraph 1.
2 What impression of biomimicry is the writer trying to convey with their word choice? Is it successful?
3 Find words in these sentences that convey a positive or negative impression of biomimicry.
   a Biomimicry seeks sustainable solutions by imitating nature's tried-and-true patterns and strategies.
   b The so-called benefits remain unconvincing.
   c The Biomimicry Institute empowers people to create nature-inspired solutions for a healthy planet.
   d Butterfly wings are undoubtedly beautiful, but nature also has a darker and more competitive side.
   e Biomimicry will catalyze a new era in design and business that benefits both people and the planet.

9 MY PERSPECTIVE

What do you think of the parallels made in the text between the natural world and human innovation? Think about ways in which the natural world might have inspired the following: flight, underwater exploration, clothing, building materials, societies.

Designers can use vapor during wind-tunnel tests to show how aerodynamic a car is.

Biological blueprints

🎧 **45** What do a Japanese bullet train and a kingfisher have in common? The answer lies in the exciting and rapidly emerging discipline called *biomimicry*. Literally meaning "imitation of life" or "copying nature,"
5 biomimicry looks to the natural world for solutions to human challenges. Increasingly, creative minds from such diverse fields as biology, architecture, engineering, and medicine are studying processes that nature has developed and streamlined over billions of
10 years and replicating them in innovative products and technologies. These include Olympic-winning sailboats and swimsuits whose surfaces mimic a shark's skin; solar cells based on the structure of a leaf; building materials inspired by bones and eggshells; and non-
15 reflective, energy-efficient windshields inspired by butterflies' wings. The questions behind such innovations are "How would nature solve this?" or "What blueprint already exists in the natural world?"

But back to the bullet train. The first train was, as the
20 name suggests, shaped like a bullet, with a rounded engine at the front. But when it entered tunnels, it created a pressure wave that resulted in a huge sonic boom, like a clap of thunder, as the train emerged at the other end. The train's designer, an engineer who
25 also happened to be an avid birdwatcher, went back to the drawing board. Observing how a kingfisher was able to move smoothly between the air and the water with minimum turbulence, he remodeled the nose of the engine using the shape of the kingfisher's beak. The
30 result? Today's super-streamlined bullet train, which travels at higher speeds than the original prototype and uses less energy.

Designs inspired by nature are not new. Da Vinci's drawings of helicopters and parachutes are clearly based
35 on observations from nature, and the Wright brothers created their first aircraft by studying the flight of birds. But in recent years, teams of engineers and researchers worldwide have been studying the characteristics of winged creatures to come up with designs for even
40 more complex vehicles, including robotic drones (unmanned aircraft) the size of hummingbirds, moths, or even tiny bees. These vehicles are programmed to avoid obstacles and to stabilize themselves after a collision, but they face the same threats as actual
45 insects, which include being eaten, caught in a spider's web, or even squashed by pedestrians.

Urban planners are also drawing inspiration from the biological world to come up with smart energy and transportation solutions. A problem with complex
50 human infrastructure, such as the electrical grid, is that its various parts don't talk to each other or monitor the whole grid. In bee colonies, by contrast, individuals can sense what jobs need to be done and do them instinctively without central organization. By identifying
55 the unifying pattern, or algorithm, underlying the bees' system, energy companies can design interconnected components that communicate with each other, thus maximizing efficiency and reducing costs.

Researchers have also discovered an exemplary case of
60 perfect traffic in nature: there is never congestion on ant tracks. Like bees, ants continuously communicate by touch and by the release of pheromones, or chemical signals, which give them an overview of the movements of the swarm as a whole. Could cars use such "swarm
65 intelligence" in the future to communicate with each other and reduce traffic? In purely technical terms it is a possibility. But radical new systems like these can only function if people are prepared to think collaboratively, and that may take some time.

7C Sustainable Cities

GRAMMAR Nominalization

1 Work in pairs. Read the text in the Grammar box about the challenges of urbanization. What do you think the other problems are? What sustainable solutions might there be?

Nominalization

A *The rapid growth of our cities has led to an increase in the world's urban population. UN predictions suggest that by 2050, about two-thirds of the world's population will be living in cities, creating a shortage of living space and other problems. Therefore, there is a desperate need to find sustainable solutions to these problems of urbanization.*

2 Text A in the Grammar box contains the same facts as Text B below, but they are expressed differently. Look at the underlined sections of Text B. How are they different from Text A?

B Our cities are (1) growing rapidly, and so the world's urban population (2) has increased. (3) The UN has predicted that by 2050, about two-thirds of the world's population will be living in cities, and there (4) won't be enough living space. So, (5) we desperately need to find sustainable (6) ways of solving the problems which will be created because so many (7) people will be living in urban areas.

3 Answer the questions about the two texts.

   1 How are the adverb + verb combinations in Text B expressed in Text A?
   2 How many clauses does each text contain?
   3 Which text has more nouns? Which has more verbs?
   4 Which text is more formal and impersonal?

Check your answers on page 140. Do Activities 4–6.

4 **PRONUNCIATION** Words with two stress patterns

   a Where do you think the main stress is in the words in bold?
      1 The population of urban areas will **increase**.
      2 There will be an **increase** in the population of urban areas.

   b Listen and check. Then choose the correct options to complete the rule. 🎧 46
   Some two-syllable words are stressed on the (1) *first / second* syllable when they are verbs and on the (2) *first / second* syllable when they are nouns.

   c Listen to five pairs of sentences. Underline the stressed syllable and write N (noun) or V (verb). 🎧 47
      1 **a** decrease   **b** decrease   _____
      2 **a** imports   **b** imports   _____
      3 **a** record   **b** record   _____
      4 **a** present   **b** present   _____
      5 **a** suspect   **b** suspect   _____

The rapid-transit system in Curitiba, Brazil, connects express buses that get around the city quickly. Its popularity has decreased traffic and helped reduce pollution.

5 Work in pairs. Complete the text about sustainable cities with these nominalizations.

change	conservation	contribution
cost	creation	decrease
disruption	improvements	need
reduction		

Transportation

In light of the widespread problems with traffic jams, there is an urgent need for a radical (1) _____ in the way people travel. We need sustainable cities. First of all, sustainable cities support the (2) _____ of communities in which amenities are built close together, so there is a reduced (3) _____ for commuting far. Other measures include (4) _____ to existing public transportation systems. For example, the Brazilian city of Curitiba, rather than accepting the huge (5) _____ of constructing a whole new subway system and the severe (6) _____ to the lives of the city's residents, decided to improve and speed up the public bus network by making it more like a subway system, with raised platforms, longer buses, and pre-paid tickets.

Energy use

An important aim of sustainable cities is to achieve a (7) _____ in the city's carbon footprint. The use of renewable energy and the introduction of energy (8) _____ measures can produce a massive (9) _____ in CO_2 emissions. Waste recycling can also make an important (10) _____ to energy production.

6 Complete the cause-and-effect sentences (1–6) by nominalizing these phrases.

it improves air quality	sea levels rise
they get healthier	they get more independent
~~they pollute the air~~	we invest in renewable energy

1 _*Air pollution*_ is largely due to vehicle emissions.
2 A reduction in car ownership could result in _____ .

3 _____ in young people could result from encouragement to walk to school.
4 Lowering the driving age to 16 could lead to _____ for young people.
5 _____ would bring about less reliance on fossil fuels.
6 Failure to tackle climate change could cause _____ .

7 Work in pairs. Read about another way of improving energy efficiency. Rewrite the text using nominalizations and verbs expressing cause and effect from Activity 6. Then compare your ideas with another pair.

More and more people are becoming interested in the idea of smart sidewalks, and they are investing more money into research. People can recycle old tires to create small electromagnetic tiles. When people walk on them, they produce energy, which can be used to power small appliances. Smart sidewalks are being installed in places such as shopping centers, concert venues, sports venues, and airports, and one day this could provide more of our energy.

8 Had you heard of smart sidewalks before? Where else do you think they could be installed to produce energy?

9 MY PERSPECTIVE

Work in groups. Discuss the initiatives from this lesson that you find most interesting, giving your reasons.

10 CHOOSE

Choose one of the following activities.

- Research how different towns around the world are becoming more sustainable. Write a report on an initiative that you find interesting.

- Work in pairs. Write a paragraph for how a town or city in your country could become more sustainable. Then read your paragraph and explain your ideas in groups.

- Work in pairs. Find four or five interesting facts in this unit. Write a multiple-choice question about each one. Then work with another pair to ask and answer your questions.

The Van Gogh–Roosegaarde bicycle path in the Netherlands is made from thousands of stones poured into concrete and covered in a material that allows them to absorb energy during daylight and glow after dark.

AUTHENTIC LISTENING SKILLS

Predicting what comes next

When people listen to a speaker, they constantly make and update predictions about what the speaker might say next. It is often possible to do this by noticing the words he or she uses, especially if they are stressed. This makes it easier to follow the flow of ideas.

1 Look at the Authentic Listening Skills box. Then read the first sentence from the TED Talk. Decide which of the topics Wanis is most likely to talk about next. Listen and check your answer. 🎧 48

One of my greatest pleasures in life is, I have to admit, a bit special.

a the speaker's life
b a description of the pleasure
c why the pleasure is special

2 Work in pairs. Read and listen to three more sentences from the talk. Predict what Wanis might talk about after these sentences. Use the stressed words in bold to help. 🎧 49

1 *Some cities are calmly industrious, like Dusseldorf or Louisville.*
2 *For decades, our remedy for congestion was simple.*
3 *But if you look at our cities, yes, we have some underground subway systems and some tunnels and bridges, and also some helicopters in the sky. But…*

3 Listen and check your ideas. 🎧 50

WATCH

4 Work in pairs. What do you know about driverless cars? What could be the advantages and disadvantages?

5 Watch Part 1 of the talk. Choose the correct options to complete these sentences. ▶ 7.1

1 Wanis sees cities as "living beings" because
   a they are full of people.
   b the roads remind him of a human body.
   c they are lively and energetic places.
2 Wanis's main complaint about traffic is that
   a there are too many vehicles on the road.
   b people make too many unnecessary trips.
   c people waste too much time traveling slowly.
3 Wanis says that a program of expanding or building new roads
   a can never solve the problem of traffic jams.
   b is only possible outside cities.
   c is possible in some cities, but not others.

6 Watch Part 2 of the talk. Are these statements *true* or *false*? ▶ 7.2

1 Wanis was first inspired by the vascular system when he was sick.
2 The body contains 16,000 miles of blood vessels.
3 Wanis believes more vehicles should travel in the air and underground.
4 The Chinese bus can travel above congested streets.
5 Commuters in Tel Aviv and Abu Dhabi are traveling in detachable pods.
6 Businesses are interested in the potential of urban flying vehicles.

7 Watch Part 3 of the talk. Complete the statements with numbers or a percentage. ▶ 7.3

1 Almost _____ of traffic in cities is caused by drivers looking for somewhere to park.
2 _____ of cars in cities contain only one passenger.
3 Every time our heart beats, it pushes _____ of red blood cells around the body.
4 More than _____ of the oxygen capacity of our blood cells is used efficiently.

8 Complete the summary.

The train Wanis describes does not need to stop because the cars (1) _____ and turn into (2) _____ buses. Then a section of the bus (3) _____ and (4) _____ to your house.

9 Watch Part 4 of the talk. Choose the correct options. ▶ 7.4

1 It is *easy / difficult* for driverless cars to learn traffic rules.
2 Driverless cities *would still need / would not need* traffic lights and traffic lanes.
3 Cars would drive *faster than / at the same speed as* they do now.
4 Cars would move according to *new rules / changing algorithms.*
5 Driverless cars *will flow freely / will not need robotic control.*
6 Wanis believes these developments could happen *now / in the near future.*

10 VOCABULARY IN CONTEXT

a Watch the clips from the TED Talk. Choose the correct meaning of the words and phrases. ▶ 7.5

b Think of an example of each of the following. Then compare your examples in pairs.
1 an *"aha" moment* you have had
2 something that has been an *eye-opener* for you
3 how a city can be *car-centric* or *people-centric*
4 an *attribute* of a healthy transportation system

CHALLENGE

Work in pairs. Imagine you have to design a transportation strategy for a sustainable city. Which three features would you prioritize? Which three would you not include? Make notes on your reasons for each.

- build more bike lanes and paths
- build tunnels and overpasses
- encourage carpooling
- encourage working from home
- only allow parking outside the city center
- expand the subway system
- encourage delivery by drones
- invest in driverless cars
- subsidize all public transportation
- widen existing roads

Now work in groups. Try to agree on a plan to include five different features.

11 MY PERSPECTIVE

Discuss in pairs. Would you want to travel in a driverless car? Why?

7E Opinion Poll

SPEAKING

1 Work in pairs. Compare the length of different trips from your home to school, the city center, and other places in your town or city.

It's a twenty-minute walk.
It's a ten-minute bus ride.
It's a three-hour drive.

2 Listen to the survey on a local bus system. Number the questions in the order you hear them. (The wording may be different.) 🎧 **51**

_____ Do you use the bus system?
_____ Why is that?
_____ How could local authorities improve the bus service?
_____ What is the bus fare to the city center?
_____ How do you normally travel?
_____ If the buses ran more frequently, would you use them more often?
_____ How often do you take the bus?
_____ If the city council subsidized the bus service, would you use it more often?

3 Listen to the interview again. Is the interviewee positive or negative about the local bus system? What indicates this? 🎧 **51**

4 Look at the Asking for information section of the Useful language box. Use these expressions to make the questions in Activity 2 more polite. Then listen again and check. What do you notice about the word order in indirect questions? 🎧 **51**

5 Work in pairs. Ask and answer the questions in Activity 2 about your own town or city. Use some indirect questions.

6 Work in pairs. Choose one of these topics and write six to eight questions about your town or city. Then ask different class members the questions and write down their answers. (You will use them later to write a report.) Use the expressions in the Useful language box.

traffic near your school / home / in the city center
conditions for cyclists / pedestrians
public transportation (e.g., buses, subway, shuttles, ferries)

Useful language

Introducing a survey

I'm conducting / carrying out a survey on…

Would you mind answering a few questions?

Asking for information

I wonder if I could / Can I ask…?

I'd like to know…

Do you happen to know / Do you have any idea…?

Giving information

I'd say… / I think… / I have a feeling…

Not offhand. / Not off the top of my head.

As far as I know / remember, …

On average, … / Generally speaking, …

Sorry, I have no no idea. / don't have a clue.

School buses in Zhengzhou, the capital of central China's Henan Province

WRITING A report

7 Are there green spaces where you live? How are they used?

8 Work in pairs. Read the report on page 152. What questions do you think the interviewers asked?

9 Work in pairs. Which of these is <u>not</u> a feature of a report? Find examples of the others in the report.

1 a title and subheadings
2 a statement of purpose
3 the background of the report
4 figures and statistics
5 a formal style
6 recommendations
7 personal opinions
8 nominalizations

10 Find phrases in the report to express the number of students with a particular opinion (e.g., *almost half*).

11 A survey asked students about a bike path to school from the town center. Complete the text with expressions of quantity from Activity 10.

	always	usually	sometimes	occasionally	never
Do you bike to school?	35%	19%	9%	11%	26%
Do you use the bike path?	90%	8%	2%	0%	0%

We surveyed the students about biking to school and found that (1) _____ biked to school at least occasionally. (2) _____ always or usually biked, and (3) _____ said that they sometimes or occasionally did. When asked if they used the bike path, (4) _____ used it all the time while (5) _____ used it most of the time. (6) _____ said they had no or little interest in using the path at all.

12 WRITING SKILL Expressions of approval and disapproval

Work in pairs. Find three ways of expressing approval and three of expressing disapproval in the report on page 152. Can you think of any other ways of writing about people's (dis)approval of something?

13 Work in pairs. Plan a report based on the findings of the survey you conducted in Activity 6. Then write the report using the features from Activities 9–12 and expressions in the Useful language box.

Useful language

Explaining the purpose

This report has been written to provide information on…

The purpose of this report is to inform the public about…

The purpose of the survey / investigation was to determine…

Explaining findings

It was found that…

The key finding is that…

Most of the people interviewed feel that / find…

Most respondents said that / reported…

A number of people commented on…

With regard to / Regarding…

In terms of…

Overall, it appears / would appear that…

8 The Real Me

IN THIS UNIT, YOU...

- talk about teenage stereotypes.

- read about Ms. Marvel, the teenage comic superhero.

- learn about how sleep patterns change in adolescence.

- listen to a TED Talk about how the teenage brain is wired.

- write an essay comparing advantages and disadvantages.

8A A typical teenager?

VOCABULARY Teenage stereotypes

Teens in South Africa practice iSbhujwa, a type of local dance, for a competition.

1 Do you think teenagers have typical characteristics and behaviors? Why? If yes, how would you describe them?

2 Take the quiz. Does it mention your ideas? Compare your answers in pairs.

> **1** How much are you **influenced by** your **peers**?
>   **a** I very often give in to **peer pressure**.
>   **b** I **follow the crowd** with some things but sometimes **do my own thing**.
>   **c** I don't pay attention to what other people do.
> **2** How self-conscious are you?
>   **a** I **couldn't care less about** what other people think of me.
>   **b** I'm aware of how I **come across** but not very worried.
>   **c** What people think of me is very important.
> **3** What is your attitude toward authority?
>   **a** I never question what other people tell me to do.
>   **b** I obey the rules, but I like to talk about them and know why they exist.
>   **c** I'm the typical rebellious teenager!
> **4** How moody are you?
>   **a** I'm usually very even-tempered.
>   **b** I'm always cheerful and in a good mood.
>   **c** My moods tend to go up and down a lot.
> **5** What is your attitude toward risk?
>   **a** I avoid danger, but I sometimes take calculated risks.
>   **b** Risky activities **give me a thrill**.
>   **c** I prefer to **play it safe** and avoid taking risks.
> **6** How impulsive are you?
>   **a** I often do things without thinking of the consequences.
>   **b** I always have a lot of self-control.
>   **c** I generally **weigh the pros and cons** before acting.

3 Work in pairs. Complete the sentences with the correct form of the words or phrases in bold in the quiz. Do you agree with them?

1 Teenagers usually compare themselves with their _____ .
2 There's a lot of _____ to wear fashionable clothes.
3 People who _____ as self-confident are usually less confident deep down.
4 Teenagers tend to be more _____ their friends than by their parents.
5 People who don't _____ when it comes to fashion tend to stand out.
6 Regardless of their own interests, parents should allow kids to _____ in their free time.
7 People who _____ about what other people think are in danger of becoming arrogant.
8 When making a decision, you'll have a better idea of what to do if you _____ .
9 You'll never learn from new experiences if you always _____ and avoid danger.
10 People tend to do extreme sports because the danger _____ .

4 Find six character adjectives in the quiz. Do they have a positive or negative meaning, or could they be either? Use a dictionary if necessary. Then describe people you know using the adjectives.

LISTENING

5 Listen to a radio show where a psychologist and a teenager talk about the teenage years. According to the speakers, are the statements *true*, *false*, or *not given*? 🎧 52

1 Teenagers tend to be the same all over the world.
2 The concept of a "teenager" is a modern invention.
3 Laura is always influenced by her peers.
4 Laura looks more self-confident than she feels.
5 There are cultural differences in attitudes to authority.
6 Many teenagers enjoy volunteering and helping others.
7 Laura prefers to avoid taking risks.
8 Laura had a difficult experience while changing trains.

6 Look at the quiz on page 93. Listen again. Find the answers that best describe a "typical teenager." For which question is it hard to generalize about a typical teenager? 🎧 52

7 MY PERSPECTIVE

Work in pairs. Discuss the questions.

1 How much do you think teenagers in your country fit the stereotypes described?
2 How are teenagers in your country portrayed in the media? Are they ever unfairly criticized?
3 What would you say to point out the positive contributions of teenagers?

GRAMMAR Adverbials

8 Look at the sentences from the radio show in the Grammar box. Underline the adverbs and adverbials. Then answer the questions.

Adverbials

Adverbials consist of one word or expressions of two or more words. They modify the meaning of a sentence or part of a sentence.

a I *definitely* like to follow the fashion.
b *Interestingly*, that depends a lot on the culture.
c I *probably* wouldn't wear anything that made me stand out.
d Teenagers will *often* engage in risky activities.
e I *really* like traveling.
f *In fact*, I have my own taste in music.
g I planned it *carefully*.
h Teenagers will have their ups and downs *from time to time*.
i *Maybe* that's another myth?
j Teenagers *also* tend to be very self-conscious.

1 What do the underlined adverbs and adverbials express: addition, attitude, degree, frequency, manner, or level of certainty?

Teenagers shopping in Hiroshima, Japan

Teenagers shopping in Poznan, Poland

2 Choose the correct option to complete the rules.

 a Adverbs expressing an attitude (e.g., **apparently**, **frankly**), **perhaps**, and **maybe** tend to be used *at the beginning / in the middle / at the end* of a clause.

 b Longer adverbials and adverbs of manner tend to be used *at the beginning / in the middle / at the end* of a clause.

 c Frequency adverbs, adverbs of degree, and others such as **probably**, **also**, and **just** tend to be used *at the beginning / in the middle / at the end* of a clause.

3 Which sentence expresses a stronger negative idea?

 a *I really don't like speaking in public.*

 b *I don't really like taking risks.*

Check your answers on page 142. Do Activities 1 and 2.

9 PRONUNCIATION *really*

 a Listen to the sentences from the radio show. Underline the words that carry the main stress. 🎧 53

  1 I really like traveling.

  2 I really don't like speaking in public.

  3 I don't really like taking risks.

 b Listen again and repeat the sentences. 🎧 53

 c Work in pairs. Talk about things you (don't) like, (don't) enjoy, or (don't) want to do. Use *really* and the correct stress in your sentences.

10 Work in pairs. Decide where to put the adverbials in parentheses in the sentences. More than one position may be possible. Then discuss if the statements are true for you.

 1 I'd enjoy backpacking around the world. (probably / very much)

 2 I wouldn't enjoy extreme sports like rock climbing. (definitely / at all)

 3 I might try to overcome an irrational fear I have. (possibly / some day)

 4 To make a balanced decision, I try to weigh the pros and cons. (just / carefully)

 5 I ask my parents and friends for guidance. (also / most of the time)

 6 I do my homework every night; I have more time for my family and friends. (as a result / usually / very quickly)

11 Complete the sentences with your own opinions. Then read them to a partner and explain your ideas.

 1 Interestingly, most people in my family…

 2 Basically, teenagers are…

 3 Strangely enough, I have never…

 4 To tell the truth, I would never risk…

 5 Honestly, I don't imagine…

 6 Apparently, most teenagers…

Teenagers shopping in Dubai, UAE

Teenagers shopping in São Paulo, Brazil

8B Teenage Superheroes

VOCABULARY BUILDING

Binomial expressions

Binomial expressions are pairs of words used together, joined by *and*. The words always appear in the same order. (For example, *peace and quiet, black and white, fish and chips*). It would sound awkward to say *quiet and peace*.

1 Work in pairs. Complete the binomial expressions with these words. Then guess what they mean.

clear	downs	ends	figures	foremost
order	sound	sweet	tear	tribulations

1 first and _____
2 odds and _____
3 short and _____
4 trials and _____
5 safe and _____
6 facts and _____
7 law and _____
8 wear and _____
9 ups and _____
10 loud and _____

2 Put these pairs of words into the correct order with *and*.

1 gentlemen / ladies
2 black / white
3 address / name
4 salt / vinegar
5 lightning / thunder
6 there / here
7 bed / breakfast
8 forth / back

3 Complete the sentences with expressions from Activity 1.

1 Their parents were relieved when the children turned up _____ .
2 We don't have much time, so let's keep this _____ .
3 He supported his argument with interesting _____ .
4 They had their _____ , but overall they had a good relationship.
5 The insurance policy doesn't cover _____ to the equipment.

READING

4 Work in pairs. Discuss the question.

Do you know any of these superheroes? Do you know any others? What are their characteristics?

Batman   Captain America   Flash   Wonder Woman   X-Men

5 Read the article about Ms. Marvel. Which of these features of superheroes are described?

a backstory	a desire to help
a secret identity	a special costume
confidence in their own abilities	extraordinary powers

6 Work in pairs. Find these words and phrases in the article and try to guess their meaning using the context to help you. Then check your ideas in a dictionary.

Paragraph 1   groundbreaking, skyrocketed
Paragraph 2   phase, reconcile
Paragraph 3   distinctive, alien
Paragraph 4   coming-of-age, overwhelming
Paragraph 5   misfit, worthy

7 Work in pairs. Answer the questions.

1 In what way is Kamala "torn between two worlds"?
2 How does Kamala's idea of what she wants out of life change?
3 How does Kamala's story reflect "every teenager's coming-of-age crisis"?
4 What is Kamala's "dual identity" and how does she "come to terms" with it?
5 What makes the book different, according to Wilson?
6 What are the similarities between Ms. Marvel and Sana Amanat?
7 What do "misfits" and superheroes have in common?
8 In what way can Ms. Marvel be "a comfort and a joyful inspiration"?

8 MY PERSPECTIVE

Work in pairs. Discuss the questions.

1 Would you like to read a Ms. Marvel comic? Why?
2 Sana says "This character is a celebration!" What do you think she means?
3 What is the value of comic superheroes to teenagers?

CRITICAL THINKING Evaluating evidence

When writers make arguments, read carefully to see what facts they give as evidence to support them. Then you can decide how much you can trust their opinions and claims.

9 Work in pairs. Answer the questions.

1 Which of the facts support the statement from the article? How strong is the evidence? How could you check it?

   The Ms. Marvel phenomenon has skyrocketed to success.

   a The first series has consistently appeared on the *New York Times* Bestseller List.
   b The first series had seven reprintings in the first year.
   c Even boys and men have become huge fans.

2 Find evidence in the article for these claims. How strong is the evidence?

   a Kamala's "dual identity" becomes her strength. (line 41)
   b That's what makes this book different. (line 47)
   c She is first and foremost a real girl. (line 56)

Ms. Marvel
Teenage comic superhero

🎧 **54** Meet Ms. Marvel—the first female Muslim-American superhero to have her own comic book series. Ever since her first appearance in 2014, the groundbreaking Ms. Marvel phenomenon has skyrocketed to success. The
5 first series has consistently* appeared on the *New York Times* Bestseller List, and it had seven reprintings in the first year alone. Even boys and men have become huge fans, with one naming her "our new Spiderman."

So who is Ms. Marvel? We first meet her as Kamala Khan, an
10 ordinary 16-year-old high school student from New Jersey in the US and the daughter of Pakistani-American immigrants. Though respectful of her heritage, she has always felt different from her more conservative parents and feels torn between two worlds. She is going through a rebellious phase
15 and struggles to reconcile being an American teenager with the demands and expectations of her parents, whom she loves but who drive her crazy, and her peers, who don't really understand what her home life is like.

Kamala is a big fan of superheroes, and her role model is
20 Carol Danvers, the original Ms. Marvel. In the first issue, Kamala has a vision of Carol asking her what she wants out of life. Kamala immediately replies, "I want to be you." All of a sudden, she finds herself transformed into Ms. Marvel, with amazing superhuman powers that allow her to change her
25 body shape and lengthen her arms and legs at will. However, as time goes on, Kamala realizes that merely looking like her hero was not what she wanted after all. She goes on to adopt her own distinctive costume, and to use her superhuman powers first to rescue a friend from drowning, and then to
30 defend New Jersey from enemy alien invaders.

Ms. Marvel is the co-creation of Sana Amanat, Director of Content and Character Development at Marvel Comics, and writer G. Willow Wilson. For Wilson, Kamala's story reflects every teenager's coming-of-age crisis. "She's so
35 young—only 16—that the normal trials and tribulations of being in high school are still very much a part of her life, even as she's becoming something different and amazing." As she grapples with* her overwhelming new powers and gradually comes to terms with her new identity, Kamala
40 realizes that it is possible to be both herself and a superhero at the same time. Wilson believes that this "dual identity" becomes her strength and makes her tough and vulnerable simultaneously. "When you try to straddle* two worlds, one of the first things you learn is that instead of defending
45 good people from bad people, you have to spend a lot of time defending good people from each other. It's both illuminating and emotionally brutal. That's what makes this book different."

Amanat, like Kamala, struggled to find her place in society.
50 The daughter of Pakistani-American immigrants, she felt like a misfit growing up in an overwhelmingly white suburban neighborhood in New Jersey. As a fan of X-Men, she discovered the power of storytelling and the "otherness" of comic superheroes to work through her own identity crisis.
55 For Amanat, Kamala is so valuable in our storytelling culture because she is first and foremost a real girl. "I wanted her to feel accessible to everyone—to be a comfort and a joyful inspiration to women of all colors and backgrounds who are struggling with high school, insecurities, identity, and growth.
60 We wanted to help girls see they are normal and worthy, no matter what they look like or where they come from. This character is a celebration!"

consistently *continuing without change*
grapples with *tries hard to understand*
straddle *be on both sides of something*

A young man naps at the Temple of Heaven in Beijing, China.

8C A Good Night's Sleep

GRAMMAR Expressing habitual actions and states

1 Work in pairs. Discuss the questions.

1 How many hours of sleep do you average a night?
2 Has this changed since you became a teenager? If so, how and why?

2 Read a post and response on a teenage health-advice website. Then answer the questions in pairs.

Problem I'm worried that I'm not getting enough sleep lately. This never used to cause me problems on such a regular basis! When I started high school, I would always go to bed at ten and sleep like a log until the alarm went off at six the next morning. I was doing well at school and getting good grades. Now I tend to not feel sleepy until after midnight. So I'll stay up texting friends or playing computer games. On an average night, I won't fall asleep until around one or two. This means that I feel sleepy and moody the next morning. I'm always losing concentration, and I even fall asleep in classes. I'm not used to feeling like this, and I'm concerned about the effect it's having on my schoolwork and homelife.

Advice I just checked this, and what you're describing is completely normal. We usually follow the pattern of being awake during the day when it's light and asleep at night when it's dark. During adolescence, there's a tendency for this pattern to shift because the body starts to produce melatonin (a hormone that makes you feel sleepy) later at night. It means that teenagers have a natural tendency to fall asleep later, and wake up later than they did as children. Generally speaking, teenagers need about nine hours of sleep. If they don't get enough, it can have a negative impact on their mood and life. But don't worry—there are solutions!

1 Have you experienced this problem with sleep?
2 What new facts did you learn?
3 Can you think of any solutions? What are they?

3 Look at the Grammar box. Then find more examples of expressing habits or regular actions in the post and response in Activity 2.

Expressing habitual actions and states

In addition to using the simple present and simple past tenses, there are many different ways to talk about present and past habits in English.

a This ***never used to cause*** *me problems on such a regular basis!*
b *I* ***would always go*** *to bed at ten...*
c *I* ***tend to not feel*** *sleepy until after midnight.*
d *I'll* ***stay up texting*** *my friends.*

4 Choose the correct options to complete the rules. Use the post and response in Activity 2 to help you.

Use:
- *used to* and *would* (*always*) + infinitive to describe repeated actions in the past. We don't use (1) *used to / would* to describe states in the past.
- the present continuous with *always* or *forever* to describe (2) *a frequent / an occasional* action.

- *will* or *won't* + the base form for repeated actions in the (3) *future / present*.
- *be used to* + the *-ing* form to describe actions that we are (4) *accustomed / unaccustomed* to.
- the verb *tend (not)* + infinitive for (5) *states and repeated actions / states but not repeated actions*.

Check your answers on page 142. Do Activities 3–5.

5 Work in pairs. Is there a difference in meaning between the two options? If there is, explain the difference.

1 I *would / used to* go to bed at 9:00 p.m. when I was a kid.
2 Most people *tend to not / don't usually* fall asleep quickly after they've been using a computer.
3 I *used to take / am used to taking* a nap in the afternoon.
4 My mother *will often get up / often gets up* before anyone else in the house.
5 I *always oversleep. / I'm always oversleeping*.
6 Most people *usually wake up / are used to waking up* with an alarm clock.
7 I *never used to / didn't use to* stay up all night.
8 *Teenagers have a tendency / There is a tendency for teenagers* to stay in bed late on weekends.

6 Work in pairs. Make the sentences in Activity 5 true for you.

7 Work in pairs. Look at the tips for improving sleep habits. Can you suggest others? Discuss if these are true for you.

Tips for a good night's sleep
Here are some ideas that those of us in the medical profession tend to suggest to teenagers with sleep problems:

- Have a regular bedtime and stick to it.
- Exercise regularly during the day.
- Listen to relaxing music before you go to bed.
- Avoid having too much caffeine.
- Don't watch horror or action movies before you go to bed.
- Don't use electronic devices right before bedtime.

8 Work in pairs. Choose some of the statements and use them to describe yourself.

When I was a child, my parents would make me eat vegetables. I used to refuse. But I've gotten used to eating them now, and I actually like them a lot.

1 I didn't use to like them, but now I do.
2 I always do that. It drives my parents crazy.
3 I'm getting used to doing it, but it's hard.
4 I'll often do that at night, but I never used to.
5 I wasn't used to doing that.

9 CHOOSE

Choose one of the following activities.

- Work in pairs. Choose one or two of the ideas in Activity 5 or Activity 7 and write questions to find out about the past and present habits of classmates. Then ask your classmates and report on the class's habits.
- Write a blog post about a problem you have with sleep, getting up, or other routine activity, like studying or getting enough exercise. Then exchange your post with a classmate and write a reply.
- Work in groups. Compare your past and present habits in one or more of these areas.

playing video games	playing sports	reading
spending and saving money	watching TV	

Experts say that using electronic devices like tablets can harm sleep patterns.

The Mysterious Workings of the Adolescent Brain

" The adolescent brain undergoes really quite profound development, and this has implications for education. "

SARAH-JAYNE BLAKEMORE

Read about Sarah-Jayne Blakemore and get ready to watch her TED Talk. ▶ 8.0

AUTHENTIC LISTENING SKILLS

Preparing to listen

Before you listen to a talk about a new or complex topic, think about what you are going to listen to. You can do this by using clues (e.g., the title or description of the talk) and by researching the topic beforehand. This lets you focus more on general listening and not just on the complex ideas.

1 Look at the Authentic Listening Skills box. Then read the descriptions of parts of the brain. What else do you know about the human brain?

The *prefrontal cortex* is an area at the front of the brain connected with higher-level thinking.

Gray matter is a substance existing throughout the brain that consists mainly of neurons (cells that carry messages to, from, and within the brain).

The *limbic system* is a complex system of nerves in the brain that is connected to instinct and emotion.

2 Read the title of the TED Talk, the quotation, and the definitions in Activity 1. Which of these topics do you expect the speaker to mention? What might she say about them? Can you predict any others?

- The structure of the brain
- How scientists study the brain
- How adults learn
- How adolescents think and feel
- How adolescents learn

WATCH

3 Watch Part 1 of the talk. Choose the correct option, according to Sarah-Jayne. ▶ 8.1

1 In the past, people thought that the brain changed mainly in *childhood / adolescence*.

2 Nowadays, we have *better equipment / more funding* to study the brain.

3 Structural MRI helps scientists study how the brain *is formed / works*.

4 Functional MRI can reveal how the brain *works in different situations / develops*.

4 Watch Part 2 of the talk. Are the statements *true* or *false*? ▶ 8.2

1 Before the photo was taken, Michael Owen had just scored a goal.

2 Most of the fans in the photo root for Owen's team.

3 The photo shows that people often react without thinking.

4 Sarah-Jayne's experiments compare how adults and adolescents understand the thoughts and feelings of others.

5 Teens and adults think in similar ways in social situations.

5 Watch Part 3 of the talk. Choose the correct option. ▶ 8.3

In the first experiment, …
1 the man behind the shelves (the director) can see *all / some* of the objects.

2 the participant can see *all / some* of the objects.

3 the *director / participant* is asked to move some objects.

4 the participant has to *think about / ask about* which objects the director can see.

In the control experiment, …
5 there is *no / a different* director.

6 participants *have to / do not have to* move objects.

7 participants have to *think about the director's perspective / remember a rule*.

The results

8 All participants make more errors when there is *a director / no director*.

9 Children get *better / worse* at doing both tasks as they grow older.

10 In adolescence, the ability to see another person's perspective is *fully developed / still developing*.

6 Watch Part 4 of the talk. Answer the questions. ▶ 8.4

1 Which of these stereotypical teenage characteristics are mentioned?

desire to be liked by friends	indecision
moodiness risk-taking	self-consciousness

2 What are the results (a–c) of the brain features (1–3)?

1 a hypersensitive limbic system _____

2 an underdeveloped prefrontal cortex _____

3 the brain is still malleable _____

a The teenage years are a great opportunity for learning and creativity.

b Teens find it more difficult to control their impulses.

c Teens get a rewarding feeling from risk-taking.

7 **VOCABULARY IN CONTEXT**

a Watch the clips from the TED Talk. Choose the correct meaning of the words and phrases. ▶ 8.5

b Think of examples of the following things. Then compare your ideas with a partner.

1 things you have *radically changed* your views on

2 errors you are particularly *prone to* making in English

3 activities that give you *a kick*

4 an activity you need to do carefully, with *split-second* timing

8 **MY PERSPECTIVE**

Work in pairs. Choose two statements you agree with and say why.

Neuroscience should be a mandatory subject for adolescents and young adults in school.

Environment and upbringing are more important than genetics in developing a person's character.

Knowing that my brain is still developing makes me more careful about things like diet, sleep, and hobbies.

Teenagers' tendency to take risks should be seen as a positive trait.

CHALLENGE

Work in pairs. Discuss the questions.

1 Sarah-Jayne describes the development of social intelligence as the ability to understand how other people are thinking and feeling. What things do you think can help you interpret this?

2 Practice saying the sentences to demonstrate some of the states in the box. Can your partner guess your mood? Use ideas from question 1 to convey your feelings. Then continue some of the conversations.

astonished	bored	delighted
embarrassed	furious	nervous
puzzled	suspicious	upset

a This isn't mine. Someone else must've left it here.

b I just found out my test score.

c We're spending our vacation at the beach again.

d I'm going climbing tomorrow.

e You're looking very sharp today.

f I've never done anything like this before.

8E Looking on the Bright Side

Useful language

Showing understanding

What a drag / a pain.

You must have been so frustrated.

How upsetting / annoying!

I'm not surprised you feel upset / irritated.

That's totally understandable.

Offering encouragement

Well, at least…

(Look) on the bright side, …

It might not be as bad as you think.

Offering help

I'm more than happy to… , if that would help.

I could… , if that's helpful.

Let me know if you need a hand with…

Would you like me to… ?

Is there anything I can do to help?

SPEAKING

1 Work in pairs. Talk about a time when you had a problem and someone offered you help or encouragement. Were they able to see things from your perspective? Did they offer you any comforting "words of wisdom"?

2 Listen to two conversations in which a friend tries to help with a problem. Answer the questions about each conversation. 🎧 55

1 What is the problem?
2 How does the friend offer to help?

3 **PRONUNCIATION** Intonation to show understanding

Listen to the expressions for showing understanding. Which word or words carry the main stress? Do the expressions end with a falling or a rising tone? Listen again and repeat. 🎧 56

4 Look at the Useful language box. Work in pairs. Listen to five people describing problems. Respond using expressions for offering understanding or encouragement. 🎧 57

5 Work in pairs. Choose two of the situations and make up conversations. Find out more information, show understanding, and offer encouragement and help.

- I'm finding it hard to choose a college course.
- I can't seem to get to school on time these days. I keep oversleeping.
- I feel stressed out about the test next week.
- My friend keeps texting me late at night. It's really annoying!!
- It's Lucia's birthday tomorrow, and I haven't gotten her anything yet.

WRITING An essay comparing advantages and disadvantages

6 Work in pairs. Read the essay question. Discuss your views on the options.

What are the advantages and disadvantages of the different options for getting advice on how to solve a problem? Which do you think is the best? Why?

Talking to your parents   *Posting a question on an online forum*

Talking to a friend   *Talking to a professional (e.g., a teacher or doctor)*

7 Read the essay on page 152. Does the writer mention the points you discussed? What other points are mentioned?

8 Work in pairs. Find expressions in the essay that describe advantages and disadvantages. Then write a paragraph about one of the other options in Activity 6. Use expressions from the Useful language box.

9 **WRITING SKILL** Interpreting essay questions

> When you write an essay, it is important to read and analyze the question carefully.
>
> **1** Read the question at least twice.
>
> **2** Look for instruction words (e.g., *explain*) and topic words (e.g., *advice*).
>
> **3** Decide what you must include and what you can include if you want.
>
> **4** Decide what is an appropriate style.
>
> **5** Check the word count and any other instructions.

Work in pairs. Read the essay question. Interpret it using the guidelines (1–5).

You have read an online article about the best living arrangement for college students. Four of the options are mentioned below, along with some of the readers' comments. Write an essay discussing the advantages and disadvantages of two of the options (1–4). You should explain which one you think is the best option. Give reasons to support your answer. You may refer to the opinions of other readers, but you should use your own words. Write your answer in 220–260 words in the appropriate style.

1 living at home with your parents   *saves a lot of money*

2 sharing an apartment   *roommates could be messy*

3 living in college dorms   *could be noisy*

4 living alone in a studio   *peace and quiet, good for studying*

10 You are going to write an essay comparing advantages and disadvantages. Make notes for a plan with four paragraphs.

11 Write your essay. Use expressions from the Useful language box.

Useful language

Introducing advantages and disadvantages

What are the benefits of… ?

There are pros and cons to…

There are many advantages to…

However, it also has some disadvantages / drawbacks.

One possible advantage / disadvantage of… is…

The main advantage / disadvantage of… is…

This has the (possible) advantage / disadvantage of…

Another plus is…

One major drawback is…

The advantages outweigh the disadvantages.

Listing points

First of all, … / First and foremost, …

Moreover, … / In addition, …

Another benefit…

Most importantly…

Finally / Lastly / Last but not least…

Many college students choose to live in cities or on a college campus because it allows them to be around other people who share their interests.

9 A Healthy Life

People around the world participate in activities to feel healthier and connect with others. These people are doing group yoga in a park in Vilnius, Lithuania.

9A How to Stay Well

VOCABULARY Health and fitness

1 Look at the photo and read the caption. What are five ways you stay fit and healthy?

2 Work in pairs. Complete the tips for staying healthy with these words and phrases. Which of your ideas from Activity 1 are mentioned?

alert	beneficial effect	carbohydrates	detrimental effect
enhance	in moderation	intake	nutrients
nutritious	obesity	protein	refined sugar
relieve stress	sedentary lifestyle	unprocessed	well-being

Have a balanced diet. You can get all the essential (1) _____ the body needs if your diet contains foods rich in (2) _____ (e.g., fish, beans, dairy products), (3) _____ (e.g., bread, potatoes, pasta), non-saturated fats, and plenty of fruit and vegetables.

Eat (4) _____ . Overeating will make you put on weight and can lead to (5) _____ .

Eat naturally. Cut down on processed foods and food containing (6) _____ and choose (7) _____ foods such as whole grain bread and brown rice, which are more (8) _____ .

Reduce your salt (9) _____ . Too much salt can have a (10) _____ on your health and is associated with high blood pressure and heart disease.

Drink plenty of water. Staying hydrated can have a (11) _____ on your energy level and also keeps your organs and skin healthy.

Stay active and get exercise. Studies suggest that a (12) _____ (e.g., spending long periods sitting in front of the computer or television) is related to a number of illnesses later in life. Staying active is also good for your heart.

Get enough sleep. A good night's sleep can (13) _____ your mood and help you stay (14) _____ throughout the day.

Relax. Activities such as yoga or meditation or taking deep breaths can (15) _____ when you feel under pressure and help you refocus.

Practice the art of appreciation. Not only is "an attitude of gratitude" good for the people around you, but it can also increase your own emotional (16) _____ .

3 Work in pairs. Write six more tips like the ones in Activity 2. Use these words.

bright colors	junk food	kindness	laugh	smile	sunscreen

4 Complete the sentences. Then work in pairs. Compare and give reasons for your answers.

1 I should reduce my intake of _____ and eat / drink more _____ .
2 If I _____ , it will be beneficial for my well-being.
3 A nutritious meal I had recently was _____ .
4 _____ can have a detrimental effect on the health of young children.
5 People who have a sedentary lifestyle should _____ .
6 Foods such as _____ are full of nutrients.

LISTENING

5 Work in pairs. Discuss the questions, giving reasons for your opinions.

_____ Is drinking coffee bad for you? _____

_____ Is it OK to skip breakfast? _____

_____ Should you exercise every day? _____

_____ Is chocolate really a superfood? _____

_____ Can exercise improve your mood? _____

6 Listen to a radio show in which an expert responds to the questions in Activity 5. Number the questions in the order you hear them. Is the answer to each one *yes*, *no*, or *it depends*? 🎧 **58**

7 Work in pairs. Match the topics with the statements. More than one answer may be possible. Then listen again and check your ideas. 🎧 **58**

a skipping breakfast
b drinking coffee
c getting exercise
d eating chocolate

1 It might prevent an illness that affects the elderly.
2 It can be done in moderation.
3 It can make you feel less stressed.
4 You may end up with a less healthy alternative.
5 It has both beneficial and detrimental effects.
6 It could lead to problems at school.
7 It has a range of benefits for the body.
8 Variety is recommended.

8 MY PERSPECTIVE

Work in pairs. Say how much you agree with the statements and why.

1 It's hard to know what is healthy because experts' advice keeps changing.
2 It's too hard to make healthy lifestyle choices because of peer pressure.

GRAMMAR Relative clauses with prepositions

9 Match the sentences with the extracts from the radio show in the Grammar box. There are some differences between 1–3 and a–c. Why do you think they are different?

1 It can also contain sugar and fat, which can both make you put on weight.
2 Exercise can relax you, wake you up, and give you confidence, which are all really important.
3 Find an activity you're interested in.

Relative clauses with prepositions

a *Ideally, young people should find an activity in which they are interested…*
b *… physical activity can relieve stress… make you feel more alert and confident, all of which are obviously important.*
c *… it also contains sugar and fat, both of which contribute to weight gain…*

10 Work in pairs. Look at the sentences in Activity 9 and in the Grammar box. Answer the questions.

1 Which sentences contain defining relative clauses? Which contain non-defining clauses?
2 In which two positions can we put a preposition in a relative clause? Why?
3 Some of the relative clauses contain a word expressing quantity. What are these words, and what positions do they appear in?

Check your answers on page 144. Do Activities 1 and 2.

11 Read the advice to teenagers. Then rewrite it in a less formal way to email to a friend.

1 It is vital to eat breakfast every day. Try to have some cereal, fruit, yogurt, or eggs, all of which contain essential nutrients for your health.
Make sure you eat breakfast every day. Have some…
cereal, fruit, yogurt, or eggs, which are all nutritious.

2 It is essential to do some physical activity each day from which you obtain some enjoyment.
You need to get some exercise everyday, …

3 It is advisable to focus more on school subjects and activities at which you are talented.
You should focus more on subjects and activities…

4 It is a sensible idea to develop a wide circle of friends with whom you can relax and be yourself.
Why don't you make some good friends…

12 Complete the article with these relative expressions.

all of whom	both of which	half of whom
in which	many of which	some of which
the most common of which		where

According to World Health Organization (WHO) estimates, physical inactivity accounts for 3.2 million deaths globally, (1) _____ could be prevented by more active lifestyles. Other studies have shown that inactivity is a major factor in many illnesses, (2) _____ are cancer, diabetes, stroke, and heart disease. Globally, around 31 percent of adults were not active enough in 2008. Furthermore, studies have established a link between activity and dementia. A study at the University of Illinois looked at a number of older adults, (3) _____ engaged in moderate aerobic exercise. Brain scans showed that brain volume increased in this half of the group, unlike in the control half.

The countries (4) _____ people are the least active are higher income countries; inactivity is linked to insufficient exercise in free time and a sedentary lifestyle, (5) _____ are more widespread in the developed world. The WHO makes specific recommendations for children aged between five and seventeen, (6) _____ should do at least 60 minutes of moderate to intense physical activity daily. The organization suggests a number of ways (7) _____ children can get exercise, including games, sports, and household chores, (8) _____ can be easily included in a more active daily routine.

13 MY PERSPECTIVE

Work in pairs. What do you think about the advice given in this lesson? What surprised you the most? Will it make you change your habits at all? Why?

A group of friends practice parkour in Gaza City while bystanders watch.

9B Live Long and Prosper

VOCABULARY BUILDING

Adjective suffixes -able and -ible

Many adjectives in English contain the suffixes -able or -ible, which mean "can be done" (e.g., *sustainable, affordable, accessible*). Adjectives ending with -able usually have a corresponding verb (e.g., *enjoy—enjoyable, afford—affordable*), but adjectives ending in -ible often do not (e.g., *horrible, visible*).

1 Choose the correct options to complete the definitions.

1 Edible mushrooms can be *cooked / eaten*.
2 Legible handwriting can be *appreciated / read*.
3 A feasible project can be *completed / explained*.
4 An audible comment can be *laughed at / heard*.
5 An accessible building can be easily *constructed / reached*.
6 A plausible excuse can be *believed / forgiven*.

2 Match the adjectives (1–10) with the nouns (a–j). Use a dictionary if you need to. More than one alternative may be possible.

1 achievable ___*a*___   **a** goal
2 curable _____   **b** battery
3 disposable _____   **c** bottle
4 inflatable _____   **d** coat
5 memorable _____   **e** disease
6 preventable _____   **f** energy
7 rechargeable _____   **g** error
8 recyclable _____   **h** trip
9 renewable _____   **i** life jacket
10 machine-washable _____   **j** razor

READING

3 Work in pairs. Look at the photo. How old do you think these people are? Can you think of any "secrets" to living a long life?

4 Read the article and check your ideas. Which statement best summarizes the article?

1 A healthy diet can increase your life expectancy.
2 Longevity (a long life) is associated with both lifestyle and diet.
3 People living on islands tend to have a healthier lifestyle.

5 Work in pairs. Are the statements *true, false,* or *not stated*?

1 People live longer than average in Ikaria and Okinawa.
2 Most people in Ikaria and Okinawa live to be 100.

3 People in Ikaria and Okinawa do not suffer from chronic illnesses.
4 The lifestyle of Ikarians has been influenced by the island's location.
5 Many Ikarians have a vegetarian diet.
6 In Ikaria, all generations work together to fund and organize local festivals.
7 Okinawans have the highest life expectancy in the world.
8 There is a higher ratio of fast food restaurants in Okinawa than in the rest of Japan.
9 Younger Okinawans have a lower life expectancy than their elders.

6 Work in pairs. Find evidence in the article to support these conclusions.

1 Be active in your daily life.
2 Have a sense of purpose.
3 Take time to relax.
4 Belong to a community.
5 Value family life.
6 Eat a plant-based diet.
7 Don't overeat.

7 MY PERSPECTIVE

Work in pairs. Discuss the questions.

1 Do you want to live to be a centenarian? Why?
2 In what ways is the lifestyle of people in Ikaria and Okinawa similar or different from that of your community?
3 Which aspects of life in Ikaria and Okinawa do you think are the most important for good health? Why?

CRITICAL THINKING Checking facts

Some websites and publications contain information that is inaccurate, out of date, or false. Check information carefully from more than one source before accepting it as true. Use this checklist.

• Who is the writer? What experience or qualifications do they have?
• What can you find out about the purpose of the website or publication?
• Does the writer present only one side of the issue or multiple perspectives?
• Does the writer state where they got their information? Can you check it?
• When was the article written? Has the information been updated?

8 Find three claims in the article that you would like to investigate. Then investigate them on two or three websites using the checklist to determine the reliability and credibility of the source.

Vasili and Eleftheria enjoy a long life in Ikaria.

THE HEALTHIEST PLACES IN THE WORLD?

🎧 **59** We know that our genes determine only about a quarter of our life expectancy. So how do we account for the rest? People have tried to find the secrets to a long and healthy life for thousands of years. In recent years,
5 however, demographers* around the world may have finally found some promising clues. What they discovered were regions around the world where life expectancy is considerably higher than the norm and where there is a high proportion of centenarians*. These places also tend
10 to have a lower rate of preventable chronic illnesses that commonly kill people in the developed world, such as heart disease, cancer, and diabetes.

Ikaria is a small Greek island whose inhabitants live eight years longer than the world average and
15 have considerably lower dementia rates. Its relative geographical and cultural isolation and low numbers of tourists mean that, so far at least, Ikaria has remained largely unaffected by a Western way of life. Islanders live on a variant of the Mediterranean diet—rich in olive
20 oil and vegetables and low in meat and dairy products (apart from goat's milk). Researchers at the University of Athens, in Greece, also point out the health benefits of the local greens and herbs that are a part of the Ikarian diet. Their vegetables are picked wild or home-grown,
25 and they also drink green herbal tea sweetened with locally produced honey rather than a lot of coffee.

Sociability and a slow pace of life are key factors in the health of the community. Ikarians tend to wake up naturally, work in the garden, have a late lunch, take a
30 nap, and visit neighbors after sunset. At local festivals in which everyone—teenagers, parents, the elderly, young children—takes part, they combine their money to buy food and drink and give what is left over to the poor. The one old people's home on the island is only used by
35 those who have lost all their family. "It would shame us to put an old person in a home," said one resident. And as another put it, "Ikaria isn't a *me* place. It's an *us* place."

Okinawa, Japan, consists of 161 small islands some
40 1,300 km (808 miles) south of Tokyo. Researchers, like the ones at the Okinawa Centenarian Study, have found that elderly people here have the longest life expectancy in Japan, which is the world's longest-lived country. Okinawans use small plates to reduce meal portions.
45 Their diet is low in meat, fish, and dairy products but rich in other forms of protein such as beans and tofu* and also includes a high proportion of plants such as seaweed and sweet potatoes. In terms of social life, each resident is assigned at birth to a *moai*—a small social
50 network whose members are responsible for one another throughout their lives. There is no word for retirement in the Okinawan language. Instead, Okinawans' lives are governed by another principle called *ikigai*, which roughly translates as "the reason why you wake up in
55 the morning." Demographers who have visited the island have encountered an 85-year-old whose lifelong passion was his work as a fisherman, an 84-year-old training for a decathlon, a 102-year-old karate grand master, and a 102-year-old woman whose greatest joy was her great-
60 great-great-granddaughter.

However, the famed longevity of Okinawans is now under threat as a generation that grew up eating a Western diet is now reaching middle age. Japan's first fast food restaurant opened in Okinawa in 1963, and
65 it now has more fast food restaurants per person than anywhere else in the country. Today, almost 30 percent of Okinawan men die before reaching 65, and nearly half of men in their forties are obese. In the 1995 census, Okinawa had the highest longevity of all 47 prefectures
70 in Japan. By 2000, it was 26th. Could it be that the secret to longevity is to be found with an earlier generation and in a traditional lifestyle?

demographer *a scientist who studies human populations*
centenarians *people one hundred years old or older*
tofu *a form of solid protein made from soy milk*

Healthy food is a key ingredient in preventing illnesses.

9C Prevention as Cure

GRAMMAR Articles

1 Work in pairs. Read the sayings from around the world in the Grammar box. What does each one mean? Do you agree with the idea in each one? Do you have similar sayings in your language?

Articles
a *Prevention is better than cure.*
b *When the heart is at ease, the body is healthy.*
c *From the bitterness of disease man learns the sweetness of health.*
d *The greatest wealth is health.*
e *Laughter is the best medicine.*
f *Diseases of the soul are more dangerous and more numerous than those of the body.*
g *A man too busy to take care of his health is like a mechanic too busy to take care of his tools.*
h *Time, not medicine, cures the sick.*

2 Read these rules about the use of articles. Then find examples of each use in the sayings in the Grammar box.

1 Use a plural noun without an article to refer to a group in general.

2 Use an uncountable noun without an article to refer to the concept in general.

3 Use *the* with an uncountable noun to make it specific, often with a phrase that specifies it.

4 Use *the* with a singular noun in more formal contexts to refer to all examples of the noun.

5 Use *a/an* to refer to a single example of a group.

6 Use *the* with certain adjectives to refer to a group of people.

Check your answers on page 144. Do Activities 3 and 4.

3 Work in pairs. Which of these health nouns can be both countable and uncountable? For those that can be both, is there a difference in meaning?

activity	checkup	cure	diet
exercise	health	illness	life
medicine	scan	well-being	youth

4 Work in pairs, A and B. Student A completes Text A, and Student B completes Text B. Use with *the, a/an,* or — (no article).

A Preventive medicine

(1) _____ preventive medicine, or (2) _____ preventive healthcare, is not about giving patients (3) _____ cure; it is about enabling (4) _____ people to stay healthy. Many traditional forms of (5) _____ medicine, such as Chinese acupuncture, are based on preventing (6) _____ illness and strengthening (7) _____ immune system. Nowadays it takes the form of giving (8) _____ information on how to live (9) _____ healthy life or (10) _____ advice on exercise and diet. (11) _____ doctors also attempt to detect (12) _____ illness before symptoms emerge, with regular checkups, for example.

B Wearable technology

More and more people are wearing technology to monitor and regulate their own health. (1) _____ wearable fitness trackers, which are worn on (2) _____ wrist like (3) _____ watch, record (4) _____ data on (5) _____ person's activities (e.g., calories burned, steps taken, hours of sleep). This is then transmitted to (6) _____ app on their smartphone. (7) _____ studies have found that in some cases, using (8) _____ wearable technology can lead to (9) _____ increase in (10) _____ physical activity of up to 25 percent and (11) _____ reduction in (12) _____ blood pressure.

5 Tell your partner about what you learned. Which way of preventing illness described in each text do you think is better? Why?

6 Now look at each other's texts. Do you agree with the articles your partner used?

7 Work in pairs. Read about other types of preventive health technology. Add *a/an* or *the* where appropriate. What conditions could these devices help with?

1 This is free, online tool which can help you create daily personalized diet. Just type in information about your age, weight, and health goals.

2 This is wearable electronic device that measures air pollution and gives warning on your smartphone when you should go inside.

3 Research is being conducted in order to develop smart contact lenses that monitor user's blood-sugar level. Lenses then send data to person's smartphone and their doctor.

4 This is small recorder that is inserted under skin to record patient's heart rhythm.

8 Work in groups. Discuss the questions.

1 What are the advantages and disadvantages of the preventive devices described in Activity 7? Which would you be interested in using? Why?

2 What other wearable technology would you like to see? Why? How would it be useful?

3 Do you wear a fitness tracker, or do you know someone who does? If so, how helpful is it? If not, would you like to wear one? Why?

9 CHOOSE

Choose one of the following activities.

- Find reliable information from two or three sources about a type of food or drink that is good or bad for you. Summarize your findings in a short report and read it to the class. Pay attention to article use.

- Work in pairs. Create either a health brochure or a poster for a campaign to promote healthy living for teenagers. Show your brochure or poster to another pair. Pay attention to article use.

- Look at some ingredients that are often promoted as essential for a happy life. Choose the three that you think are the most important, thinking of examples from your own life or the lives of people you know. Work in groups and discuss your ideas.

ability to deal with life's difficulties	awareness
being part of something bigger	exercise
focusing on positive emotions	giving to other people
having a clear purpose	learning new things
self-acceptance	strong relationships

Young runners check their fitness trackers before a run.

of technology to change lives for the better. "

KENNETH SHINOZUKA

Read about Kenneth Shinozuka and get ready to watch his TED Talk. ▶ **9.0**

AUTHENTIC LISTENING SKILLS

Understanding fast speech

When you listen to fast speech, listen for key words that can help you understand the gist (main idea). If you are listening to or watching a recording (e.g., online videos or streamed TV or movies), play a short part several times. See if you can understand more each time. Remember that weak forms of common words (e.g., *the, a, an, of, at, to*) are often said very quickly.

1 Look at the Authentic Listening Skills box. Then predict which words complete the extract from the TED Talk.

My family (1) _____ experienced firsthand
(2) _____ struggles (3) _____ caring
(4) _____ Alzheimer's patient. Growing up
(5) _____ family (6) _____ three generations,
I've always been very close (7) _____ my grandfather.

2 Listen and check your ideas. How are the missing words pronounced? ∩ **60**

3 Listen to three more extracts from the TED Talk. You will hear each section several times. Complete what Kenneth says. Try to guess the words you can't hear. ∩ **61**

1 As the number of Alzheimer's patients _____ overwhelming societal challenge.
2 When I was _____ suddenly got lost.
3 My aunt _____ the bed.

WATCH

4 Work in pairs. Discuss the questions.

1 What do you know about Alzheimer's disease?
2 What challenges might people who care for those with Alzheimer's face?

5 Watch Part 1 of the talk. Are the sentences *true, false,* or *not stated*? ▶ **9.1**

1 Alzheimer's disease is currently the biggest health problem among old people in America.
2 By the middle of this century, there will be twice as many Alzheimer's patients as now.
3 Kenneth's family did not know his grandfather had Alzheimer's until he got lost.
4 His grandfather's illness has gotten worse in the last two years.
5 Kenneth was worried about both his grandfather and his aunt.
6 Kenneth's invention involves sending a signal from a sock to a smartphone.
7 Kenneth wanted his grandfather to be able to sleep better.

6 Watch Part 2 of the talk. Number the statements in the order that Kenneth mentions them. ▶ **9.2**

_____ Kenneth was too young to implement his plan.
_____ An elderly friend was badly hurt in a fall.
_____ Kenneth was inspired to use sensors to help the elderly.
_____ Kenneth designed a system to detect falls.

TEDTALKS

7 Watch Part 3 of the talk. Match the stage in the invention process with things that Kenneth used. There may be more than one for each stage. ▶ 9.3

1 He created a sensor to put on patients' feet. _____
2 He designed an electric circuit. _____
3 He coded a smartphone app. _____

a YouTube
b a small battery
c ink particles that conduct electricity
d a thin material
e textbooks
f Bluetooth technology

8 Watch Part 4 of the talk. Complete the summary. Then watch again to check your answers. ▶ 9.4

Kenneth designed two different (1) _____ for his device. One was designed to fit inside a (2) _____ , and the other was designed to be worn on the patient's (3) _____ . Since his grandfather started using the device, it has had a 100 percent (4) _____ . Kenneth has tested his invention at residential homes and now hopes to make it into a (5) _____ . He has discovered that not everybody is willing to (6) _____ at night. He is now conducting research into how often patients (7) _____ at night, and how this relates to their (8) _____ during the day. He still remembers how his invention helped him know when his grandfather (9) _____ out of bed, and this has inspired him to use (10) _____ to change people's lives and help them to be healthier.

9 VOCABULARY IN CONTEXT

a Watch the clips from the TED Talk. Choose the correct meaning of the words and phrases. ▶ 9.5

b Think of an example of the following things. Then compare your ideas with a partner.
1 something you have *experienced firsthand* that has taught you a useful lesson about life
2 people who used to *keep an eye on* you
3 an interest that *stems from* shared family activities
4 a skill you have learned from an online *tutorial*

10 MY PERSPECTIVE

Work in pairs. Discuss the questions.
1 In what ways have your grandparents or older relatives helped you and your family throughout your life?
2 What do you do, or what could you do, to improve their quality of life?

CHALLENGE

Work in groups. Read the situation. Discuss the pros and cons of each option. What would you advise your family to do? Why?

Your grandparent lives alone, is getting less mobile and more frail, and finds it hard to do everyday tasks. Your parents work full-time, and there is no spare room in your house. Your grandparent has two more children; one, who is single, lives in a distant city where your grandparent knows no one, and the other, who does not work, is in poor health and has little contact with the family. Your grandparent could:

a come and live with your family.
b live with another relative.
c share living arrangements among the relatives.
d move into a residential care home.
e continue to live at home with specialist help.

9E Stronger Together

WRITING A proposal

1 How much involvement do elderly people have in your school? How could this be increased? What could the benefits be?

2 Work in pairs. Read the proposal on page 153. Answer the questions.

1 What concerns did the elderly people express?
2 What opportunities did they identify?
3 How do the proposal's suggestions benefit both the elderly and the young?
4 Is the situation that the writer describes similar in your country?

3 **WRITING SKILL** Impersonal style

> In reports, proposals, and academic writing, it is common to use impersonal structures instead of personal pronouns such as *I*, *we*, or *you*. These include: passive verbs, a gerund (*-ing* form) as subject, *there is / are*, and *it is / would be* + adjective.

a Find examples of impersonal structures in the proposal on page 153.

b Rewrite these sentences in a more impersonal style using the words in parentheses.
1 Perhaps we could schedule regular movie nights. (possible)
2 We don't have enough volunteers. (a lack)
3 We should speak clearly and loudly in case they are hard of hearing. (helpful)
4 If we organized events, they could meet more people. (organizing)
5 We could devote one day a month to visiting people. (devoted)

4 Choose one of these topics to write a proposal about. Discuss problems with the current situation and make suggestions for improving it. Use phrases from the Useful language box.

- Providing healthier food at your school cafeteria
- Creating a buddy system between older and younger students
- Making the school or local community feel more like an *us* place

SPEAKING Talking about proposals

5 Work in pairs. Look again at the proposal on page 153. Can you think of any potential problems or issues with it?

6 Listen to someone describing and answering questions about the proposal. What three issues or potential problems are mentioned? What solutions are proposed? 🎧 62

7 Listen again. Which expressions from the Useful language box do you hear? How did the speakers respond enthusiastically to suggestions? 🎧 62

8 **PRONUNCIATION** Intonation in responses

a Listen to someone responding to proposals. Which word or words are stressed? Does the speaker's voice fall or rise at the end? Why? 🎧 63
1 That's a great idea!
2 What a fantastic idea!
3 I really like the idea of taking them on trips.
4 That sounds like an excellent way of helping!
5 It's a good idea in principle, …
6 Yes, but the problem is…
7 You'd need to keep in mind that…
8 It's worth remembering that…

b Listen to the sentences again. Repeat the intonation. 🎧 63

9 Work in pairs. Use phrases from the Useful language box to respond to these comments on the proposal on page 153.
1 Some older people may have difficulty hearing.
2 Some students don't know what to say to older people.
3 How could students visit older people in their homes?
4 We'd need to organize a schedule.
5 Some older people may have difficulty getting up or around.

10 Work in groups. Take turns describing the proposals you wrote in Activity 4. You should respond to each other's ideas and ask questions. Use phrases from the Useful language box. Decide which proposal you like best and why.

> **Useful language**
>
> **Summarizing proposals**
> *Basically / In essence what we're aiming to do is…*
> *Our goal is to…*
> *What we're proposing to do, specifically, is…*
> *Our first / second recommendation is…*
>
> **Responding to proposals**
> *It's a good idea in principle, provided that…*
> *Yes, but the problem is…*
> *You'd need to keep in mind that…*
> *It's worth remembering that…*
> *I wonder how feasible it would be to…*

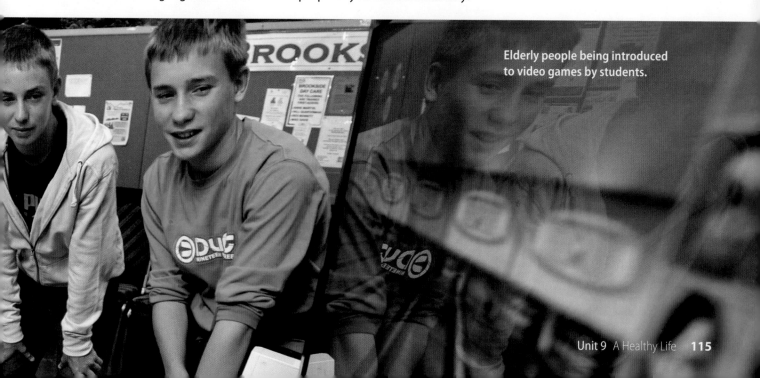

Elderly people being introduced to video games by students.

10 Ideas

IN THIS UNIT, YOU...

- talk about how to express ideas.
- read about the power of photography to change people's perspectives.
- learn about how people respond to new ideas.
- watch a TED Talk about the secret to giving an excellent talk.
- write a review about a performance that changed your perspective.

People line up to speak and ask questions at a TED event in Banff, Canada.

10A Expressing Ideas

VOCABULARY Making your point

1 Work in pairs. Look at the photo and read the caption. When and where do you normally ask questions? Have you ever asked questions in public?

2 Read the quiz about expressing ideas. Match the meanings (1–10) with the words or phrases in bold in the quiz. There are six extra words and phrases. What do these words mean? Use a dictionary if necessary.

1 specialized vocabulary	**6** hand or body movements
2 support	**7** in a few words
3 forget my point	**8** give more information
4 exact	**9** comparisons explaining something
5 say again with different words	**10** get across

1 How do you make sure your listeners understand you?
  a I **make eye contact** to make sure they haven't tuned me out.
  b I ask questions to make sure they are still with me.
  c I don't. I just keep talking and hope for the best.

2 What do you do to **convey** your ideas to listeners?
  a I speak clearly and **concisely** with examples to **back up** my ideas.
  b I avoid **jargon** and explain any difficult words.
  c I use **analogies** to explain complex ideas.

3 How good are your communication skills?
  a I use **gestures** and **facial expressions** to help get my point across.
  b I vary my intonation to **engage** my listeners' **attention**.
  c I try to be open-minded and listen to others' points of view.

4 How do you react if someone misunderstands or **misinterprets** you?
  a I **rephrase** my answer using simpler and more **precise** words.
  b I **elaborate on** my point with different examples.
  c I tend to freeze, and my **mind goes blank**.

5 What do you do if someone interrupts or makes an irrelevant comment?
  a I try to **stick to the point** and not get distracted.
  b I sometimes panic and **lose my train of thought**.
  c I pause to think of the best way to respond.

3 Work in pairs. Answer the questions in Activity 2 so they are true for you. You can agree with more than one answer. Then compare your answers.

4 Listen to six extracts. Choose the correct statement to describe each extract.
🎧 **64**

_____ She lost her train of thought.
_____ His mind went blank.
_____ She elaborated on her idea.
_____ He was concise and to the point.
_____ She rephrased her idea.
_____ He used jargon.

5 MY PERSPECTIVE

Work in pairs. Discuss the questions.

1 Has your mind ever gone blank when you were trying to express an idea? What did you do?
2 How can someone convey confidence or a lack of confidence nonverbally?
3 What effect does other people's body language have on you?

LISTENING

6 Work in pairs. You are going to listen to Dr. Emily Grossman talk about how she explains the concept of electricity to students. Study the description of electricity. Label the diagram with the underlined words.

Electricity is a kind of energy caused by the movement of <u>electrons</u>, which are tiny parts of an atom, around a <u>circuit</u>. A circuit is a closed path that allows an electric charge to move from one place to another. One way of creating energy is by attaching a <u>battery</u> to the circuit. The flow of electricity around the circuit is called the <u>current</u>, and the rate of flow is measured in units called *coulombs*. The size of a current depends partly on the voltage of the battery. *Voltage* refers to the amount of power in the electricity flow (and it is measured in units called *joules*).

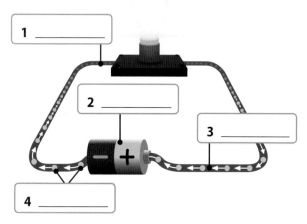

1 _____

2 _____

3 _____

4 _____

7 Listen to the interview. Answer the questions. 🎧 **65**

1 What three tips for conveying ideas does Emily give?
2 What analogy does Emily use to describe electricity? What do you remember about it?
3 Does she think that analogies are more effective than examples or visuals?

8 Work in pairs. Match the parts of the analogy to the scientific terms. Use a dictionary if necessary. Listen and check your ideas. 🎧 **66**

1 racetrack _____
2 a horse _____
3 hairs _____
4 horses per second _____
5 stable ___f___
6 bales of hay _____
7 number of bales of hay _____

a electrons
b circuit
c a coulomb
d current
e voltage
f battery
g joules

9 Listen to the end of the interview again. What types of visuals does Emily mention? Why is each effective? 🎧 **67**

10 Work in pairs. How successful was Emily's analogy for you? Do you feel like you understand electricity more?

GRAMMAR Advanced question types

11 Look at the questions from the interview in the Grammar box. Can you remember the answers?

Question forms

a *How do you think people can get their ideas across most effectively?*

b *Could you tell us how you use analogies to help you explain things?*

c *You do what?*

d *Isn't it hard to think of analogies for some situations?*

e *You think analogies work better than, say, examples or visuals, don't you?*

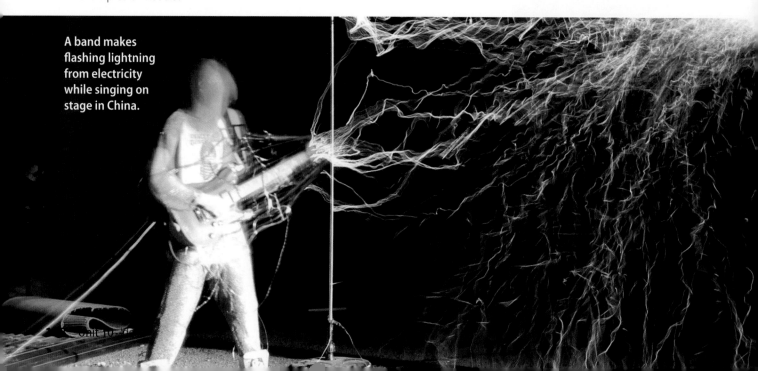

A band makes flashing lightning from electricity while singing on stage in China.

12 Match the questions in the Grammar box with a question type.

1 a tag question _____
2 an echo or reply question _____
3 a negative question _____
4 a polite indirect question _____
5 an indirect opinion question _____

13 Work in groups. What do you know about these question types? Answer the questions.

1 How is the tag question in the Grammar box different from most tag questions? What answer does this expect?
2 What kind of answer do we expect to an echo question?
3 How do we make negative questions? Does the negative question in the Grammar box expect a *yes* or *no* answer?
4 How does the word order change in indirect questions? Do they always have a question mark?
5 Is there anywhere else you could place *do you think* in the indirect opinion question?

Check your answers on page 146. Do Activities 1–3.

14 Complete these questions with one or two words. Then listen to an interview and compare your answers. 🎧 68

1 _____ think that gestures are international?
2 _____ tell us something about differences in the meaning of gestures?
3 So you'd say the biggest issue with using the wrong gesture is causing confusion, _____
4 I'm sorry, _____ considered what?
5 We aren't necessarily conscious of our gestures, though, _____
6 What do _____ the answer is?

15 PRONUNCIATION   Question intonation

a Listen to the questions. Does each one end with a rising or falling tone? 🎧 69

b What can a rising tone and a falling tone mean? Match meanings to the questions in Activity 14. You can use some more than once. 🎧 69
_____ I'm surprised by this.
_____ I really want information.
_____ I'm quite sure of this, but I'd like confirmation.
_____ I'm asking for agreement.

16 Listen to the interview again. Take notes on the answers to the questions in Activity 14. 🎧 68

17 Work in pairs. Ask and answer the questions in Activity 14 to recreate the interview.

18 Rewrite the sentences to make one of the question types in Activity 12. Use the words in parentheses.

1 Do you use many gestures when you speak? (Could you?)
2 I'm sorry. I'm not sure I understand what you said exactly. (what?)
3 Why do these gestures help people to understand? (do you think?)
4 It's easier just to rely on speech when we explain something, right? (Isn't?)
5 So, would you use fewer gestures when you talk to someone from another country? (you would)

19 Work in pairs. Make a list of gestures you frequently use when you speak and what they mean. Then discuss your gestures with another pair. Try to use three of the questions from Activity 18 or similar questions.

10B Iconic Images

VOCABULARY BUILDING

Adjectives ending in -ful and -less

Some English adjectives end in -ful or -less (e.g., thankful – full of thanks; homeless – without a home). Some are paired (e.g., powerful / powerless; hopeful / hopeless), and some are not. We can say skillful (with a lot of skill) but not ~~skillless~~, and jobless (without a job) but not ~~jobful~~.

1 Which of these words can be followed by a) both -ful and -less, b) only -ful, or c) only -less?

doubt	event	fear	forget	fruit
heart	meaning	point	regret	tact
taste	thought	waste	worth	

2 Work in pairs. Tell your partner about one of the options.

1 an eventful / fruitless journey you have taken
2 a time when you felt doubtful / regretful
3 a fruitful / pointless discussion you have taken part in
4 a tactless / meaningful remark someone made to you
5 someone you know who is forgetful / thoughtful
6 a place you know with tasteful / tasteless decor

READING

3 Work in pairs. Look at the photo. Answer the questions.

1 What does the photo show?
2 What do you think is special about it?
3 Why do you think it is called "Earthrise"?
4 What thoughts and feelings does the photo inspire in you?

4 Read the article. Check your answers to Activity 3, questions 1–3.

5 Work in pairs. Read the article again. Choose the option that is <u>not</u> indicated in the article.

1 The writer says that photographs can _____
   a show beautiful and poetic images.
   b help us see beyond our normal experiences.
   c change our beliefs and attitudes.

2 The Apollo crew _____
   a was the first to travel around the moon.
   b had been told not to take photographs of the Earth.
   c were surprised by the Earth's beauty.

3 The "Earthrise" photograph _____
   a was the first photo of the Earth taken on the mission.
   b was shot without planning or preparation.
   c showed the Earth as more beautiful than the moon.

4 After seeing the Earth from space, crew members _____
   a turned their attention to the scheduled mission.
   b felt a longing to return to Earth.
   c experienced strong emotions.

5 "Earthrise" has become an iconic image because _____
   a it was widely distributed and viewed.
   b it showed the effects of pollution and loss of resources.
   c it made people think about the planet in a new way.

6 Work in pairs. Answer the questions.

1 Why is "Earthrise" described as "groundbreaking"?
2 What new perspective on the Earth did it give?
3 What is the powerful message that it conveys?
4 Why did it inspire people to protect the planet?
5 What did you find most surprising or inspiring?

CRITICAL THINKING Understanding quotations

Writers sometimes quote other opinions to back up or elaborate on a point. The words used to introduce the quotation can also persuade readers that the opinion is true. Read carefully and make up your own mind whether or not to agree with an opinion. Use the evidence presented.

7 Work in pairs. Answer the questions.

1 Read the sentences beginning with "According to…" (line 6) and "As National Geographic photographer…" (line 15). Which way of introducing the quotation suggests that the writer agrees with it?

2 Choose the more persuasive option.
   a He explains / suggests that "images speak a universal language."
   b She argues / demonstrates that "photographs can transport us to other worlds."
   c He says / points out that "the best images help us see our lives from a different perspective."

3 Find more quotes by Lovell and Borman in paragraphs 3 and 4. How persuasively are their opinions presented? Do you agree with them? Why?

8 MY PERSPECTIVE

Work in pairs. Tell each other about a photo that is special to you or that you are proud of.

The photo "Earthrise" was taken from the Apollo 8 spacecraft on the morning of December 24, 1968.

EARTHRISE

🎧 70 A picture, so the saying goes, is worth a thousand words. But in a world in which millions of photographs are taken and uploaded every minute and we are exposed to a daily avalanche of pictures
5 on our computer screens, what is the value of a single image? According to Martin Barnes, Senior Curator of photographs at the Victoria and Albert Museum in London, "Great photographs are like visual poetry. They neatly capture and express a situation or emotion
10 that transcends the everyday." By capturing a single moment and holding it absolutely still, a photograph can convey a powerful idea in a universal language. But more than that, images can transport us to new places and help us see our lives from a different
15 perspective. As National Geographic photographer Aaron Huey says, "Photography has the power to undo your assumptions about the world."

Nowhere is this more clearly illustrated than in "Earthrise," the groundbreaking picture which, though
20 not the first ever photo of the Earth from space, transformed people's attitudes to a world they had taken for granted up to that point. It all started on the morning of December 21, 1968, when the crew of Apollo 8—Frank Borman, Jim Lovell, and Bill Anders—
25 set out for humanity's first manned mission to orbit the moon. With the excitement of lunar exploration, photographs of Earth were not included at all in the official NASA plans. Yet when, on Christmas Eve, and on their fourth orbit, the crew emerged from behind
30 the moon's dark side, they saw in front of them an astounding sight—an exquisite blue sphere hanging in the blackness of space.

"Look at that picture over there. Here's the Earth coming up. Wow! That is pretty!", exclaimed Anders. It
35 is thought that at this point Borman snapped a black-and-white image of the scene. "Hey, don't take that. It's

not scheduled," Anders joked. He then added, "Hand me that roll of color, quick." After a brief scramble to find the film, Anders shot a color photograph. It
40 showed the Earth as a blue planet, partially covered by white swirling clouds and contrasting starkly with the empty backdrop of space and the dead, gray lunar surface, which Borman described as "a vast, lonely, forbidding expanse of nothing." Looking back on the
45 mission, Anders observed, "I was immediately almost overcome by the thought that here we came all this way to the moon, and yet the most significant thing we're seeing is our own home planet." Borman also said that glimpsing Earth was "the most beautiful,
50 heart-catching sight of my life, one that sent a torrent of nostalgia, of sheer homesickness, surging through me."

The true power of photographs lies in what is done with them after they are created. Within just a few
55 months of the shot being taken, millions of people on Earth had seen the picture, which soon became one of the most iconic images of the century. "Earthrise" gave a new perspective on the planet at a time of great social and political unrest. As Borman
60 remarked, "Raging nationalistic interests, famines, wars, pestilences don't show from that distance. From out there, it really is 'one world.'" Moreover, many people credit the birth of the environmental movement and the first Earth Day celebration in 1970, to this view of
65 the planet from outer space—a view that showed its smallness, fragility, and vulnerability. People realized there was no other sanctuary in the solar system, and so they needed to conserve Earth's resources and protect it from pollution and destruction. Lovell
70 concluded, "It was the most beautiful thing there was to see in all the heavens. People down here don't realize what they have."

Albert Einstein at home

10C Ideas Worth Spreading

GRAMMAR Subordinate and participle clauses

1 Work in pairs. Read about new ideas. Discuss the questions.

New ideas are often met with resistance and criticism, or even rejected, when they are first proposed. For example, when Thomas Edison first had the idea for the electric light bulb, experts in the scientific community couldn't imagine why it would ever work. Even Einstein's theory of relativity was initially ridiculed.

1 Can you think of other ideas (in science, society, or everyday life) that are now widely accepted, but which were initially rejected?

2 What can people do nowadays to gain widespread acceptance of their ideas?

2 Read the text. Could Ignaz Semmelweis have done more to gain acceptance of his idea?

Please wash your hands

Ignaz Semmelweis, known as "the savior of mothers," was a nineteenth-century Hungarian physician. Having worked for a number of years as Director of Maternity Care at Vienna General Hospital, Semmelweis became concerned with the high number of mothers dying at the hospital shortly after childbirth. Since he had noticed that fewer mothers died when giving birth in hospital wards run by midwives,* he wondered if this might be due to infection being spread by doctors who were working with dead bodies before delivering babies. He therefore proposed the radically simple idea that doctors should wash their hands before they delivered babies. Once implemented, this practice drastically reduced the mortality rate. However, his colleagues were offended by his idea, refusing to believe they could be responsible for the deaths of their patients. Not being able to persuade his colleagues, Semmelweis argued with many of them and eventually left the hospital.

Although his hypothesis was supported by the statistical analysis he conducted in the 1840s, Semmelweis did not publish his results until 1861, only a few years before his death in 1865. Later in the century, scientists such as Pasteur and Koch proved the link between germs and disease, leading to the request now repeated every day across the world: "Please wash your hands."

midwives *people trained in helping women give birth*

3 Work in pairs. Look at the examples from the text in the Grammar box. Answer the questions.

Subordinate and participle clauses

a *Having worked for a number of years as Director of Maternity Care, ...*

b *... the high number of mothers dying at the hospital...*

c *Since he had noticed that...*

d *... fewer mothers died when giving birth in hospital wards run by midwives, ...*

e *... doctors should wash their hands before they delivered babies.*

f *Once implemented, this practice drastically reduced the mortality rate.*

g *..., refusing to believe they could be responsible for the deaths of their patients.*

h *Not being able to persuade his colleagues, ...*

1 Which examples are participle clauses? Which are subordinate clauses? What are the differences between them?

2 Which of the participle clauses are active? Which are passive? What is the rule?

3 Which example is negative? How do we make participles negative?

4 Which participle indicates the past?

5 Which ones are reduced relative clauses?

6 The two subordinate clauses express a notion (e.g., purpose, contrast). Which notions do they express? Do the participle clauses express notions?

Check your answers on page 146. Do Activities 4–6.

4 Work in pairs. Delete the incorrect option in the sentence. Why is it incorrect?

1 *Having worked / Worked* as a physician, Semmelweis noticed that many mothers were dying after childbirth.

2 *Offended / Having offended* by his idea, people rejected it as untrue.

3 His colleagues refused to wash their hands, not *realizing / realized* the danger.

4 *Discouraging / Discouraged* by the hostile reception to his views, he left the hospital.

5 *Proved / Being proved / Once proved* by scientific evidence, the link between germs and disease was widely accepted.

5 Complete the text about an innovative businesswoman with the correct form of the verbs in parentheses. There may be more than one correct answer.

Born and (1) _____ (raise) in Monterrey, Mexico, Blanca Treviño is one of Latin America's most well-known business innovators. (2) _____ (study) computer science in Monterrey, she joined Softtek, the Mexican IT company, which, (3) _____ (lead) by Treviño as its President, has become the most prominent IT company in Latin America. The company is now also (4) _____ (enjoy) success in the United States. (5) _____ (promote) both Latin American information technology and women in business, Treviño has become a popular speaker at international conferences. She was also once (6) _____ (feature) in CNN's Leading Women series. Now (7) _____ (know) beyond her home country, Treviño has been identified by several media publications as one of the most influential executives in Latin America.

6 Work in pairs. Student A looks at the A prompts, and Student B looks at the B prompts. Using the prompts and any other information you can find, write "The story of an idea." Then read your story to your partner. What are the similarities and differences?

A discovery of penicillin—Alexander Fleming / returned from vacation / accidentally left dish with bacteria open / green mold growing / bacteria hadn't spread / mold not poisonous / turned into penicillin / saved many lives

B how Cornflakes came about—Dr. John Kellogg / worked in US hospital / patients on strict diets and bland food / Kellogg cooked wheat / left for too long / went stale / not much money for meals / flattened wheat and toasted it / served to patients / proved very popular

7 CHOOSE Choose one of the activities below.

- Research a famous "person of ideas" (for example, Gabriel Garcia Marquez, Mary Wollstonecraft, King Sejong, Muhammad Yunus, Ellen Ochoa, or somebody else). Make a poster and include a short description of the person's life and the development of their ideas.

- Write a short story called "A change of mind." Answer these questions. Then read your story to a partner.

  Who had the idea? What was it? Why was it good? How did the person pursue it? What was the final result?

- Work in pairs. Think of an idea that people disagree about nowadays (for example, the use of animals in science). Make notes about the idea. Then discuss it with another pair.

**Blanca Treviño, President of
Mexican IT company Softtek**

AUTHENTIC LISTENING SKILLS

Collaborative listening

Often when you listen, you aren't alone. People naturally discuss what they have just heard because it is common for different members of an audience to hear and remember different things. By comparing notes and ideas, you can find that as a group you understand something better than any one individual.

1 Look at the Authentic Listening Skills box. Then work in groups. Listen to the beginning of the TED Talk. 🎧 **71**

Student A: listen and note any references to ways of giving a TED Talk

Student B: listen and note any references to Chris's experience

Student C: listen and note any information you want

2 Compare your notes. Listen again and check. 🎧 **71**

3 Listen to another extract from the talk without taking notes. Then compare what you heard in your groups. Did you remember the same information? Listen again and check. 🎧 **72**

WATCH

4 Watch Part 1 of the talk. Make notes to answer the questions. ▶ **10.1**

1 What is the danger of trying to follow a fixed formula?
2 What "gift" do successful speakers give their audience?
3 What do Haley's and the listeners' brains have in common?

4 What are the components of the idea in Haley's mind?
5 How is Haley's idea "teleported" into people's minds?
6 How does Chris define "an idea"?

5 Watch Part 2 of the talk. Match the speakers with their topics. Two topics are not used. ▶ **10.2**

1 Sir Ken Robinson _____
2 Elora Hardy _____
3 Chimamanda Adichie _____

a an innovation in construction
b the importance of literature
c understanding cultural complexity
d how to raise stronger children
e how to improve schools

6 Complete the summary. Watch Part 2 again to check your answers. ▶ **10.2**

Chris Anderson says that everyone's mind contains many ideas which are (1) _____ to create an individual (2) _____ . The different (3) _____ of this make people react and see things differently, so they should be very (4) _____ . It is important to convey ideas clearly because they can (5) _____ the way people understand reality and (6) _____ both their behavior and civilization as a whole.

7 Watch Part 3 of the talk. What are the four key ingredients of a good TED Talk? ▶ **10.3**

8 Watch Part 3 of the talk again. Choose the correct options to complete ideas from Chris's guidelines. ▶ 10.3

1 You should focus on *a single idea / a few important ideas*.
2 It's helpful to *elaborate on / check that the audience understands* your main idea.
3 You should *present your idea logically / help listeners realize what they don't know*.
4 You should *explain your concepts carefully / build on the audience's current knowledge*.
5 Metaphors can *be very helpful / sometimes be confusing*.
6 It's a good idea to *edit your talk carefully beforehand / rehearse your talk*.
7 An idea worth sharing is *practical for / relevant to* your audience.
8 A good idea is one that *inspires large or small changes / changes everything*.

9 **VOCABULARY IN CONTEXT**

a Watch the clips from the TED Talk. Choose the correct meaning of the words and phrases. ▶ 10.4

b Think of examples of the following things. Then compare your ideas in pairs.
1 the elements that *make up* a good story
2 a piece of news or an event you found *startling*
3 a time when someone *saw through* an excuse you made
4 how you might *bridge the communication gap* when speaking to someone who doesn't speak your language

10 **MY PERSPECTIVE**

Look back at the TED Talks you have seen in this course. Choose your favorite talk. Work in pairs. Explain why you have chosen that talk.

CHALLENGE

Look at the strategies for giving a good presentation. Choose the five you consider to be the most important and think about how to justify your ideas.

- Keep it short and simple.
- Think about your audience.
- Use visual aids (pictures, objects, charts, or slides with key phrases).
- Anticipate questions.
- Rehearse and time your presentation.
- Speak at a normal speed and volume.
- Look at the audience and vary your eye contact.
- Vary your intonation.
- Explain key words.
- Check understanding.
- Relax and be aware of your body language.
- Use gestures to help explain your ideas and connect with the audience.

Work in groups and compare your ideas.

10E Changing Perspectives

Useful language

Introducing your presentation

I'm going to talk to you / tell you about…

I want to share with you…

Starting

Put your hands up if…

I want to start by asking…

So, let's start by looking at…

Highlighting important points

Now, …

So, why / what…? Well, …

As you can see, …

The really interesting / strange thing is that…

And / But more than that, …

Finishing

Thank you for listening.

If you have any questions, I'll do my best to answer them.

Are there any questions?

SPEAKING

1 Work in pairs. Discuss the questions.

1 Have you ever kept a diary? What did you write about? When did you write it? Do you still write it?
2 What could be the rewards and challenges of keeping a diary?

2 Listen to a talk about keeping a diary. Answer the questions. 🎧 **73**

1 How does the speaker engage the audience's attention and interest?
2 Label the sections of the presentation in the order you hear them.

_____ research on keeping a diary

_____ a life-changing experience

_____ the writer's first diary

3 Work in pairs. Discuss what you can remember about each section. Then listen again to check your ideas and add more information. 🎧 **73**

4 Match the signpost expressions with their uses. You can use one more than once.

1 Turning now to (research), …
2 To elaborate on that, …
3 To expand a little on that…
4 To digress for a moment, …
5 To go back to (my diary), …
6 To summarize, …
7 To illustrate that, …

a to give an example
b to start a new section
c to return to an earlier point
d to repeat the main points
e to talk about an unrelated topic
f to give more information

5 **PRONUNCIATION** Intonation of signpost expressions

Listen to the expressions in Activity 4. Does the speaker's voice go up or down at the end of each one? Listen again and repeat. 🎧 **74**

6 Plan a presentation. Follow this procedure.

1 Think of an experience you've had which has changed your perspective.
2 Decide on the content for your talk and structure it clearly. Use the four suggestions from Chris's TED Talk. Use expressions from the Useful language box.
3 Think of a good opening line.

Singer Juan Luis Guerra performs onstage during the 16th Latin GRAMMY Awards in Las Vegas, Nevada.

7 Work in groups. Give your presentations. Ask questions at the end.

WRITING A review

8 Work in pairs. Talk about a concert, play, or sports event you have been to that made an impression on you. What made it special?

9 Read the review of a concert on page 154. How did the concert change the writer's perspective on life and why?

10 **WRITING SKILL** Reference

> Like *the*, you can use *this* or *these* to refer back to something you have just mentioned (e.g., *this* in line 9 refers back to *a new song*). *This*, *these*, and *such* / *such a(n)* (meaning *of this kind* or *like this*) can also be followed by a summarizing noun (e.g., *these musicians* refer back to the group 440, and *such versatility* refers back to Guerra's musical abilities).

Work in pairs. Complete the sentences with *this*, *these*, or *such* followed by these summarizing adjectives.

classic songs	concert	encore	energy	solos	stage presence

1 I was struck by the young musician's confidence and rapport with the audience. _____ is rare in a performer of his age.

2 After finishing the set, the band returned and played two more songs. _____ lasted over fifteen minutes.

3 The singer left the stage while the drummer and guitarist each played for several minutes. _____ were greeted with loud applause.

4 The band played non-stop for four hours. I don't know where they found _____ .

5 I saw the group live two years ago. _____ was their first gig in this country.

6 The audience was singing along to old favorites. _____ included hits from their first album.

11 Write a review based on the ideas you discussed in Activity 8. Use the expressions in the Useful language box.

Useful language

Giving background details
The concert was held / given…
The play starred… / was put on by…

Describing the effect of the performance
The band energized / amazed the audience.
The actor gave a powerful / electric performance.
The audience was moved to tears.

Evaluating the performance
Highlights included… / For me the highlight was…
The most impressive aspect of the performance was…
A disappointing part of the concert was…
It was an unforgettable concert.
I came away feeling…
It is well worth seeing.

MODALS OF PERMISSION AND OBLIGATION

Permission is expressed by *can* or *am/is/are allowed to*.
*Girls **can wear** pants, and they**'re allowed to wear** jewelry.*

For the past, use *could* or *was/were allowed to*.
*In elementary school we **could wear** whatever we wanted, and in kindergarten we **were** even **allowed to bring** toys to school.*

May for permission is more formal.
*Visitors **may leave** their belongings in the staff room.*

Obligation can be expressed by *must, have to, need to, should, ought to,* and *be supposed to*. *Must* and *have to* express strong obligation.
*We **have to wear** a uniform, and we **must** always **carry** ID.*

Must is usually more formal than *have to*, but often they are interchangeable.
*We **have to keep** all personal details confidential.*
*You **must show** your ID to get in.*

There is no past form of *must* for obligation, so the past is always expressed by *had to*.
*Every day, we **had to wait** until our parents came to pick us up.*

Need to is used in a similar way to *must* and *have to* but can express a more physical necessity.
*You **need to take** a break every two hours to be productive.*

For less strong obligation *should, ought to,* or *be supposed to* are used. These often suggest that the obligation is not followed.
*We **should/ought to/are supposed to do** our homework during our study period, but we usually just talk.*

For the past, use *was/were supposed to* + base form or *should have* + past participle.
*We **were supposed to study** three times a week.*

Should have can suggest the action didn't happen.
*We **should have studied** three times a week.*

For strong prohibition, use *can't* or *not be allowed to*.
*The students **can't run** in the hallways.*
*We **aren't allowed to use** our phones at school.*

Use *shouldn't* and *not be supposed to* for less strong prohibition and to suggest that sometimes we do the prohibited action.
*We **aren't supposed to leave** early, but sometimes we do.*

For the past, use *couldn't, wasn't/weren't allowed to* or *wasn't/weren't supposed to*.
*We definitely **couldn't leave** the school at lunchtime.*

Shouldn't have + past participle suggests that the action was done.
*You **shouldn't have yelled** at him; you'll get in trouble.*

Use *doesn't/don't have to* or *doesn't/don't need to* when something isn't necessary.
*In the last two years of school, we **don't have to wear** a uniform.*

For the past, use *didn't have to* or *didn't need to* + past participle.
*In elementary school, we **didn't have to/didn't need to carry** any books around; they were all in the classrooms.*

PASSIVE *-ING* FORMS AND INFINITIVE

The present passive *-ing* form and present passive infinitive are formed with a past participle.

-ing form = *being* + past participle: ***Being taught** by a real actor is amazing!*

infinitive = *to be* + past participle: *They don't want **to be given** any credit.*

As with the active voice, the passive *-ing* forms are used after certain verbs and prepositions and in non-finite clauses.
*The important thing is **being recognized** for your work.*

The passive infinitive is used after certain verbs, in adjective constructions, and in infinitive clauses.
***To be voted** "teacher of the year" is a great honor.*

Form the past passive *-ing* form and past passive infinitive with *been* + past participle.

-ing form = *having been* + past participle: *I regret **never having been given** the opportunity to go to college.*

infinitive = *(to) have been* + past participle: *I would like **to have been invited**, but I wasn't.*

Use the past passive *-ing* form and past passive infinitive in the same constructions as in the present.
***Having been exposed** to the hot sun, he got heatstroke.*
*It was impossible not **to have been affected** by the recession.*

1 Choose the two options that are possible in each sentence.

1 The girls in our school aren't very happy with the rule that they *can't / don't have to / aren't allowed to* wear pants.

2 We all understand the dangers of bullying; the principal *wasn't supposed to give / didn't need to give / didn't have to give* us a lecture about it!

3 Punishment *can / may / must* be given after three unexcused school absences if the principal considers it necessary.

4 Disruptive behavior will result in losing privileges. Respect *should / can / needs to* be shown in all areas of school life.

5 The school *can't / shouldn't / isn't allowed to* suspend students without warning.

2 Complete the text with these modal expressions. Use each expression once.

are supposed to	don't have to	don't have to
have to	have to	should
should	shouldn't	

If you're looking for innovative solutions to engage both children and teachers in the learning process, you (1) _____ look any further than Finland, and, in particular, the elementary school run by Jussi Hietava, a teacher and teacher trainer. In this school, neither the students nor the teacher (2) _____ rely on technology to make the school day interesting and fulfilling. Students (3) _____ move around during classes, and they (4) _____ take endless tests and exams or do a lot of homework. However, they currently (5) _____ assess themselves and their peers, offering constructive feedback. They also take outside play breaks of fifteen minutes up to four times a day. Their teachers believe that they (6) _____ take these breaks in order to maximize their learning. Similarly, the teachers are freer than in many schools. Hietava believes that they (7) _____ feel restricted by rules and regulations but (8) _____ feel able to experiment with new styles of teaching and learning.

3 Complete the second sentence so that it means the same as the first. Use the word in parentheses.

1 Fortunately, it wasn't necessary for me to get a master's degree in education to become a teacher. (need)
I _____ a master's degree in education to become a teacher.

2 We obviously weren't supposed to skip school, but we sometimes skipped gym class. (shouldn't)
We obviously _____ school, but sometimes we skipped gym class.

3 It wasn't necessary for the younger children to wear the school uniform. (to)
The younger children _____ the school uniform.

4 We brought all the ingredients for the cooking class, but it wasn't necessary since the class was canceled. (have)
We _____ all the ingredients for the cooking class since the class was canceled.

4 Complete the text with one word in each space. You can repeat words.

Having long (1) _____ considered one of the best education systems in the world, the system in Singapore has also been criticized in the past for being too dependent on formal testing. An initiative to (2) _____ implemented in the next few years will change the system to a broader view of achievement. Exams (3) _____ already been abandoned in elementary schools, with students now (4) _____ encouraged to learn a wider range of skills. While students would have (5) _____ recognized individually for their achievement in the past, the emphasis is now more on group achievement and on students (6) _____ rewarded for overcoming challenges and for improving. The former emphasis on memorization (7) _____ largely been dropped and soon (8) _____ be fully replaced with more applied learning, based on real-life topics and situations.

5 Complete the second sentence so that it means the same as the first. Use a passive form.

1 The school administration may suspend any student who exhibits poor behavior.
Any student who exhibits _____ .

2 Only teaching assistants with a college education can monitor advanced-level classes.
Advanced-level classes _____ .

3 The emphasis on testing young children regularly will be reconsidered next year.
The emphasis on young children _____ .

4 Given this new information, we should have adopted a different approach.
A different approach _____ .

5 Having abandoned the recent trial, the team will now move on to a new project.
The recent trial _____ .

ELLIPSIS AND SUBSTITUTION

Ellipsis

Ellipsis is leaving out an element of a clause because the meaning can be understood without it. This avoids repetition.

These parts of a clause can be omitted in speech and writing.

A repeated noun/pronoun in a second clause starting with *and* or *but* can be omitted. However, it cannot be omitted after a subordinating conjunction (e.g., *because, if, although*).

(< > = words that can be omitted)

I learned to drive and <I> took the test when I was 17.

Adjectives can be omitted after the verb *be*.

They say it's really crowded there. Yes, it is <crowded>.

The main verb can be omitted after auxiliaries and modal verbs.

A *I think they're bringing in traffic reduction measures.*
B *They are <bringing in traffic reduction measures>, but not yet.*
A *They said it would lower pollution, and we're sure that it will <lower pollution>.*

With complex verb phrases (more than one auxiliary), just the main verb or one or more of the auxiliaries can be omitted.

A *The new road should have been completed weeks ago.*
B *Yes, it should have been <completed weeks ago>. / Yes, it should have <been completed weeks ago>. / Yes, it should <have been completed weeks ago>.*

Infinitive clauses can be omitted, ending the sentence with *to*.

A *They expect to increase the number of bus routes next month.*
B *Good. They need to <increase the number of bus routes>.*

Substitution

Substitution replaces one part of a clause with something else.

Like personal pronouns (*he, us, them*, etc.) which substitute for nouns, quantifiers such as *any, both, few*, and *much* are commonly used as pronouns.

*There used to be a lot of smog, but there isn't as **much** now.*

The pronoun *one* is used only with countable nouns and can be made plural.

*We use electric cars, but we still have some gas **ones**.*

An adjective can't be used on its own to substitute for a noun.

My car doesn't meet the emissions standards, so I'll have to buy a new.

After some verbs usually followed by a *that*-clause (e.g., *be afraid, appear, believe, expect, guess, hope, suppose, think), so* or *not* can be used to substitute for the clause.

A *Can we drive into this part of the city?*
B *I guess **so**.*

The negative of *be afraid* and *hope* is usually formed with *not* after the verb; most of the other verbs form the negative with auxiliary *do + not +* verb, but in more formal contexts verb + *not* can be used.

*It was thought that most teachers wanted on-site parking, but it would appear **not**.*

With the simple present and simple past, the auxiliary *do* is used as a substitute for the main verb.

*Asked if he drove here, he said that he **did**.*

Use *do it/that/so* to substitute a whole clause.

*We didn't use to recycle our old clothes, but at school they encouraged us to **do it** / **do so**.*

NOMINALIZATION

Nominalization is the creation of nouns, often abstract, from verbs and sometimes adjectives.

*The committee **decided** to close the school, which angered all the students' parents. ⟶ The **decision** of the committee to close the school angered all the students' parents.*

*The artist's creation was **perfect**, and critics praised it. ⟶ The **perfection** of the artist's creation was praised by critics.*

Nominalization is very common in more formal and academic writing. The focus is more on ideas than actions.

Some verbs convert easily to nouns (e.g., *grow ⟶ growth, develop ⟶ development*). For others, equivalents are used (e.g., *build ⟶ construction, buy ⟶ purchase*), although the *-ing* form of the verb can be used (e.g., *build ⟶ building*).

*It took years to build the new station. ⟶ The **construction/ building** of the new station lasted a long time.*

Nominalizations can be followed by a prepositional phrase, often *of* + noun.

*People are consuming more energy. ⟶ The **consumption** of energy is rising.*

With widely used concepts, compound nouns are often formed (e.g., *energy consumption, air pollution*).

Nominalization is often used as a way of expressing an idea from a previous sentence in one word.

*More people are biking to work. This **trend** is reducing pollution.*

1 Cross out all of the words that could be left out to avoid repetition.

1 I had been warned that the transportation system in the city was very confusing, and it was very confusing.
2 The changes were introduced to encourage people to take public transportation, and, after a few months, it became clear that they had encouraged people to take public transportation.
3 **A** We could bike into town.
　　B We could bike into town, but where will we leave the bikes?
4 The government first introduced a traffic tax on weekdays, and then they introduced the traffic tax on weekends, too.

2 Read part of a text about the transportation system in Rio de Janeiro during Carnival. Write what the pronouns and verbs in italics are substitutes for.

Once you arrive in Rio, you'll notice that the transportation system (1) *there* is easy to use. You can choose between buses, the subway, taxis, and for (2) *those* brave enough to rent and ride a bike, there are plenty of places to (3) *do so*.

Taking the bus is cheap, but it's smart to use (4) *them* only during the day. Another option is the subway. (5) *It* has only two lines, and you might need to take a shuttle bus to get to your destination. If you intend to use the subway during Carnival, check your routes carefully before you (6) *do*.

1 _____Rio_____	2 _____	3 _____
4 _____	5 _____	6 _____

3 Read the rest of the text from Activity 2. Replace the underlined words with these substitute phrases.

another	do it	do so	not	one	~~these~~

For a lot of tourists, however, the best way to travel in Rio is by taxi. Unlike in some cities, (1) taxis in Rio are cheap. Remember, though, that during Carnival many streets are closed, so you should give yourself plenty of time. If (2) you don't give yourself plenty of time, you might arrive late. Taxis here have two rates—(3) a rate for daytime and (4) a rate at night. If you're staying in a hotel and can book your taxis through them, you should (5) book your taxis through them, as they will know the best companies.

Rio is wonderful at Carnival time, so if you get the opportunity to visit then, (6) visit!

1 _____these_____	2 _____	3 _____
4 _____	5 _____	6 _____

4 Rewrite the sentences as nominalization + preposition. Use a dictionary if necessary.

1 Can you clarify the meaning? —→ a __*clarification of*__ the meaning
2 They changed plans. —→ a _____ plans
3 They created new green spaces. —→ the _____ new green spaces
4 The idea originated here. —→ the _____ the idea
5 We've integrated all the suggestions. —→ the _____ the suggestions
6 He justified the expense. —→ his _____ the expense

5 Complete the text with these nominalizations.

commute to	donations	food production
for sale in	the creation of	the cultivation of
the use of	volunteer labor	

The town of Todmorden in West Yorkshire, England, has become known for its "Incredible Edible" project—part of which refers to (1) _____ pieces of abandoned land around the town for (2) _____ vegetables and fruit (3) _____ the town's stores and supermarkets. (4) _____ in Todmorden has become a community project, using (5) _____ and (6) _____ from local businesses. A typical program in the town was (7) _____ the garden in the Health Center parking lot, which focuses on plants with medicinal uses. Even businesspeople on their (8) _____ work can help by pulling weeds out of the garden on the train station platform!

6 Complete the text by making nominalizations from the words in parentheses.

Sustainable cities aim to be as self-sufficient as possible in terms of (1) *resource management / the management of resources* (manage / resources) and (2) _____ (produce / food). They encourage grassroots initiatives such as (3) _____ (create / urban farms), as well as smart solutions such as (4) _____ (monitor) energy use to maximize resource efficiency. Other priorities include (5) _____ (create / jobs), (6) _____ (develop) community-based businesses, (7) _____ (prevent / crime), and (8) _____ (encourage) strong community links, in order to cause (9) _____ (improve) in the quality of life of their inhabitants.

ADVERBIALS

Adverbials are both single-word adverbs (e.g., *quickly, perhaps*) and longer phrases with an adverbial function (e.g., *on time, at the end of the day*).

Adverbials can express different meanings and can appear in different positions in the clause/sentence.

Front position

Adverbials of attitude (e.g., *perhaps, basically, honestly, in fact*) and some time adverbs (e.g., *then, later, suddenly*) are put at the beginning of the sentence.

Honestly, I don't agree.

Then we need to consider the changes happening at this time.

Text connectors of addition, result, contrast, etc., are also put at the beginning (e.g., *in addition, as a result, however*).

That is one idea. However, there are others.

Some adverbs can also be moved from other positions to the beginning of a sentence to foreground them.

Occasionally, we all do something that we later regret.

Mid position

Adverbs of frequency (e.g., *always, often, rarely*), adverbs of degree (e.g., *very, really, almost*), and adverbs of certainty (e.g., *definitely, probably*) are usually put in the middle of the clause.

We've almost finished the study on risk-taking in teens.

The adverb comes before the verb in simple tenses, but it follows *be*. In compound tenses, it comes between the auxiliary and the verb.

He always agrees with us / He is always in agreement with us / He has always agreed with us.

In the negative, the adverb usually follows the negative auxiliary.

He doesn't always agree / He isn't always in agreement / He hasn't always agreed.

Notice the word order with adverbs of certainty in the negative.

He definitely doesn't agree with everything we say.

We probably wouldn't want to stay up all night.

Note the difference in meaning with *really* in different positions in negative sentences.

We wouldn't really want to do that. (slight reluctance)

We really wouldn't want to do that. (strong reluctance)

While most frequency adverbs can come at the beginning for emphasis, *always* has to be placed with the verb, and negative

adverbs of frequency (*never, hardly, rarely*) need subject-verb inversion if they are placed at the beginning.

End position

Adverbs of manner (e.g., *quickly, carefully, well, fully*) can go before or after the verb + object.

We planned the experiment carefully.

We carefully planned the experiment.

Longer adverbial phrases of place and time usually go at the end of the clause, following the order manner, then place, then time.

We waited patiently outside the theater for hours.

EXPRESSING HABITUAL ACTIONS AND STATES

Use the present and past continuous, often with an adverb such as *always, forever*, or *constantly*, to express habitual actions.

Mom's constantly telling me to sit up straight.

This form can describe an emotional reaction to a habitual action, often annoyance, but also other emotions (e.g., pleasure).

The puppy was so sweet; he was always following me around.

Use *will* for present habits and *would* for past habits, sometimes with *always*.

My younger sister will keep working at the restaurant.

I would always borrow my sister's clothes as a child.

To suggest annoyance in speech, *will* or *would* can be stressed.

Note that *always* is not used to express habits in the negative because this expresses "sometimes."

My best friend wouldn't always invite me to go with her. (= sometimes she invited me, but not every time)

Use *used to* + base form to express past habits or states.

I used to bite my nails when I was a child.

Use *didn't use to* or *never used to* (more emphatic) for the lack of a habit.

You never used to take me to school!

Note the difference between *used to* + base form and *be/get used to* + *-ing* form. This refers to actions or states that the speaker is or is becoming accustomed to.

I never used to like it, but now I'm getting used to living here.

Use *tend to* + base form or, more formally, expressions like *have a tendency* + infinitive or *there is a tendency* + infinitive.

Teenagers tend to / have a tendency to worry a lot.

1 Correct the mistake in each sentence.

1 People often think that when you're a teenager you follow foolishly the crowd without making up your own mind.
2 My brother always disturbs me when I've finished almost my homework.
3 If I had more self-confidence, I wouldn't probably give in to peer pressure.
4 People think I'm rebellious, but that's just because of what I say; I often don't act badly.
5 I totally had misunderstood what was needed for the chemistry assignment last week.
6 I'm completely out of cash at the moment. I bought a really expensive pair of boots last Friday stupidly.

2 Put the words and phrases in the correct order.

1 most teenagers / influenced by / aren't / their peers / easily / in fact
2 people / maybe / better / more openly / if we spoke / would understand us / about our emotions
3 acting / instead of / impulsively / weigh / the pros and cons / carefully / you should
4 definitely / our parents / on Saturday night / to go to / the club / wouldn't want
5 stereotypes / annoy me / thought-through / frankly / badly / really / of the moody teenager
6 sensibly / don't / of their brains / developed / young people / always / as certain aspects / fully / aren't / behave

3 Choose the correct options to complete the post on a teenage health-advice website.

Problem I'm really starting to get concerned about the amount of time I'm spending online, especially on social media sites. Every day after school, (1) *I'll / I'd* go straight to my room and go online and then again after dinner. My parents think I'm doing my homework, but I'm sure my mom suspects something because she (2) *'s always asking / always asks* me if I'm finished. I (3) *'m used to / tend to* follow a lot of people that I don't really know on social media, and I know it isn't good. I (4) *used to tell / 'm always telling* myself "just another ten minutes," but that ten minutes turns into an hour, then two. The worst thing is that I (5) *used to get / 'm used to getting* really good grades at school, and I (6) *will / would* hang out with a great group of friends after school, but now my grades are slipping and my friends (7) *would get / are getting* used to me making excuses and disappearing after school. Mom often asks about my friends, but I (8) *'m used to / 'll* just blow her off by saying we're all busy with the exams coming up. In fact, I really don't know what I'm going to do when the exams come along and my parents see how badly I do. Please help me!

4 Complete the response to the problem with these expressions. There is one you do not need.

always following	getting used to	have a tendency
there is a tendency	used to be	will tend to

Advice Young people can (1) _____ to do things in extremes, but I think you do have a problem. From what you say, you (2) _____ an outgoing and hardworking student, and the fact that this has changed is a cause for concern. Spending a lot of time online in itself may not be such an issue. Your parents may not see it this way because (3) _____ for older people to see online time as wasted time, which isn't necessarily the case. What concerns me more is that you appear to be (4) _____ people you don't know online rather than interacting with friends. I think you should start by talking to your friends about this. They may be (5) _____ you disappearing after school, but my guess would be that they're concerned about you. Ask them what they do online and how they control their time, and see if you can change your habits.

5 Complete the second sentence so that it means the same as the first. Use the word in parentheses.

1 My little brother takes my things without asking! (taking)
My little brother is _____
_____ !
2 Older people tend to spend far less time online than younger people. (tendency)
There _____
_____ .
3 I'm used to communicating with my friends by text. (tend)
I _____
_____ .
4 When my parents were my age, they'd spend hours watching TV. What's the difference? (to)
My parents _____
_____ ?
5 Teenagers tend to need more sleep than adults. (tendency)
Teenagers _____
_____ .

RELATIVE CLAUSES WITH PREPOSITIONS

The use of prepositions with relative clauses is the same in both defining and non-defining relative clauses.

In informal language, the preposition is placed at the end of the relative clause.

Defining: *It's your health **that** smoking has a detrimental effect **on**.*

Non-defining: *For breakfast I have a big bowl of cereal, **which** I add extra nuts and berries **to**.*

In formal language, the preposition is placed at the beginning of the relative clause, in front of the relative pronoun.

Defining: *One has to be aware that it's one's own health **on which** smoking has a detrimental effect.*

Non-defining: *For breakfast, we recommend cereals with high fiber, **to which** extra nuts and berries can be added.*

When *who* comes after a preposition, it can become *whom*.

*There are people **for whom** a sedentary lifestyle is unavoidable.*

Note that prepositions are not used before the relative pronoun *that*.

Some words can be placed before the preposition (usually *of*) in formal, non-defining relative clauses. The most common of these are quantifiers (e.g., *all, several, none, both*).

*Try to eat green leafy vegetables, **most of which** are rich in vitamins and minerals.*

*The patient visited several specialists, **all of whom** were puzzled by her symptoms.*

Note that in less formal contexts the quantifiers may have to be changed.

*I visited a lot of doctors, **who** were **all** puzzled by my symptoms.*

Superlatives are placed before *of which/whom*.

*Berries are a good addition to any diet, **the most nutritious of** **which** is possibly blueberries.*

There are also a number of useful set phrases following this pattern (e.g., *the majority of which, a number of whom*).

ARTICLES

The indefinite article (*a/an*) is used to introduce a singular countable noun for the first time. It is used to refer to something indefinite (i.e., not specified).

*There's **a pharmacy** in the shopping center.* (any pharmacy, not a specific one)

It can also be used for an example of a group.

An antibiotic is a type of medicine that fights infection.

Note that singular countable nouns are almost always preceded by the indefinite or definite article or another determiner.

The definite article (*the*) precedes a singular countable noun when both speaker and listener know which one it is.

*Go to **the pharmacy** in the shopping center. It's open late.*

Here, *pharmacy* is made specific by the prepositional phrase that follows it. It could also be specified by a relative clause or a previous mention.

*He works in **the pharmacy** that opened last year.*

*A new doctor started at the clinic last week. **The doctor** is a specialist in heart disease.*

The definite article is also used when it is assumed that the listener knows "which one" the speaker is talking about.

*It would be a good idea to take **the medicine**, wouldn't it?*

In relatively formal contexts, the definite article can be used to refer to a single object that represents the whole group or class of the object or a species.

*Exercise is good for **the heart**.* (i.e., all hearts)

***The tiger** has been hunted for decades.*

The + adjective is also used to refer to some groups of people.

***The sick** and **the elderly** are the most vulnerable groups in society.*

The zero article (i.e., no article) is used with plural nouns when referring to the group in general and uncountable nouns when referring to the concept in general.

*Humans' immune systems can fight off most minor **illnesses**.*

***Health care** is high on the agenda of most governments these days.*

When either a plural noun or an uncountable noun is made specific by a relative clause or a prepositional phrase, use the definite article.

***The minor illnesses that we all suffer in childhood** can be prevented by vaccinations.*

***The health of people living into old age** is a hot topic for governments these days.*

There are many fixed uses of articles. Some illnesses take the indefinite article (e.g., *a heart attack, a cold*), while others don't take an article (e.g., *diabetes*).

The possessive adjective (*my, his*, etc.) is usually used with parts of the body.

*I broke **my wrist**.*

1 Complete the text using one or two words in each blank.

The human body needs a variety of minerals to stay healthy, some (1) _____ which we need to be careful about. One of these is salt, a substance (2) _____ many of us put on our food without thinking. Adults should eat no more than six grams of salt a day. That's approximately a teaspoon. Too much salt can increase the possibility of heart disease, (3) _____ which millions of people in the developed world die each year.

An easy way of reducing salt intake is to identify the types of food (4) _____ which we regularly add salt—fries, tomatoes, eggs, for example—and try to avoid these foods. More problematic is packaged food like soups or sauces (5) _____ a lot of salt is added to enhance the flavors because it is not always easy to read the salt content on the label. Busy people, for (6) _____ shopping is a chore to be completed as fast as possible, are unlikely to check the salt content of every item they choose. Fortunately, in many countries there are clearer food labels today, (7) _____ of which use color coding to indicate levels of particular substances in the food.

If you are one of the many people (8) _____ salt is an essential aid to flavor, try experimenting with other seasoning likes pepper, garlic, or lemon juice, none (9) _____ are as detrimental to our health as salt.

2 Rewrite the sentences with relative clauses so that they mean the same thing. The relative clauses all contain a preposition. Write a formal (F) or informal (I) sentence, as in the examples.

1 Do you know a good physical therapist? Can I go to them? (I)

Do you know a good physical therapist (that) I can go to?

2 We have just received a delivery of medical supplies. Payment is required for them. (F)

We have just received a delivery of medical supplies for which payment is required.

3 Professor Harris is unable to attend the lecture on nutrition. She was invited to it last week. (F)

4 There's a podcast on teenagers' health. You should really listen to it. (I)

5 What happened to that brochure on obesity? I saw it the other day. (I)

6 Patients should not become close to counselors. They might become dependent on them. (F)

7 Do you remember Samia, the medical student? I introduced you to her at the party. (I)

8 His new book is on a new treatment for asthma. There is currently no cure for it. (F)

3 Choose the correct option to complete the sentences. (–) means no article is needed.

1 If you aren't feeling right, go to – / the doctor and ask for a / the checkup.

2 The / – mental health is a / the huge concern for many societies today.

3 Some doctors believe that an / the aspirin a day is good for – / the heart.

4 Too much time using – / a computer without taking a break can result in injury to the / a wrist.

5 My / The ankle really hurts. I think I must have injured it when I was on – / the running track.

6 – / The elderly need a very specific type of a / – medical attention.

7 Some of the / – most common medical problems suffered by the / – teenagers are the / – asthma, allergies, and fatigue.

8 One of – / the major priorities for any government is the / – health of the / a nation.

4 Complete the text with the definite article, the indefinite article, and the zero article.

With (1) _____ advances in (2) _____ medicine and better nutrition, (3) _____ people are generally living longer these days, and more people are living to be older than 100. While (4) _____ official record for (5) _____ oldest person to have lived goes to Frenchwoman Jeanne Calment, who died at 122 in 1997, Carmelo Flores, (6) _____ Bolivian man who died in 2014, is said to have lived to (7) _____ ripe old age of 124. However, this claim has not been verified. (8) _____ problem is that (9) _____ birth certificates didn't become official in Bolivia until 1940, so there isn't (10) _____ official record of Flores's birth.

Even in his final years, Flores lived alone in (11) _____ hut high in (12) _____ Andes. He believed that (13) _____ diet was (14) _____ very important ingredient in his recipe for long life, in particular (15) _____ mushrooms and quinoa*.

quinoa *a seed grown in the Andes*

ADVANCED QUESTION TYPES

Tag questions are formed by changing a statement to a tag (i.e., from positive to negative, or negative to positive).

You **haven't followed** the argument at all, **have** you?

The positive can also be used in both the statement and the tag. This usually asks for confirmation.

You **would** agree the smile is universal then, **would** you?

Other less common forms of tag questions are:

Someone misled you about that gesture, didn't **they**?

Explain that to me again, **would you**? / **will you**? / **could you**?

Indirect questions can be asked to be polite or to soften a question. These start with an introductory phrase (e.g., *Can you tell me / I'd like to know…*) .

What **would you use** here? ⟶ **Can you tell me** what **you'd use** here / **I'd like to know** what **you'd use** here.

In the simple present and simple past, *do/does/did* is omitted in the indirect question.

Does the journal use a lot of jargon? ⟶ Do you know if **the journal uses** a lot of jargon?

Did the lawyer clarify the wording? ⟶ Could you tell me if **the lawyer clarified** the wording?

There is a second type of indirect question which asks for an opinion with *do you think*.

Why **do you think** these gestures have an offensive meaning?

Negative questions are formed by using the negative form of the auxiliary verb.

Why **haven't** these ideas **become** more universally accepted?

Yes/no questions in the negative are often used to ask for confirmation.

Didn't you **notice** the expression on her face?

Echo questions are used to show surprise at a piece of information, or to ask someone to repeat something. The appropriate question word is used to ask about the piece of information.

A We went to the Eden Project last month.

B You went **where**?

SUBORDINATE AND PARTICIPIAL CLAUSES

Subordinate clauses add information to the main clause in a sentence and start with a subordinating conjunction (e.g., *since*).

⟵———— main clause ————⟶
Doctors have been washing their hands regularly

⟵———— subordinate clause ————⟶
since *Semmelweis noticed the problem.*

Subordinate clauses are finite (i.e., the verb contains information about tense and person).

The subordinating conjunction provides a meaning connection between the main and subordinate clauses (i.e., in the example above, the meaning is one of time: *since*). Other meanings conveyed are reason (*because, as*), result (*so*), purpose (*so that*), and concession (*although*).

Although he proved his theory, he didn't publish it.

The subordinate clause can come first, usually followed by a comma.

Participial clauses are similar to subordinate clauses, but the verbs in them are non-finite (i.e., they don't show tense or person). There are different types of participial clauses.

Present participial clauses use the present participle and have an active meaning. When they precede the main clause, they often express the idea of cause.

Noticing that fewer mothers died when giving birth at home, he decided to investigate…

When they follow the main clause, they often express result.

Pasteur and Koch proved the link between germs and disease, **leading** *to the request… (which led to…)*

Note that present participial clauses can also be introduced by subordinating conjunctions.

Noticing that fewer mothers died **when giving** *birth at home…*

Past participial clauses use the past participle and have a passive meaning. They can be used alone or after subordinating conjunctions *when, once, until, although, if,* and *unless.*

Discouraged by the hostile reception, he decided to leave.

Although abandoned, the building still showed potential.

Perfect participial clauses use the present participle *having* + past participle. They have an active meaning and refer to the past.

Having left the hospital, he returned to Hungary.

The negative of a participial verb is made by putting *not* in front of the participle.

Not wanting to accept responsibility for the deaths, the doctors rejected the argument.

1 Rewrite the basic question or statement in the question form given in parentheses.

1 Do you know what this facial expression means? (negative question)

_____

2 What does this facial expression mean? (indirect question)

_____

3 Do you understand what this facial expression means? (positive tag question)

_____

4 What does this facial expression mean? (indirect opinion question)

_____

5 I don't understand what it means. (echo question)

_____

2 Put the words in the correct order to make questions.

1 You / *tip* and / understand / don't / *tongue* / you / ?
2 fascinating / differ / Isn't / how / it / languages / ?
3 the / Sorry, / what / on / ?
4 think / English / When / you / you / do / speak / I'll / like / ?
5 what / you / tell / expressions / mean / Can / kind of / you / me / ?

3 Complete the dialog with the questions from Activity 2.

A I know lots of expressions about the mind in English.
B (a) _____ I don't really know any.
A Yeah, well, something like "my mind goes blank," or the one I like is "on the tip of my tongue."
B (b) _____
A On the tip of my tongue.
B Oh, tongue. OK. But what does it mean?
A You don't know? (c) _____
B Yes, of course, but together I don't have a clue.
A I assumed you would because Spanish has a similar expression. It's like, when you can almost remember something, but not quite. So I could say "What's that actor's name? It's on the tip of my tongue."
B Ah, yes, we do have a similar expression, but it translates literally as "It's under my tongue."
A Oh, OK. (d) _____ Really interesting.
B (e) _____ I've been here for ages!

4 Rewrite the sentences using a subordinate clause instead of the participial clause.

1 Understanding the link between germs and infection now, doctors are much more careful.

Because they understand the link between germs and infections now, doctors are much more careful.

2 Not being healthy enough to go home, the patients had to remain in the hospital.
Because _____ .
3 Left to his own thoughts, the researcher realized where he was going wrong.
When _____ .
4 Having taken her final exams, she started working in the local hospital.
After _____ .
5 Antibiotics are being overused today, resulting in more resistant bacteria.
_____ , which _____ .

5 Complete the text with these words and phrases.

being used	breaking	depending on
having realized	Initially discovered	Not having
not using	Viewed	

I was recently in a remote area in East Africa when I fell, (1) _____ my leg badly. (2) _____ immediate access to an X-ray machine, I started to think about this vital tool that the developed world takes for granted. (3) _____ by Roentgen in 1895, the simple X-ray now contributes to speedy diagnosis in much of the modern world. Roentgen, (4) _____ the potential importance of his discovery, started testing it by X-raying his wife's hand. (5) _____ by many at first as an invasion of privacy, X-rays soon became used in medicine and by the military, (6) _____ on the battlefield as a way of locating bullets in soldiers who had been shot. However, (7) _____ harmful radiation for the clear imaging, it became obvious that X-rays needed to be used sparingly. It was only in the 1970s that a safe alternative to X-rays was found: (8) _____ dangerous radiation, magnetic resonance imaging allows clear images of the body without serious risk and is now the diagnostic tool of choice in many medical arenas.

6 Complete the second sentence so it means the same as the first.

1 I had a brilliant idea and wanted to tell the world!
Having _____ .
2 But since I'm not well-known in my field, I knew I'd have to find someone to advise me.
But not _____ .
3 After I'd identified the leading scientist in the field, I decided to write to her.
Having _____ .

IRREGULAR VERBS

INFINITIVE	SIMPLE PAST	PAST PARTICIPLE
arise	arose	arisen
beat	beat	beaten
become	became	become
bend	bent	bent
bet	bet	bet
bite	bit	bitten
blow	blew	blown
break	broke	broken
breed	bred	bred
bring	brought	brought
broadcast	broadcast	broadcast
build	built	built
burn	burned	burned
burst	burst	burst
cost	cost	cost
cut	cut	cut
deal	dealt	dealt
dig	dug	dug
dream	dreamed	dreamed
fall	fell	fallen
feed	fed	fed
fight	fought	fought
flee	fled	fled
forget	forgot	forgotten
forgive	forgave	forgiven
freeze	froze	frozen
grow	grew	grown
hang	hanged/hung	hanged/hung
hide	hid	hidden
hit	hit	hit
hold	held	held
hurt	hurt	hurt
keep	kept	kept
kneel	kneeled	kneeled
lay	laid	laid
lead	led	led
lend	lent	lent
let	let	let
lie	lay	lain
light	lit	lit
lose	lost	lost
mean	meant	meant

INFINITIVE	SIMPLE PAST	PAST PARTICIPLE
mislead	misled	misled
misunderstand	misunderstood	misunderstood
must	had to	had to
overcome	overcame	overcome
rethink	rethought	rethought
ring	rang	rung
rise	rose	risen
sell	sold	sold
set	set	set
shake	shook	shaken
shine	shone	shone
shoot	shot	shot
shrink	shrank	shrunk
shut	shut	shut
sink	sank	sunk
slide	slid	slid
smell	smelled	smelled
spell	spelled	spelled
spend	spent	spent
spill	spilled	spilled
split	split	split
spoil	spoiled	spoiled
spread	spread	spread
stand	stood	stood
steal	stole	stolen
stick	stuck	stuck
strike	struck	struck
swear	swore	sworn
tear	tore	torn
throw	threw	thrown
undergo	underwent	undergone
undertake	undertook	undertaken
upset	upset	upset
wake	woke	woken
win	won	won
withdraw	withdrew	withdrawn

WRITING
UNIT 6 An opinion essay

In an opinion essay, state the arguments for and against different views, including one that is different from your own.

In the second paragraph, explore the arguments against your own point of view.

Support general statements with examples from your own experience.

In the third paragraph, outline your own views on the topic, using the language of personal opinions.

In the final paragraph, summarize both sides of the argument and state your own opinion.

Schools have so many different functions that it is difficult to identify one single aim. On the one hand, it is probably true that, for many students the main purpose of their education is to find work. In my country, there is a great deal of unemployment among young people. As a result, there is increasing competition to obtain high scores on exams in order to go to a great college and have a successful career. On the other hand, most schools have other important goals as well.

There are strong arguments for the view that preparation for work is the key function of a school. Young people need skills to enter the workplace, so all students need to leave school with a good level of language and mathematical literacy and IT skills. Moreover, schools should equip young people to make a contribution to society. My school, for example, provides internships and vocational training that prepare students for the job opportunities that are available.

However, I would question whether preparing students for work is the most important job of schools. I strongly believe that one of the key goals of education should be personal development, in other words helping students to reach their potential. In particular, schools should help students discover their strengths and passions, consider their aims in life, and set goals for the future. In my case, it was in an after-school club that I developed a strong interest in local wildlife. Now I am hoping to study ecology in college and work in nature conservation after I graduate.

In conclusion, it seems to me that although vocational training and academic success are important, the central focus of schools should be on personal development. Schools should enable students to develop their individual talents and interests; only in this way can they choose the right career path for the future and become valuable members of society.

UNIT 7 A report

Give your report a clear and informative title and use sub-headings for each section.

In the first paragraph, state the purpose of the report and summarize the questions asked.

Summarize the findings in the body of the report, using a variety of quantity expressions.

Use formal language (e.g., *expressed dissatisfaction with,* not *complained about*).

Use the final paragraph to summarize the findings and make a brief recommendation.

A report on the use of parks and green spaces

Purpose of the report
This report has been written to provide information on the results of an investigation into parks and recreation spaces in the town. Improvements have been introduced to these spaces over the last few years to make them more accessible and appealing to young people. The purpose of the survey was to determine how well the updates are meeting the needs of young people and to suggest further possible improvements. Students from schools and colleges across the town were asked about how they use the parks, their satisfaction with them, and their suggestions for improvements.

Use of the parks
It was found that the parks are used on a regular basis by just over half the students interviewed. The majority use the parks for exercise and sports, while approximately a third use the spaces as inexpensive and convenient meeting places. Virtually no one views the spaces as an escape from town life.

Opinions of interviewees
The vast majority greatly value the parks with sports facilities, in particular Breakspear Park with its swimming pool and soccer field. About half of the girls rated the cafe in Highfield Park very highly, and just over a third of all interviewees spoke approvingly about the parks that offered shelter against bad weather. Most interviewees expressed dissatisfaction with the less formal open spaces, which they felt were more appropriate for dog walkers. A sizeable minority of the interviewees were deeply disappointed that the running track in Taunton Park was overgrown. Virtually all of the interviewees heavily criticized the early closing times of the parks.

Recommendations
Overall, it appears that young people are relatively satisfied with the facilities at the parks, with the main exception of closing times. It is suggested that the parks should be closed two hours later, particularly in the summer, and that maintenance of the running track should be resumed as soon as possible.

UNIT 8 An essay comparing advantages and disadvantages

When comparing the advantages and disadvantages of two options, mention both options in the first paragraph.

In the second paragraph, list both the pros and cons of the first option.

In the third paragraph, list the pros and cons of the second option.

Finish by saying which of the two options you think is better, giving clear reasons for your choice.

There are many times in life when we struggle to find a solution to a problem. In these situations, it can be very helpful to talk the issue over with a good friend or to discuss it on an online forum. There are pros and cons to both alternatives.

There are many benefits to talking to a friend. First and foremost, a friend knows you very well and is concerned about your happiness and well-being. Another benefit is that they can easily understand what you are going through, because they are from the same generation. However, one possible disadvantage is that they may not question your attitude because they want to make you happy. Most importantly, a friend may not be experienced enough to give the right advice.

The main advantage of online forums is that they are anonymous, so it is easier to be open about your problem. Moreover, in an online forum you have the chance to read a variety of opinions from many different people. However, this has the possible disadvantage of creating confusion, so it is necessary to consider the advice critically. Another significant drawback is that people who post in online forums can sometimes write cruel and hurtful things.

Of course, no one can solve a problem for you; nonetheless, it is always helpful to get different perspectives on an issue. My own view is that the advantages of talking to a friend outweigh the disadvantages, as it is more personal, and by sharing a problem, you can feel less stressed out about it.

UNIT 9 A proposal

As in a report, give your proposal a title and use sub-headings.

Making links between the school and elderly people in the community

Introduction

This proposal is based on the results of a survey in which 35 people, all over the age of 65, were asked about their concerns and suggestions for greater involvement in our community. It outlines both difficulties experienced by the elderly and contributions they could make. It concludes by making recommendations on how the school could make positive links with older local residents.

In the introduction, briefly state what the proposal includes: the research, the findings, and recommendations.

Challenges and opportunities

The main difficulties that need to be addressed are loneliness and isolation. Many elderly people tend to feel out of touch with the local community and find it difficult to get out, either due to difficulties in getting around by walking or a lack of reliable public transportation. They would appreciate more support for their caregivers. In terms of opportunities, they are excited to share skills and support the school.

In a proposal, the *Recommendations* section is longer than in a report.

Recommendations

There are several steps that the school could take in order to involve local elderly residents in the community.

Use bullet points to list your recommendations.

- First of all, it would be useful to devote a certain number of school hours every month to visiting elderly people in their homes. This would build relationships and enable their visitors to learn more about their needs.

Use a variety of language to give recommendations. Use impersonal expressions and a formal style.

- Secondly, it is recommended that elderly people be invited to the school to give talks, on local history for example, or to teach practical skills such as knitting or woodwork. In this way, the community would benefit from their skills and experience.

Give concrete examples (*for instance, such as, like* …).

- Third, students could provide support for families who have older family members living with them, for example, in the form of rides to the doctor.
- Finally, the school might consider scheduling a small number of field trips to local attractions, where students could volunteer and accompany the elderly people.

Conclusion

By implementing these suggestions, the school could make positive links with elderly people. These are not just old people in need of help, they are people with amazing life experiences and talents to share. Involving students in this plan would benefit not only the older people, but also the students themselves.

Finish by stating the improvements that could be made if the proposal is implemented.

UNIT 10 A review

A giant of Latin Music

Begin your review with a strong opening sentence to engage the reader's attention (e.g., describing the performer, the type of music or play, or the performance).

Last weekend's sell-out concert by Juan Luis Guerra proved beyond any doubt that he is a giant of Latin music. In the concert, given to launch his new album *Todo tiene su hora,* the singer from the Dominican Republic gave a thrilling performance, mixing nostalgia and novelty. The city stadium was packed with 9,000 fans of all ages who were loving every moment, singing along with old favorites and dancing to the infectious rhythms of salsa, merengue, and bachata.

In the first paragraph, give background information about the performer(s), the performance, and the audience.

Guerra opened the two-hour set by emerging theatrically from an old-fashioned telephone booth on stage and singing a new song, "Cookies & Cream," featuring catchy lyrics and a strong, energetic beat. This was followed by an exhilarating mixture of new tunes and classic hits such as "La bilirrubina" and "Ojalá que llueva café," accompanied by the artist's talented backing group, 440. These musicians also entertained the crowd during a break by Guerra with powerful instrumental solos and exciting choreography. Guerra ended the concert with a lengthy encore to satisfy his loyal fans, some of whom had crossed continents for a once-in-a-lifetime glimpse of the superstar.

In the second paragraph, focus on interesting details about the performance, using a variety of adjectives to convey your opinion.

In the final paragraph, evaluate the performance and give a personal opinion.

Describe the impact the performance had on you and how it has changed your ideas or feelings.

For me, the most impressive aspect of Guerra's performance was his ability not only to energize the audience with the dance tunes, but also to move them with tender romantic ballads and social commentary. Such versatility is for me the hallmark of a great performer. Through his joyful music and lyrics, his modest stage presence, and his effortless rapport with the audience, Guerra conveys the message that life is good. I came away feeling uplifted and optimistic about the power of music to bring people together. It was an unforgettable and life-enhancing evening with a must-see performer. Don't hesitate to catch another concert on the tour if you can.

Make a recommendation about whether to see the performance or not.

UNIT 6

accessories (n)	/əkˈsɛsəriz/
advice on (phr)	/ədˈvaɪs ɔn/
approach to (phr)	/əˈproʊtʃ tu/
assumption (n)	/əˈsʌmpʃən/
attitude to (phr)	/ˈætɪˌtud tu/
ban on (phr)	/ˈbæn ɔn/
be given a warning (phr)	/bi ˌgɪvən ə ˈwɔrnɪŋ/
be punctual (phr)	/ˌbi ˈpʌŋktʃuəl/
bully (v)	/ˈbʊli/
bullying (n)	/ˈbʊliɪŋ/
challenge to (phr)	/ˈtʃæləndʒ tu/
change in (phr)	/ˈtʃeɪndʒ ɪn/
clash (n)	/klæʃ/
clash between (phr)	/ˈklæʃ bɪˌtwin/
clear up (v)	/ˌklɪr ˌʌp/
comparison between (phr)	/kəmˈpærɪsən bɪˌtwin/
comprehensive (adj)	/ˌkɑmprɪˈhɛnsɪv/
conclude (v)	/kənˈklud/
conflict between (phr)	/ˈkɑnflɪkt bɪˌtwin/
counterpart (n)	/ˈkaʊntərˌpɑrt/
damage to (phr)	/ˈdæmɪdʒ tu/
decrease in (phr)	/ˈdikris ɪn/
detention (n)	/dɪˈtɛnʃən/
difference between (phr)	/ˈdɪfrəns bɪˌtwin/
disruptive (adj)	/dɪsˈrʌptɪv/
distinct (adj)	/dɪˈstɪŋkt/
drastic (adj)	/ˈdræstɪk/
enforce (v)	/ɪnˈfɔrs/
fast forward (v)	/ˌfæst ˈfɔrwərd/
five consecutive years (phr)	/ˌfaɪv kənˈsɛkjətɪv ˌjɪrz/
focus on (phr)	/ˈfoʊkəs ɔn/
gap between (phr)	/ˈgæp bɪˌtwin/
give a punishment (phr)	/ˈgɪv ə ˈpʌnɪʃmənt/
have a very long way to go (phr)	/ˌhæv ə ˈvɛri lɔŋ ˌweɪ tə ˌgoʊ/
impact on (phr)	/ˈɪmpækt ɔn/
improvement in (phr)	/ɪmˈpruvmənt ɪn/
inappropriate (adj)	/ˌɪnəˈproʊpriət/
increase in (phr)	/ˈɪnkris ɪn/
influence on (phr)	/ˈɪnfluəns ɔn/
innovative (adj)	/ˈɪnəˌveɪtɪv/
insight (n)	/ˈɪnsaɪt/
literacy (n)	/ˈlɪtərəsi/
misbehave (v)	/ˌmɪsbiˈheɪv/
misbehavior (n)	/ˌmɪsbiˈheɪvjər/
need for (phr)	/ˈnid fɔr/
norm (n)	/nɔrm/
offensive (adj)	/əˈfɛnsɪv/
peer (n)	/pɪr/
principle (n)	/ˈprɪnsəpəl/
punishment for (phr)	/ˈpʌnɪʃmənt fɔr/
radically (adv)	/ˈrædɪkli/
regime (n)	/reɪˈʒim/
respect for (phr)	/rɪˈspɛkt fɔr/
responsibility for (phr)	/rɪˌspɑnsəˈbɪləti fɔr/
restorative approach (n)	/rɪˌstɔrətɪv əˈproʊtʃ/
rise in (phr)	/ˈraɪz ɪn/
set the tone (phr)	/ˌsɛt ðə ˈtoʊn/
show disrespect (phr)	/ˌʃoʊ ˌdɪsrɪˈspɛkt/
skip class (phr)	/ˈskɪp ˈklæs/
suspend (v)	/səˈspɛnd/
take away privileges (phr)	/ˌteɪk əˈweɪ ˈprɪvəlɪdʒɪz/
talent for (phr)	/ˈtælənt fɔr/
threat to (phr)	/ˈθrɛt tu/
thrive (v)	/θraɪv/
unthinkable (adj)	/ʌnˈθɪŋkəbəl/
vandalism (n)	/ˈvændəˌlɪzəm/
vocational (adj)	/voʊˈkeɪʃənəl/
what is on their minds (phr)	/ˌwʌt ɪz ˌɔn ðeər ˈmaɪndz/
workplace (n)	/ˈwɜrkˌpleɪs/

UNIT 7

aha moment (phr)	/ɑhɑ ˌmoʊmənt/
attributes (n)	/ˈætrɪˌbjuts/
breakdown (n)	/ˈbreɪkˌdaʊn/
car-centric (adj)	/ˌkɑr ˈsɛntrɪk/
carpool (v)	/ˈkɑrˌpul/
collaborate (v)	/kəˈlæbəreɪt/
communicate (v)	/kəˈmjunɪkeɪt/
commute (n/v)	/kəˈmjut/
commuter (n)	/kəˈmjutər/
commuting (n)	/kəˈmjutɪŋ/
component (n)	/kəmˈpoʊnənt/
congested (adj)	/kənˈdʒɛstɪd/
congestion (n)	/kənˈdʒɛstʃən/
connection (n)	/kəˈnɛkʃən/
consumption (n)	/kənˈsʌmpʃən/
crossing (n)	/ˈkrɔsɪŋ/
drop someone off (phr v)	/ˌdrɔp sʌmwʌn ˈɔf/
electrify (v)	/ɪˈlɛktrɪfaɪ/
eye-opener (n)	/ˈaɪ ˌoʊpənər/
formulate (v)	/ˈfɔrmjəˌleɪt/
fumes (n)	/fjumz/
gridlock (n)	/ˈgrɪdˌlɑk/
happen to (phr v)	/ˈhæpən ˌtu/
imitate (v)	/ˈɪmɪteɪt/
imitation (n)	/ˌɪmɪˈteɪʃən/
infrastructure (n)	/ˌɪnfrəˈstrʌktʃər/
innovate (v)	/ˈɪnoʊveɪt/
innovation (n)	/ˌɪnoʊˈveɪʃən/
journey (n)	/ˈdʒɜrni/
justify (v)	/ˈdʒʌstɪfaɪ/
lengthen (v)	/ˈlɛŋθən/
maximize (v)	/ˈmæksɪmaɪz/
memorize (v)	/ˈmɛməraɪz/
obstacle (n)	/ˈɑbstəkəl/
originate (v)	/əˈrɪdʒəneɪt/
overview (n)	/ˈoʊvərˌvju/
paradox (n)	/ˈpærədɑks/

prioritize (v)	/praɪˈɔrɪtaɪz/
purely (adv)	/ˈpjʊrli/
purify (v)	/ˈpjʊrɪfaɪ/
radical (adj)	/ˈrædɪkəl/
rate (v)	/reɪt/
regulate (v)	/ˈrɛgjəˌleɪt/
replicate (v)	/ˈrɛplɪkeɪt/
restless (adj)	/ˈrɛstləs/
restrict (v)	/rɪˈstrɪkt/
resume (v)	/rɪˈzum/
rush hour (n)	/ˈrʌʃ ˌaʊər/
shaped (adj)	/ʃeɪpt/
shuttle service (n)	/ˈʃʌtəl ˌsɜrvɪs/
simplify (v)	/ˈsɪmplɪfaɪ/
smog (n)	/smɑg/
stabilize (v)	/ˈsteɪbəlaɪz/
strengthen (v)	/ˈstrɛŋθən/
stuck (adj)	/stʌk/
subsidize (v)	/ˈsʌbsɪdaɪz/
subway (n)	/ˈsʌbˌweɪ/
transportation (n)	/ˌtrænspɔrˈteɪʃən/
underlying (adj)	/ˌʌndərˈlaɪɪŋ/
unify (v)	/ˈjunɪfaɪ/
urbanize (v)	/ˈɜrbənaɪz/
utilize (v)	/ˈjutɪlaɪz/
vehicle (n)	/ˈviɪkəl/
walker (n)	/ˈwɔkər/

UNIT 8

adolescent (n)	/ˌædəˈlɛsənt/
assignment (n)	/əˈsaɪnmənt/
bed and breakfast (n)	/ˌbɛd ænd ˈbrɛkfəst/
believe it or not (phr)	/bɪˈliv ɪt ɔr ˌnɑt/
black and white (adj)	/ˌblæk ænd ˈwaɪt/
brothers and sisters (n)	/ˌbrʌðərz ænd ˈsɪstərz/
brutal (adj)	/ˈbrutəl/
cheerful (adj)	/ˈtʃɪrfəl/
come across (phr v)	/ˌkʌm əˈkrɑs/
conservative (adj)	/kənˈsɜrvətɪv/
consistently (adv)	/kənˈsɪstəntli/
couldn't care less (phr)	/ˌkʊdənt kɛr ˈlɛs/
distinctive (adj)	/dɪˈstɪŋktɪv/
do my own thing (phr)	/ˌdu maɪ ˌoʊn ˈθɪŋ/
drawback (n)	/ˈdrɔˌbæk/
dual (adj)	/ˈdul/
engage in (phr v)	/ɪnˈgeɪdʒ ˌɪn/
even-tempered (adj)	/ˌivən ˈtɛmpərd/
facts and figures (phr)	/ˌfækts ən ˈfɪgərz/
first and foremost (phr)	/ˌfɜrst ænd ˈfɔrˌmoʊst/
fish and chips (n)	/ˌfɪʃ ænd ˈtʃɪps/
follow the crowd (phr)	/ˈfɑloʊ ðə ˈkraʊd/
foremost (adj)	/ˈfɔrˌmoʊst/
generalization (n)	/ˌdʒɛnərələˈzeɪʃən/
give me a thrill (phr)	/ˌgɪv mi ə ˈθrɪl/
here and there (phr)	/ˌhɪr ænd ˈðɛr/
humility (n)	/hjuˈmɪləti/
husbands and wives (n)	/ˌhʌzbəndz ænd ˈwaɪvz/

impulsive (adj) /ɪmˈpʌlsɪv/
influenced by peers (phr) /ˌɪnfluənst baɪ ˈpɪrz/
insecurities (n) /ˌɪnsəˈkjʊrɪtiz/
kick (n) /kɪk/
law and order (n) /ˌlɔ ænd ˈɔrdər/
loud and clear (phr) /ˌlaʊd ænd ˈklɪr/
men and women (n) /ˌmɛn ænd ˈwɪmɪn/
moody (adj) /ˈmudi/
name and address (n) /ˌneɪm ænd əˈdrɛs/
nonetheless (adv) /ˌnʌnðəˈlɛs/
odds and ends (n) /ˌɑdz ænd ˈɛndz/
outweigh (v) /ˈaʊˌtweɪ/
overwhelming (adj) /ˌoʊvərˈwɛlmɪŋ/
peace and quiet (phr) /ˌpis ænd ˈkwaɪət/
peer pressure (n) /ˈpɪr ˌprɛʃər/
perspective (n) /pərˈspɛktɪv/
phenomenon (n) /fəˈnɑməˌnɑn/
play it safe (phr) /ˌpleɪ ɪt ˈseɪf/
prone to (adj) /ˈproʊn ˌtu/
rebellious (adj) /rɪˈbɛljəs/
reconcile (v) /ˈrɛkənˌsaɪl/
safe and sound (adj) /ˌseɪf ænd ˈsaʊnd/
self-conscious (adj) /ˌsɛlf ˈkɑnʃəs/
self-controlled (adj) /ˌsɛlf kənˈtroʊld/
short and sweet (phr) /ˌʃɔrt ænd ˈswit/
stereotype (n) /ˈstɛrioʊˌtaɪp/
thunder and lightning (n) /ˌθʌndər ænd ˈlaɪtnɪŋ/
torn between (phr) /ˈtɔrn bɪˌtwin/
transition (n) /trænˈzɪʃən/
trials and tribulations (phr) /ˌtraɪəlz ænd ˌtrɪbjʊˈleɪʃənz/
undergo (v) /ˌʌndərˈgoʊ/
ups and downs (phr) /ˌʌps ænd ˈdaʊnz/
wear and tear (n) /ˌwɛər ænd ˈtɛər/
weigh the pros and cons (phr) /weɪ ðə ˌproʊz ænd ˈkɑnz/
within a split second of (phr) /wɪðˌɪn ə ˌsplɪt ˈsɛkənd əv/
worthy (adj) /ˈwɜrði/

UNIT 9

account for (phr v) /əˈkaʊnt ˌfɔr/
achievable (adj) /əˈtʃivəbəl/
address (v) /əˈdrɛs/
affordable (adj) /əˈfɔrdəbəl/
alert (adj) /əˈlɜrt/
assign (v) /əˈsaɪn/
audible (adj) /ˈɔdəbəl/
beneficial (adj) /ˌbɛnɪˈfɪʃəl/
carbohydrate (n) /ˌkarboʊˈhaɪˌdreɪt/
chronic (adj) /ˈkrɑnɪk/
commonly (adv) /ˈkɑmənli/
correlation (n) /ˌkɔrəˈleɪʃən/
curable (adj) /ˈkjʊrəbəl/
detrimental (adj) /ˌdɛtrɪˈmɛntəl/

disposable (adj) /dɪˈspoʊzəbəl/
drink plenty of water (phr) /ˌdrɪŋk ˈplɛnti əv ˈwɔtər/
eat naturally (phr) /ˌit ˈnætʃərəli/
edible (adj) /ˈɛdɪbəl/
enhance (v) /ɛnˈhæns/
enjoyable (adj) /ɛnˈdʒɔɪəbəl/
experience firsthand (phr) /ɪkˈspɪriəns ˌfɜrstˈhænd/
feasible (adj) /ˈfizəbəl/
get enough sleep (phr) /gɛt ɪˌnʌf ˈslip/
have a balanced diet (phr) /hæv ə ˌbælənst ˈdaɪət/
horrible (adj) /ˈhɑrəbəl/
in moderation (phr) /ˌɪn ˌmɑdəˈreɪʃən/
inflatable (adj) /ɪnˈfleɪtəbəl/
intake (n) /ˈɪnteɪk/
isolation (n) /ˌaɪsəˈleɪʃən/
keep an eye on (phr) /ˌkip æn ˈaɪ ɔn/
label (v) /ˈleɪbəl/
legible (adj) /ˈlɛdʒəbəl/
lifelong (adj) /ˈlaɪfˌlɔŋ/
loneliness (n) /ˈloʊnlinəs/
longevity (n) /lɑnˈdʒɛvəti/
machine-washable (adj) /məˌʃin ˈwɑʃəbəl/
memorable (adj) /ˈmɛmərəbəl/
moderate (adj) /ˈmɑdərət/
moderation (n) /ˌmɑdəˈreɪʃən/
nap (n) /næp/
nutrient (n) /ˈnutriənt/
nutritious (adj) /nuˈtrɪʃəs/
obese (adj) /oʊˈbis/
obesity (n) /oʊˈbisəti/
occasional (adj) /əˈkeɪʒənəl/
outlet (n) /ˈaʊtˌlɛt/
plausible (adj) /ˈplɔzəbəl/
practice the art of appreciation (phr) /ˌpræktɪs ðə ˌart əv əˌpriʃiˈeɪʃən/
preliminary (adj) /prɪˈlɪmɪnɛri/
preventable (adj) /prɪˈvɛntəbəl/
protein (n) /ˈproʊtin/
rechargeable (adj) /riˈtʃardʒəbəl/
recyclable (adj) /riˈsaɪkləbəl/
reduce (v) /rɪˈdus/
refillable (adj) /riˈfɪləbəl/
refined sugar (n) /rɪˌfaɪnd ˈʃʊgər/
refundable (adj) /rɪˈfʌndəbəl/
relax (v) /rɪˈlæks/
relieve stress (phr) /rɪˌliv ˈstrɛs/
renewable (adj) /rɪˈnuəbəl/
specifically (adv) /spəˈsɪfɪkli/
stamina (n) /ˈstæmɪnə/
stay active (phr) /ˌsteɪ ˈæktɪv/
stem from (phr v) /ˈstɛm ˌfrəm/
unaffected (adj) /ˌʌnəˈfɛktɪd/
unprocessed foods (phr) /ənˈprɑˌsɛst fudz/
visible (adj) /ˈvɪzəbəl/
well-being (n) /ˌwɛl ˈbiɪŋ/

UNIT 10

analogy (n) /əˈnælədʒi/
analytical (adj) /ˌænəˈlɪtɪkəl/
back up (phr v) /ˌbæk ˈʌp/
backing (adj) /ˈbækɪŋ/
bundle (n) /ˈbʌndəl/
circuit (n) /ˈsɜrkɪt/
concisely (adv) /kənˈsaɪsli/
contrast (v) /kənˈtræst/
convey (v) /kənˈveɪ/
cookies (n) /ˈkʊkiz/
doubtful (adj) /ˈdaʊtfəl/
doubtless (adj) /ˈdaʊtləs/
elaborate on (phr v) /ɪˈlæbəˌreɪt ɔn/
empathy (n) /ˈɛmpəθi/
engage (v) /ɪnˌgeɪdʒ/
eventful (adj) /ɪˈvɛntfəl/
exclaim (v) /ɪkˈskleɪm/
exquisite (adj) /ɪkˈskwɪzɪt/
facial expression (n) /ˌfeɪʃəl ɪkˈsprɛʃən/
fearful (adj) /ˈfɪrfəl/
fearless (adj) /ˈfɪrləs/
forget one's point (phr) /fərˌgɛt wʌnz ˈpɔɪnt/
forgetful (adj) /fərˈgɛtfəl/
fruitful (adj) /ˈfrutfəl/
fruitless (adj) /ˈfrutləs/
gesture (n) /ˈdʒɛstʃər/
get across (phr v) /ˌgɛt əˈkrɑs/
giggle (v) /ˈgɪgəl/
glimpse (n) /glɪmps/
heartless (adj) /ˈhartləs/
homeless (adj) /ˈhoʊmləs/
hopeful (adj) /ˈhoʊpfəl/
hopeless (adj) /ˈhoʊpləs/
infectious (adj) /ɪnˈfɛkʃəs/
jargon (n) /ˈdʒargən/
jobless (adj) /ˈdʒɑbləs/
lengthy (adj) /ˈlɛŋθi/
lose my train of thought (phr) /ˌluz maɪ ˌtreɪn əv ˈθɔt/
make eye contact (phr) /ˌmeɪk ˈaɪ kɑntækt/
make up (phr v) /ˌmeɪk ˈʌp/
meaningful (adj) /ˈminɪŋfəl/
meaningless (adj) /ˈminɪŋləs/
metaphor (n) /ˈmɛtəfɔr/
mind goes blank (phr) /ˌmaɪnd goʊz ˈblæŋk/
misinterpret (v) /ˌmɪsɪnˈtɜrprɪt/
neatly (adv) /ˈnitli/
nostalgia (n) /nɔˈstældʒə/
novelty (n) /ˈnɑvəlti/
partially (adv) /ˈparʃəli/
pointless (adj) /ˈpɔɪntləs/
powerful (adj) /ˈpaʊərfəl/
powerless (adj) /ˈpaʊərləs/
precise (adj) /prɪˈsaɪs/
raging (adj) /ˈreɪdʒɪŋ/
rational (adj) /ˈræʃənəl/

regretful (adj)	/rɪˈgrɛtfəl/
rephrase (v)	/ˌriˈfreɪz/
republic (n)	/rɪˈpʌblɪk/
run around (phr v)	/ˌrʌn əˈraʊnd/
scramble (n)	/ˈskræmbəl/
sheer (adj)	/ʃɪr/
see right through (phr verb)	/ˌsi ˌraɪt ˈθru/
skillful (adj)	/ˈskɪlfəl/
snap (v)	/snæp/
stable (n)	/ˈsteɪbəl/
startling (adj)	/ˈstɑrtəlɪŋ/
stick to the point (phr)	/ˌstɪk tu ðə ˈpɔɪnt/
summarize (v)	/ˈsʌməraɪz/
surge (v)	/sɜrdʒ/
sync with (phr verb)	/ˈsɪŋk ˌwɪð/
tactful (adj)	/ˈtæktfəl/
tactless (adj)	/ˈtæktləs/
tangle (n)	/ˈtæŋgəl/
tasteful (adj)	/ˈteɪstfəl/
tasteless (adj)	/ˈteɪstləs/
tender (adj)	/ˈtɛndər/
thankful (adj)	/ˈθæŋkfəl/
thoughtful (adj)	/ˈθɔtfəl/
thoughtless (adj)	/ˈθɔtləs/
unrest (n)	/ʌnˈrɛst/
wasteful (adj)	/ˈweɪstfəl/
weave together (phr v)	/ˌwiv təˈgeðər/
worthless (adj)	/ˈwɜrθləs/

PERSPECTIVES 4

Workbook

NATIONAL GEOGRAPHIC
LEARNING

Australia · Brazil · Mexico · Singapore · United Kingdom · United States

NATIONAL GEOGRAPHIC
L E A R N I N G

Perspectives 4

Publisher: Sherrise Roehr

Executive Editor: Sarah Kenney

Project Manager and Editor:
  Katherine Carroll

Senior Technology Product Manager:
  Lauren Krolick

Director of Global Marketing: Ian Martin

Product Marketing Manager: Anders Bylund

Sr. Director, ELT & World Languages:
  Michael Burggren

Production Manager: Daisy Sosa

Senior Print Buyer: Mary Beth Hennebury

Composition: Lumina Datamatics, Inc.

Cover/Text Design: Brenda Carmichael

Art Director: Brenda Carmichael

Cover Image: © Alexander Remnev / Aurora
  Photos

For product information and technology assistance, contact us at
Cengage Learning Customer & Sales Support, cengage.com/contact

For permission to use material from this text or product,
submit all requests online at **cengage.com/permissions**
Further permissions questions can be emailed to
permissionrequest@cengage.com

Perspectives Workbook 4

ISBN: 978-1-337-29732-5

National Geographic Learning
20 Channel Center Street
Boston, MA 02210
USA

National Geographic Learning, a Cengage Learning Company, has a mission to bring the world to the classroom and the classroom to life. With our English language programs, students learn about their world by experiencing it. Through our partnerships with National Geographic and TED Talks, they develop the language and skills they need to be successful global citizens and leaders.

Locate your local office at **international.cengage.com/region**

Visit National Geographic Learning online at **NGL.Cengage.com/ELT**
Visit our corporate website at **www.cengage.com**

Printed in China
Print Number: 01   Print Year: 2018

CONTENTS

6 Education

6A Play by the Rules

VOCABULARY School rules

1 Review Match the words to make collocations about education.

1	attend	**a**	exams
2	develop	**b**	homework
3	take	**c**	skills
4	get	**d**	good grades
5	learn	**e**	how to speak English
6	receive	**f**	an education
7	study	**g**	science
8	take	**h**	school

2 Review Complete the paragraph with words about education.

The **(1)** _____ stands at the front of the class and writes the class assignment on the **(2)** _____. The **(3)** _____ sit at their **(4)** _____ and take notes in their **(5)** _____ using their **(6)** _____. In this class, they **(7)** _____ biology. They study one chapter of their textbook each week. Then the **(8)** _____ gives them a short **(9)** _____ every Friday.

3 Review Choose the correct options to complete the sentences.

1 Ana is fifteen. She attends *high school / elementary* school.
2 Some *schools / jobs* are *public / education* schools and others are *private / online learning* schools.
3 One benefit of having a small *class size / number of tests* is that the teacher has more time to spend with each student.
4 Taking classes in the arts allows students to *be creative / be hard-working*.
5 If a student *gets bad grades / develops skills*, teachers, administrators, and parents can work together to find solutions to help the student improve.

4 Complete the sentences with these words and phrases.

a detention	a warning	disruptive
inappropriate	offensive	punctual
shows disrespect	skip class	warning

1 No _____ behavior in the classroom will be tolerated. It _____ for your teacher and your classmates.
2 The use of _____ language will result in _____ .
3 You will be given _____ for _____ behavior of any type on school grounds.
4 Be _____. If you _____ , you will have to stay after class and catch up on the lessons you missed.
5 If you misbehave, you will first be given a _____ and then we will contact your parents.

5 Choose the correct options to complete the sentences.

1 It is the teacher's responsibility to deal with students who show _____ in the classroom.
   a misbehavior   **c** detention
   b disrespect   **d** behavior
2 _____ or any other disrespect for school property will result in serious consequences.
   a A detention   **c** Vandalism
   b Bullies   **d** Privileges
3 One example of poor behavior is _____.
   a skipping class   **c** warning
   b being punctual   **d** taking away
4 Repeatedly breaking school rules can lead to being _____ from school.
   a absent   **c** skipping
   b warning   **d** suspended

6 Cross out the word or phrase that does <u>not</u> belong.

1 *respecting others / show disrespect / be given a warning*
2 *vandalize / behave / bully*
3 *skip class / disruptive / punctual*
4 *be offensive / be on time / be punctual*
5 *disruptive / appropriate / punctual*

7 Complete the chart.

Adjective	Noun	Verb
–	**(4)**	behave
–	**(5)**	bully
(1)	–	disrupt
–	suspension	**(8)**
–	**(6)**	misbehave
(2)	–	offend
(3)	punctuality	–
–	**(7)**	vandalize

8 Put the words in the correct order to make sentences.

1 give / behavior / in / the classroom / causes / the teacher / Disruptive / to / a / detention / a student / .

_____

_____

2 disrespect / shows / people's / Vandalism / other / for / property / .

_____

_____

3 less / being / class / is / Skipping / than / a / bully / serious / .

_____

_____

4 avoid / be / and / punctual / warning / you / will / a / Always / .

_____

_____

9 Extension Listen and complete the text. 🎧 **48**

If you want to **(1)** _____ ,
consider the following advice:
Don't **(2)** _____ by waiting
to study until the night before an exam.
(3) _____ and study for
small amounts of time for several days. You should
(4) _____ for each study period.
Choose a quiet place to study and
(5) _____ , like your phone and
the television. **(6)** _____ on the
goals you set for the given study period. And remember to
(7) _____
and **(8)** _____!

10 Extension Match the two parts of the sentences.

1 In an attempt to overachieve, _____
2 Some teachers offer extra credit _____
3 Attend all your classes _____
4 Pace yourself _____
5 You will remember more _____
6 To learn all the material, _____

a if you eliminate distractions.
b set specific goals while studying.
c you may in fact hinder your achievement.
d and be prepared to take notes.
e during an exam.
f to help you improve your grade.

LISTENING

11 Listen to a talk on Malala Yousafzai. Which message do you think is the most important for Malala? 🎧 **49**

a fight terrorism
b respect your parents
c believe in yourself
d free education for all

12 Listen again and choose the correct answers to the questions. 🎧 **49**

1 Based on the talk, how would you describe Pakistani society?
  a female-dominated
  b equal for both sexes
  c male-dominated
  d youth-oriented

2 Why do you think Malala was awarded the Nobel Peace Prize?
  a She stopped the war in Pakistan.
  b She made a remarkable movie.
  c She stopped an assassination.
  d She was viewed as a role model.

3 What did Malala co-found?
  a an education fund
  b an education blog
  c an education prize
  d an education movie

4 Based on what the speaker says, when do you think most Pakistani girls get married?
  a when they're ten
  b in their teens
  c in their twenties
  d in their thirties

5 What does Malala attribute her courage to?
  a her parents
  b her close friends
  c her teachers
  d herself

6 What do you think Malala considers her role to be?
  a an inspiration for others
  b a role model for others
  c a leader for others
  d a voice for others

13 Listen and complete the sentences. 🎧 **50**

1 Six-year-old Ruby Bridges had to walk past _____ to integrate the elementary school.
2 Ruby's parents were courageous because they wanted to see _____ .
3 Ruby thought the _____ people were like those at a parade.
4 Advancing social justice and racial harmony is the _____ of her foundation.
5 Ruby helps children by drawing from her _____ .
6 Ruby doesn't think we pay enough attention to the _____ work of children.

14 Listen again. Are the sentences true (T) or false (F)? 🎧 **50**

1 Before 1960, public schools in the American South weren't integrated. _____
2 Ruby Bridges and Malala Yousafzai have both founded educational organizations. _____
3 Ruby's parents lost their lives because of their bold sacrifices. _____
4 Mardi Gras is celebrated in New Orleans with a parade. _____
5 Integration meant an equal number of black and white children in school. _____
6 Ruby's school has been designated as a building of historic importance in the US. _____
7 Ruby would like to see people taking notice of the work of children. _____

GRAMMAR Modals of permission and obligation

15 Match the sentences with a similar meaning.

1 We have to be on time for work. _____
2 I must tell my boss if I'm going to be late. _____
3 We're supposed to be on time for work. _____
4 We aren't supposed to leave early. _____
5 We may take an hour to eat lunch. _____
6 We need an hour to eat lunch. _____

a We can take an hour to eat lunch.
b I have to tell my boss if I'm running late.
c We must not be late for work.
d We have to have an hour to eat lunch.
e We shouldn't leave early.
f We should be on time for work.

16 Complete the sentences with these words and phrases.

allowed to	can	can't	don't have to
have to	need to	supposed to	

1 My manager is really nice, so we are _____ leave at one on Fridays.
2 I _____ be at work before ten, so I try to sleep in most days.
3 We're _____ refill the printer with paper if it runs out, but no one ever does.
4 We _____ take more than five days' vacation at a time without approval from a manager.
5 If my boss is away on business, I _____ use her office to make phone calls and have meetings.
6 If I _____ leave work early because I don't feel well, I can do that without a problem.
7 I _____ sign the forms before I can officially start work on Monday.

17 Cross out the option that is not correct.

1 In Ireland, drivers *have to / can / must* drive on the left side of the road.
2 All drivers *must / need to / could* have a valid driver's license.
3 No one *may / is allowed to / could* drive without wearing a seat belt.
4 Drivers *are allowed to / should / ought to* slow down on rural roads because there are often tractors nearby.

18 Choose the correct options to complete the sentences.

1 My dad _____ wear a uniform for his job as a security officer at the airport.
   a can
   b has to
   c have to
   d could

2 He _____ called his mother to let her know he'd be home late, but he didn't.
   a ought have
   b can have
   c must have
   d should have

3 While at our hotel, guests _____ worry about a thing. We will take care of everything.
   a should
   b can't
   c must
   d must not

4 I'm _____ stay out past eleven, but sometimes my parents say it's OK for a special occasion.
   a not supposed to
   b not have to
   c not supposing to
   d cannot

5 Everyone _____ make time to vote in the upcoming election.
   a needs
   b can
   c should
   d should have

6 No one _____ swim in the local swimming pool last summer because it was closed for repairs.
   a can
   b should have
   c could
   d couldn't have

19 Put the words in the correct order to make sentences.

1 school / The / allowed / charge / to / isn't / for / school supplies / parents / .
   _____

2 not / You / have / been / should / highway / on / speeding / the / .
   _____

3 the members / managers / All / to / their / team / of / supervise / have / .
   _____

4 sign in / office / Visitors / must / at / school's / the / .
   _____

5 employees / the building / may / All / access / days / week / a / seven / .
   _____

6B Redefining Education

VOCABULARY BUILDING Nouns and prepositions

1 Complete the text with these prepositions. The prepositions may be used more than once.

between	for	in	on	to

Around the world, there has been a marked increase
(1) _____ the use of technology in
classrooms. Attitudes **(2)** _____ this change
vary widely. Though it is certain that technology is having
an impact **(3)** _____ learning, educators
disagree as to whether this impact is positive or negative.
In many schools, there is a clash **(4)** _____
teachers and administrators who favor traditional methods,
and educators who want to incorporate technology more.
Education expert Lucia Roig offers this advice
(5) _____ this important issue:

"Teachers should remember that technology is a
powerful tool to motivate students. Where technology
is incorporated appropriately, there is often a rise
(6) _____ test scores. Positive changes
have also been observed **(7)** _____ areas
such as student happiness. On the other hand, there is a
difference **(8)** _____ letting students
use technology **(9)** _____ everything
and using it in a structured way. Instituting a ban
(10) _____ personal devices such as cell
phones and tablets is a good idea, because doing so helps
students focus more **(11)** _____ their
work. Every school should develop a clear technology
policy that all teachers and students are willing to follow."

READING

2 Read the article and match the two parts of the sentences. There is one sentence ending you don't need.

1 Ricardo Semler is a former CEO _____
2 At the Lumiar Schools, students _____
3 Learning how to build a bicycle _____
4 The Brazilian national curriculum _____
5 Semler's theories about the way _____

a involves learning about mathematical concepts like Pi.
b who has become a prominent contemporary educator.
c expects seventeen-year-old students to have mastered certain skills.
d company grew from $4 million to $212 million.
e work together on projects of their own choosing.
f children learn have proven to be correct.

3 Match the information (a–g) with the paragraphs (1–6). You may use numbers more than once.

a Semler's decision to apply business practices to education _____
b some of the difficulties affecting Semler's firm _____
c details about the role of tutors and mentors in the schools _____
d Semler's goals for his new educational methods _____
e details about Semler's business approach _____
f some examples of classes that are offered at Lumiar _____
g an explanation of how mentors design their classes _____

4 Choose the correct answers to the questions.

1 Which of the following statements about Ricardo Semler is not true?
  a He was a CEO who decided to run his company in a creative way.
  b He reduced the size of Semco to focus on the most responsible workers.
  c He delivered a presentation about the success of his innovative approach.

2 Which advantages of Semler's schools are specifically mentioned in the article?
  a reduced costs and more efficiency
  b improved hiring practices and applicability
  c stronger motivation and overall success

3 Which of the following lessons is not specifically mentioned in the article?
  a reviewing the work of contemporary artists
  b learning geometry and other mathematical skills
  c understanding rhythm and timing

A Brazilian Businessman Redefines Education

1 In the early 1990s, Brazilian entrepreneur Ricardo Semler set about implementing a series of unusual business practices. He had recently been named CEO* of a manufacturing firm called Semco. The firm was struggling and it looked like many employees were going to lose their jobs. Semler decided that the solution was to give employees more freedom and responsibility. He let workers make more decisions, choose their own hours and bosses, and even set their own salaries. Experts predicted that the company would fail immediately. Instead, the project was a success. Over the next twenty years, the company hired thousands of new employees and revenue* grew from $4 million to $212 million. Semler spoke about his approach in his 2015 TED Talk, "How to run a company with (almost) no rules."

2 After his experience at Semco, Semler decided to found a school. He thought that what had worked for his company could also work in education. Why not give children the freedom to pursue their own interests and decide what they wanted to learn? After all, children are naturally curious. Semler thought that by giving students more control over their education, kids would retain their innate love of learning and would want to study as much as they could.

3 With this philosophy in mind, Semler opened the first Lumiar School in São Paulo in 2003. One of Semler's first ideas was to reinvent the role of the teacher. Instead of having traditional teachers, Lumiar students are assigned tutors and mentors. Tutors look after students' emotional well-being, and mentors come in and teach things they are passionate about. Many mentors are senior citizens and have decades of experience in specialized areas. Because they really believe in what they are teaching, they are able to motivate their classes. Mentors design their classes based on students' needs and interests. If no mentor is knowledgeable about something a student wants to learn, the school brings in someone new.

4 Semler's second change was in the way classes are organized. Rather than divide kids by age, he decided to group them according to subject. At Lumiar, if a six-year-old is interested in the same subject as an eleven-year-old, they can be in the same class. Semler believes that this system has two advantages. First, it eliminates problems such as cliques* and bullying that exist in traditional schools. This is because students mix constantly and get to know each other. Second, students work hard, because they have chosen what they want to learn. Students feel more responsibility for their education, just as the employees of Semco felt more committed to the company.

5 Examples of classes offered at Lumiar are building a bicycle, reggae, and World Cup soccer. Everything students do in these classes is a learning experience. For instance, when students try to build a bike, they quickly realize that mathematical knowledge is essential. This is because it isn't possible to construct the wheels unless they understand the concept of Pi. So students learn math, but they learn it in a way that is immediately applicable to a practical skill. Similarly, in reggae, students realize that music is all about timing. They also learn the history of the genre and practice English as they analyze the lyrics of popular songs. World Cup soccer is an opportunity to study geography and world cultures. Fascinating new classes are invented at Lumiar all the time.

6 Semler's ideas about education turned out to be correct. By the time his first students had turned seventeen, they had studied roughly 600 different topics and had learned everything the Brazilian national curriculum* expected them to know. However, at no point were they forced into studying anything.

CEO *the head of a company (Chief Executive Officer)*
revenue *the money a company earns*
clique *a group of people, often students, who do not allow others to join them*

national curriculum *the topics students are required to study in a country's school system*

6C Education Initiatives

GRAMMAR Passive *-ing* forms and infinitives

1 Do these sentences contain an active infinitive (A) or a passive infinitive (P)?

1 He's hoping to be president. _____
2 He's hoping to be elected president. _____
3 I expect to be given the award. _____
4 I expect to get the award. _____
5 To be "Student of the Year" is a great honor. _____
6 To be named "Student of the Year" is a great honor. _____
7 There's work to be done! _____
8 There's work to do! _____
9 Some of my classmates don't want to be helped. _____
10 I want to help my classmates. _____

2 Underline the passive infinitives.

1 She would like to be talking to the audience by 3 o'clock. _____
2 I prefer to be driven when I'm in cities I don't know well. _____
3 They expected to be told what to do before the meeting. _____
4 He was expecting to have been given an award by now. _____
5 He wanted to be notified if the plans changed. _____
6 We were intending to have gone by now. _____
7 The winner is not likely to have been revealed yet. _____
8 Students will be instructed to leave their electronic devices at home. _____

3 Match the sentences in Activity 2 with the infinitive form (a–d).

a active infinitive
b passive infinitive
c active perfect infinitive
d passive perfect infinitive

4 Match the words in bold in the sentences (1–8) with the verb structures (a–d).

1 I'd like **to congratulate** Juan on his award. _____
2 I don't think there's anything that could **have been done** to prevent him from resigning. _____
3 Applications must **be submitted** by June 1st. _____
4 The book is believed **to have been written** by his father. _____
5 I need these books **to be taken** to the library. _____
6 There isn't much **to be done**. We just have to wait for the award committee to decide. _____
7 I wanted him **to have finished** by three. _____

8 By the time I'm 40, I want my photographs **to have been published** in *National Geographic*! _____

a active infinitive
b passive infinitive
c active perfect infinitive
d passive perfect infinitive

5 Choose the correct options to complete the text.

Many high-school students in rural parts of Patagonia live too far from the closest high school and have **(1)** _____ by their parents or take a bus. Even though there are many elementary schools in rural areas, most high schools are located in urban areas. In addition, most high schools provide a general curriculum that does not meet the needs of students in rural areas, who, in addition to learning the regular school subjects, need **(2)** _____ practical skills for rural life and future employment in a rural setting.

That's where organizations like Fundación Cruzada Patagónica come into play. Since **(3)** _____ in 1979, this particular organization has worked to promote rural education in Patagonia. It currently operates two boarding high schools, where teenagers who live up to 300 miles (500 km) away study and live. Students can expect **(4)** _____ in tasks like farming, farm equipment maintenance and operation, carpentry, and bee keeping. That's in addition to **(5)** _____ regular school subjects, such as Spanish, math, and history.

One of the two schools also offers elementary education to adults and teenagers over fourteen years old. Graduates from this program are very happy **(6)** _____ the opportunity to complete their elementary education.

1 **a** to drive   **c** being driven
   b to be driven   **d** to have been driven
2 **a** to be taught   **c** to have been taught
   b being taught   **d** having been taught
3 **a** being founded   **c** have founded
   b was founded   **d** has been founded
4 **a** being trained   **c** to have been trained
   b they train   **d** to be trained
5 **a** having been taught **c** being taught
   b teach   **d** teaching
6 **a** to have been given **c** be given
   b to give   **d** were given

6 Rewrite these sentences using a passive *-ing* form (or gerund) in place of the words in bold.

1 I remember **that they told me** to enroll early.

_____

_____

2 I remember **that they took me** there when I was very young.

_____

_____

3 **I was taught** three languages as a child. I am now fully trilingual.

_____

_____

4 He regrets **that he was never given** the opportunity to learn a second language as a child.

_____

_____

5 I remember **that they asked many of my friends** to go to school on Saturdays.

_____

_____

7 Complete the second sentence so that it means the same as the first sentence. Use the word in parenthesis and no more than four other words.

1 I want someone from the committee to recommend me for the summer job.
I want _____ (be) for the summer job by someone from the committee.

2 He did really well in the audition because he'd been taking dance lessons from the time he was a small child.
_____ (having) how to dance from a very young age, he did really well in the audition.

3 I was really hoping they'd accept my application to the summer course, but they didn't.
I would like _____ (to) to the summer course, but I wasn't.

4 They voted him "Student of the Month," which is a great honor.
_____ (be) "Student of the Month," is a great honor.

5 He wanted someone to remind him about the application deadline.
He wanted _____ (be) about the application deadline.

6 He remembers that someone told him about the application requirements.
He remembers _____ (having) about the application requirements.

8 Complete the text with the correct passive gerund (*-ing* form) or passive infinitive of the verbs in parentheses.

Meet five of the top ten Global Teacher Prize finalists for 2017

Salima Begum is from Pakistan. She has helped promote women's education. She believes classroom activities should **(1)** _____ (inspire) by real-life situations. Over 7,000 teachers across her province are estimated **(2)** _____ (train) by her.

David Calle is from Spain. More than ten years ago, he started uploading math, physics, and chemistry videos online. So far, tens of millions of students are confirmed **(3)** _____ (help) by his videos.

Raymond Chambers is from the UK. He can probably **(4)** _____ (credit) with revolutionizing how computer science is taught. The computer science curriculum went from **(5)** _____ (consider) traditional and undeveloped to being engaging and innovative.

Marie-Christine Ghanbari Jahromi is from Germany. She uses sports and physical activity to promote self-esteem, motivation, and empathy among students. She believes all students, even if they're not into sports, can **(6)** _____ (inspire) by physical education rather than **(7)** _____ (make) to feel left behind.

Wemerson da Silva Nogueira is from Brazil. He has developed a method to make science teaching more interesting and motivating. After **(8)** _____ (label) a low-performing school for many years, his school is now considered to be one of the best in his city.

6D How to Fix a Broken School? Lead Fearlessly, Love Hard

TEDTALKS

AUTHENTIC LISTENING SKILLS

1 Listen to the TED Talk extracts. Then, match the words with their definitions. 🎧 **52**

1	principal	**a**	a large metal container for trash
2	outburst	**b**	very high quality
3	top-notch	**c**	special help for students with difficulties
4	bulletin board		
5	dumpster	**d**	a person in charge of a school
6	reallocate	**e**	a board hung in a public place to post messages
7	remediation		
8	unwavering	**f**	a sudden spoken expression of a strong feeling
		g	strong and steady in spite of opposition or problems
		h	to change the use of

WATCH ▶

2 Complete the sentences. Use no more than two words.

1 Cliatt-Wayman says that people gave many excuses for why the school was low-performing and _____.

2 Only six percent of the students were _____ in algebra.

3 One of Cliatt-Wayman's slogans is, "So what. _____?"

4 Cliatt-Wayman realized that her primary responsibility was to eliminate _____.

5 The teachers changed the way they taught so that their students' _____ needs were met in the classroom.

6 After one year, the _____ revealed that student test scores had grown by over 100 percent.

3 Choose the correct options to complete the sentences.

1 Before *becoming / to become* a school principal, Linda Cliatt-Wayman had been a special education teacher.

2 Cliatt-Wayman believes that it's important *treating / to treat* all her students with love and compassion.

3 She made it clear that excuses would not *be tolerated / to tolerate*.

4 After *hearing / to hear* Ashley say, "this is not a school," Cliatt-Wayman realized that she felt the same way.

5 Cliatt-Wayman asked for her leadership team's help in *resetting / to reset* all of the locker combinations.

6 The teachers expected students *behaving / to behave* responsibly at all times.

7 Cliatt-Wayman held monthly town hall meetings *listening / to listen* to students' concerns.

8 The teachers have recognized the importance of *setting / set* consistent expectations for students.

VOCABULARY IN CONTEXT

4 Match the phrases in bold in the sentences (1–6) with the phrases (a–f).

1 Cliatt-Wayman knew it was important to **make it clear how she was going to run the school** on the first day.

2 **Skipping ahead a few years**, she saw a dramatic improvement in students' test scores and attendance rates.

3 The school had been underperforming **every year for five years without a break**.

4 Even though we have seen some meaningful improvements in student outcomes, we **definitely have not achieved our goal** yet.

5 Cliatt-Wayman holds town hall meetings with the students so that they can share **what they are worried about** with the rest of the school.

6 Cliatt-Wayman believes that it's important to communicate clearly and honestly with students, in order to **clarify any misunderstandings** that they may have.

a for five consecutive years
b fast-forwarding
c clear up any misconceptions
d set the tone
e have a very long way to go
f what is on their minds

6E Testing Times

SPEAKING

1 Listen to the statements and match them with the descriptions (a–e). There is one description that you don't need. 🎧 **53**

Statement 1 _____   Statement 3 _____
Statement 2 _____   Statement 4 _____

- **a** a person who is praising what someone did
- **b** a person who is challenging an argument
- **c** someone who only partially agrees with a decision
- **d** someone who completely agrees with a proposal
- **e** a person who is trying to settle an argument

2 Complete the conversation with these expressions. There are two expressions you don't need.

a complex issue	agree to differ
are you really saying that	couldn't
don't you	I know what you mean
no easy answers	on your mind
really feel that	what you're saying

A: Thanks for taking the time to meet with me.

B: Don't worry, it's my pleasure. What's
(1) _____?

A: Well, I **(2)** _____ class sizes in my department are too big. In the average biology class, there are 32 students. There isn't enough laboratory equipment for the students to carry out their experiments.

B: **(3)** _____ , but there isn't anything I can do. At least not right now…

A: **(4)** _____ the school hire another teacher? It would make an enormous difference.

B: I hear **(5)** _____ , but at this point in the year, it's really too late.

A: **(6)** _____ we have to put up with this situation until June?

B: It's **(7)** _____ with
(8) _____.

3 Read the sentences. Write one response where you partially agree and another where you challenge the statement.

1 Students should have less homework.

Partially agree: _____
_____

Challenge the statement: _____
_____

2 All schools should offer drama and music classes.

Partially agree: _____
_____

Challenge the statement: _____
_____

3 Digital whiteboards should be used in all classrooms.

Partially agree: _____
_____

Challenge the statement: _____
_____

4 All schools should be bilingual.

Partially agree: _____
_____

Challenge the statement: _____
_____

4 Read the questions and make notes about how you would speak about the topic. Then listen to the sample answer and compare your ideas. 🎧 **54**

1 Compare your education to your parents' education. Talk about the subjects that are (or were) taught and how teaching methods have changed over time. What is the most important difference you see between the past and today?

2 Should there be computers in school classrooms? Talk about what school computers can be used for and whether the cost of installing and maintaining them is worth it.

PRONUNCIATION Rise-fall-rise intonation

> Remember that sometimes when we stress words we use a rise-fall-rise intonation. Our voice rises, falls, and then rises again.

5 Listen to the sentences and underline the stressed words. Then practice saying the sentences. 🎧 **55**

1 I see your point, but there's more to it than that.
2 I agree to a certain extent, but I'm not completely convinced.
3 I hear what you're saying, but there are other options.
4 I agree to a degree, but that's not the whole story.
5 I hear what you're saying, but I can't agree with you.
6 I know what you mean, but it's more complicated than that.

WRITING An opinion essay

6 Choose the correct options to complete the text.

Opinion essays discuss a particular topic and offer various opinions on it. A good opinion essay will provide a **(1)** *balanced / biased* range of opinions for and against the essay topic. The **(2)** *expert / writer* also includes his or her personal opinion on the topic.

Like many essays, opinion essays should have a **(3)** *four-paragraph / five-paragraph* structure which consists of an introduction, main body, and conclusion.

The first paragraph is the **(4)** *introduction / argument*. It states the topic of the essay and provides **(5)** *a lot of detail / some background*. The main body begins with the **(6)** *first / second* paragraph. Although the opinions can be presented in more than one way, a good approach is to first cover opinions **(7)** *related to / in favor of* the topic. The main body then continues with the third paragraph, where opinions against the topic can be discussed. It is important to **(8)** *support / mention* the expressed opinions with reasons and examples.

The final paragraph is the conclusion, which **(9)** *sums up / introduces* the main points of the essay and finishes with the writer's **(10)** *other / own* opinion.

7 Read the sentences. Are they discussing an opposing opinion (O), expressing a personal opinion (P), or concluding (C)?

1 I strongly believe that teachers who inspire can make a real difference to their students' lives. _____

2 To sum up, school uniforms generally offer more advantages than disadvantages. _____

3 On the one hand, exams are necessary. On the other hand, some students find them quite stressful. _____

4 All in all, changes to the school curriculum have been welcomed by most education boards. _____

5 While some people may find math difficult, it is certainly the case that it is an essential subject. _____

6 It seems to me that learning something by heart doesn't necessarily mean you understand it. _____

7 Taking all these arguments into consideration, compulsory gym class should be continued in schools. _____

8 I would argue that longer school days would simply make students feel tired and bored. _____

9 However, there are also strong arguments for the view that classroom discipline is improving. _____

8 Put the paragraphs (a–d) in the correct order to complete the essay.

a On the other hand, there are many critics of homeschooling. For one thing, some experts feel that it limits the social development of children and young people. Not having the opportunity to participate in daily group activities may prevent them from learning to interact with others. Furthermore, they are deprived of memorable experiences such as school trips. There are also strong arguments for the view that students outside a traditional classroom have less incentive to learn and are less competitive. _____

b Parents who homeschool their children claim there are several worthwhile benefits. First of all, they can give their child a great deal of individual attention during the learning process. Generally, it is not possible to provide the same level of support in a traditional classroom with large numbers of students vying for the teacher's attention. In addition, parents can offer personalized learning, in other words, they can adapt lesson plans to suit the speed at which their child naturally learns, as well as concentrating on their child's areas of interest. Finally, some parents prefer to educate their child away from potential school-playground bullying and in the safe environment of home. _____

c To sum up, it is my personal view that we cannot simply designate homeschooling as a good thing or a bad thing. I believe it has significant benefits to offer, but that it is not for everyone. In conclusion, the traditional school system is probably the best place for the vast majority of students, but homeschooling may provide an excellent solution on a case-by-case basis. _____

d The practice of homeschooling, that is, when a parent educates his or her child at home rather than sending them to school, has become a growing trend. In the UK alone, there was a 65 percent homeschooling increase in a recent six-year period. And a recent survey in the US estimates that around one and a half million students are now being homeschooled. While a variety of reasons contribute to the decision to homeschool, not everyone agrees that it is a good option. _____

9 Write at least 250 words on the topic below. Include any relevant examples from your own knowledge or experience.

Some people believe that homework improves student achievement. Others feel that it is not beneficial and should be banned.

What is your view?

Review

1 Match the words to make phrases.

1 receive		**a** class	
2 be		**b** other students	
3 be given		**c** disrespect	
4 break		**d** behavior	
5 inappropriate		**e** a warning	
6 offensive		**f** punctual	
7 skip		**g** school rules	
8 bully		**h** language	
9 show		**i** detention	

2 Choose the correct options to complete the paragraph.

The best **(1)** _____
(2) _____ learning a new language is
through immersion. Studies show that surrounding
yourself with a language in a country where it is
spoken will have the most **(3)** _____
(4) _____ how well and how fast you
learn it. To see the most **(5)** _____
(6) _____ your skills, keep away from
speakers of your native language and put a
(7) _____ **(8)** _____
reading newspapers and websites, listening to music,
and watching TV and movies in your own language as
well. Ultimately, the **(9)** _____
(10) _____ learning another language is
your own.

1	**a** influence		**c** attitude	
	b approach		**d** advice	
2	**a** in		**c** on	
	b for		**d** to	
3	**a** clash		**c** impact	
	b change		**d** gap	
4	**a** in		**c** on	
	b for		**d** to	
5	**a** improvement		**c** threat	
	b comparison		**d** challenge	
6	**a** in		**c** on	
	b for		**d** to	
7	**a** gap		**c** ban	
	b clash		**d** conflict	
8	**a** in		**c** for	
	b between		**d** on	
9	**a** influence		**c** impact	
	b responsibility		**d** difference	
10	**a** in		**c** on	
	b for		**d** to	

3 Read the letter and underline the modal verbs. Then rewrite the letter using different modals so that it has the same meaning.

Welcome to Camp Sachem Mountain! Campers have to arrive before noon on Saturday, July 6th. Campers should find their assigned group leader and may then leave their belongings in their room. There is a lot of free time on the first day, so campers may swim in the lake or visit the ponies at the barn. If you have any questions, you should contact the camp office before arrival. See you soon!

4 Choose the correct options to complete the sentences.

1 This can _____ very inexpensively.
   a you can do   **c** to be done
   b be done

2 I wasn't expecting _____ to next week's party. That's great!
   a to have been invited   **c** to be invited
   b to being invited

3 There is still a lot of work that needs
_____.
   a to do   **c** to be done
   b being done

4 He was truly delighted _____ to speak at the conference.
   a to have been invited   **c** to invite
   b to being invited

5 The problem must _____ before the app is released.
   a be solved   **c** being solved
   b to be solved

6 I really hate _____ obvious questions.
   a be asked   **c** being asked
   b having been asked

7 Please hurry! She doesn't like _____ waiting.
   a having been kept   **c** to being kept
   b to be kept

7 Moving Forward

7A Getting There

VOCABULARY Everyday commutes

1 Review Choose the correct options to complete the sentences.

1 *Voyaging / Carpooling / Commuting* to school by electric bus is convenient and environmentally friendly.
2 Be sure to arrive at the airport two hours before the departure of your *cruise / ride / flight*.
3 Some people say that life is not about the *expedition / excursion / destination*, but about the journey.
4 If you don't leave now, you'll *miss / catch / lose* the train!
5 The *route / ride / voyage* we took to the hotel was really complicated.
6 After I graduate, I plan to go *cruising / backpacking / commuting* across Europe for the summer.
7 When you get *to / on / off* the bus, walk down Main Street toward the park.
8 During their *expedition / destination / excursion* in Antarctica, scientists will collect important data about climate change.

2 Review Complete the chart with these words to make phrases about travel.

| a bike ride | a different route | a ride | a taxi | an hour |
| home | lost | school | the airport | work |

get	get to	go for	take

3 Review Unscramble the letters to make words about travel.

1 d i r e ___ ___ ___ ___
2 u r i e x s n c o ___ ___ ___ ___ ___ ___ ___ ___ ___
3 n t n e d s i i o a t ___ ___ ___ ___ ___ ___ ___ ___ ___ ___ ___
4 t e o u r ___ ___ ___ ___ ___
5 g t i l f h ___ ___ ___ ___ ___ ___
6 s c u e i r ___ ___ ___ ___ ___ ___
7 p e n i d t x i e o ___ ___ ___ ___ ___ ___ ___ ___ ___
8 y e v a o g ___ ___ ___ ___ ___ ___

4 Listen and complete the text. 🎧 56

(1) _____ in urban areas during
(2) _____ can be time-consuming and stressful. Traffic (3) _____ or vehicle
(4) _____ may cause people to be
(5) _____ in (6) _____ for long periods of time. Instead of driving,
(7) _____ might consider taking public (8) _____, like the
(9) _____ or train. Some companies or business parks even offer a (10) _____ that picks workers up and (11) _____ at stations. Public transportation options have predictable schedules and allow you to relax during your
(12) _____. You may even save time!

5 Match the words (1–8) with their definitions (a–h).

1 carpool
2 congested
3 connection
4 fumes
5 gridlock
6 rush hour
7 smog
8 stuck

a air pollution
b smoke and gas from fuel or chemicals
c taking turns to drive to school or work
d crowded or blocked
e a change of transportation to continue a trip
f busy times of day when many people travel
g not able to move
h roads full of so many cars that traffic can't move

6 Complete each sentence with the correct word formed from the verb in parentheses.

1 The train was packed with _____ and I didn't get a seat. (commute)

2 The new plans aim to reduce traffic _____ in the area. (congest)

3 A shuttle service _____ employees to the business park and takes them back to the station at the end of the day. (transport)

4 If this flight doesn't arrive on time, I'm going to miss my _____ . (connect)

5 My car broke down so I had to use public _____ . (transport)

6 She has a daily _____ of over two hours. (commute)

7 Roads in central London are always heavily _____ . (congest)

7 Complete the phrases about journeys.

1 stuck in g __ __ __ __ __ __ __

2 c __ __ __ __ __ __ to school every day

3 take the s __ __ __ __ __ __ s __ __ __ __ __ __

4 traffic c __ __ __ __ __ __ __ __ __

5 vehicle b __ __ __ __ __ __ __

6 make a c __ __ __ __ __ __ __ __

7 d __ __ someone off

8 unpleasant car f __ __ __ __

8 Correct the mistake in each sentence.

1 Alexa is commuter to school by bus this year.

_____

2 Congested in our neighborhood has increased since they closed the bridge for repairs.

_____

3 My flight arrived late and consequently I missed my connecting.

_____

4 I usually put the kids off at school on my way to work.

_____

5 The company provides a shuttle bus to and from the train station.

_____

6 Their offices are in the suburbs so it's difficult to get there by people transportation.

_____

9 **Extension** Complete the text with these words and phrases.

carbon footprint	lane	obey the speed limit
pick up a friend	ride a bicycle	share a car
sharing transportation	shuttle bus	

If you're aiming to reduce your **(1)** _____ , begin by choosing more environmentally friendly ways to commute. Instead of driving, take public transportation, like the metro or bus, or **(2)** _____ to school or work. If that isn't possible, then consider **(3)** _____ . Take a **(4)** _____ or **(5)** _____ on your daily commute. **(6)** _____ and you can ride in the "High Occupancy Vehicle" (HOV) **(7)** _____ together. If you do drive, **(8)** _____ because, believe it or not, speeding uses more fuel!

10 **Extension** Choose the correct options to complete the sentences.

1 Many car manufacturers are currently working with technology companies to create *high-occupancy vehicles / self-driving cars*.

2 An added benefit to *carpooling / cycling* to work is that you get regular exercise.

3 If you *share a car / share a trip* on your daily commute, you'll have someone to talk to.

4 *Pollution / A carbon footprint* from cars creates problems like greenhouse gases and smog.

5 When driving in urban areas, it's very important that you don't *obey / exceed* the speed limit.

LISTENING

11 Listen and complete the sentences. Then practice saying the sentences. 🎧 57

1 The UN predicts that by 2050, half the world's population will be living in _____.

2 We need _____ to the problems of urbanization.

3 Finding ways to _____ will improve air quality for everyone.

4 Renewable energies can help reduce our reliance on _____.

5 Climate change could lead to _____, threatening coastal areas.

6 Many members of the millennial generation are _____.

7 The city is taking an _____ to solving urban issues.

8 Large-scale _____ need cutting-edge technologies.

12 Listen to a talk about Las Vegas, Nevada, and choose the correct answers to the questions. 🎧 58

1 What aspect of Las Vegas does the speaker mainly discuss?
   a water conservation
   b gambling and hotels
   c urban development
   d convention space

2 What does the speaker imply when he says "The oft repeated theme of Las Vegas is 'what happens in Vegas stays in Vegas.' In the case of urban development, perhaps we should hope that it doesn't."
   a There shouldn't be more urban development in Las Vegas.
   b Valuable lessons can be learned from development in Las Vegas.
   c Las Vegas is not a good example of sustainable development.
   d Urbanization issues are especially problematic in Las Vegas.

13 Listen again. Match the two parts of the phrases. 🎧 58

1	urban	a development
2	environmentally conscious	b project
3	eco-rated	c approach
4	cutting-edge	d urban developments
5	green	e areas
6	eco-friendly	f buildings
7	millennial	g city
8	large-scale	h generation

14 Listen again and choose the correct answers to the questions. 🎧 58

1 According to the speaker, what kind of reputation does Las Vegas have?
   a eco-friendly
   b excessive
   c excellent

2 How do we know that buildings are eco-rated?
   a certifications
   b licences
   c regulations

3 What expression does the speaker use meaning "to have a small environmental impact"?
   a go gingerly
   b live simply
   c tread lightly

4 Why is water conservation especially important in Las Vegas?
   a It's in a very dry environment.
   b It has many large conventions.
   c There are many water features.

5 Why does being eco-friendly make business sense to Mr. Murren?
   a 12,000 employees work in the development.
   b Many millennials are environmentally aware.
   c The complex has bars, shops, and restaurants.

6 What example of environmental awareness does Mr. Murren give?
   a organic menus
   b solar technology
   c recycling food

7 What criticism of City Center is given by Mr. Roch?
   a The size and magnitude of the development is excessive.
   b Natural resources were not recycled during the project.
   c Creating new buildings has a negative impact on the environment.

8 What does the saying "what happens in Vegas, stays in Vegas" mean?
   a Las Vegas is an unusual place to stay.
   b What you do in Las Vegas is your own business.
   c There is always a lot happening in Las Vegas.

GRAMMAR Ellipsis and substitution

15 Are the answers to the questions correct or incorrect? Correct those that are incorrect.

1 **A:** Do you like your courses this term?
 B: They're better than they were.

 _____

2 **A:** Are you going to the concert next weekend?
 B: I'm not sure, but I hope.

 _____

3 **A:** Why did you arrive so early for the debate?
 B: I arrived at eight because I was told to.

 _____

4 **A:** Do you think you might decide to go to college in France?
 B: I'm not sure, but I might to.

 _____

5 **A:** Do you want to come on vacation with my family this summer?
 B: I wish I could!

 _____

6 **A:** I told Miguel that he needs to start coming to the lesson on time.
 B: Yes, he needs.

 _____

16 Choose the sentence that is most likely to follow.

1 You should start exercising more often, even though you don't want to.
 a I guess so.   **b** I hope so.

2 The forecast is saying there's going to be a storm tonight.
 a I hope not.   **b** I believe not.

3 Is she really that sick?
 a I'm afraid so.   **b** I hope so.

4 Can you lend me the money I need to buy those shoes?
 a I'm afraid so.   **b** I suppose so.

5 Do I need to turn right to get to the doctor's surgery?
 a I expect so.   **b** I think so.

6 Do you think we could ask the teacher to give us an extension on the assignment?
 a I hope so.   **b** It appears so.

17 Write what the words in bold refer to in the text.

Would you like to visit Roosevelt Island in New York City while enjoying amazing views? Try taking the Roosevelt Island tram. **(1) It** travels on cables high over the East River between Roosevelt Island and Manhattan, carrying commuters and tourists. The tram is part of the public transportation system, so you can pay with a Metro Card like on the subways and buses. If you don't have **(2) one**, you should definitely buy **(3) one** when you arrive. Roosevelt Island residents love the tram because they can commute to Manhattan without using the subway, and **(4) that** can be dirty and crowded. If the weather is nice during your visit and you haven't ridden the tram yet, you should definitely **(5) do so**. Does your city have a tram similar to the **(6) one** in New York City?

1 _____   4 _____

2 _____   5 _____

3 _____   6 _____

18 Complete the sentences using the correct forms of the auxiliary *do*.

1 When asked if they ate in the school cafeteria, most students said they _____.

2 If you haven't tried snowboarding yet, you should

 _____.

3 I told Jen she should sign up for the school play and she said she already had _____.

4 If a stranger asks you to give them money, be sure to think carefully before you _____.

5 **A:** Do you play in the band?
 B: I don't, but my best friend _____.

6 **A:** Shouldn't you have called home to say you were going to be late?
 B: Yes, I should've _____.

7 I asked her if she wanted to marry me and she said she
 _____!

7B Going Car Free

VOCABULARY BUILDING Verb suffixes

1 Complete the text with these words. There are two words you don't need.

collaborate	deteriorate	devastate
eliminating	estimated	formulate
justify	maximize	operate
prioritize	simplify	strengthen
subsidized	utilize	

Rural train networks are expensive to **(1)** _____.
In many remote areas, very few people **(2)** _____
train services, which means that ticket sales are not
enough to offset the cost of operations. Consequently,
rural train networks often have to be **(3)** _____.
It can be hard for governments to **(4)** _____
this expense and critics argue that elected officials
should **(5)** _____ urban transportation
networks instead. However, there are strong arguments
for maintaining efficient rural train networks. First, they
serve to **(6)** _____ isolated communities.
They enable villages to **(7)** _____ with one
another on business ventures and social events. Second,
rural train services **(8)** _____ local tourism.
Studies have shown that tourists prefer to travel in
the countryside by train rather than by car and it has
been **(9)** _____ that, in some areas,
(10) _____ rural train services could reduce
tourism by almost two thirds. Needless to say, this would
(11) _____ many local economies. Finally,
rural train networks are good for the environment. Without
them, more people would drive cars and air quality would
(12) _____.

READING

2 Read the article and match the questions (a–d) with the sections (1–4). You may use a number more than once.

Which transportation solution…

a is similar to Masdar City because
it will be very modern? _____
b is similar to Chengdu because it
promotes exercise? _____
c is older than the other projects described? _____
d will have an impact on air travel? _____

3 Choose the correct answers to the questions.

1 How did Car Free Days change in the year 2000?
  a Cities thought of new ways to promote them.
  b They started becoming more popular.
  c Their environmental impact was demonstrated.
  d They received official recognition in France.

2 Which of the following options is <u>not</u> a goal of
Car Free Days?
  a encouraging people to use bicycles
  b promoting a healthy lifestyle
  c reducing traffic congestion
  d lowering the cost of public transportation

3 According to the article, in what way are Chengdu Great
City and Masdar City similar?
  a Residents in both cities will use PRTs.
  b The two places are roughly the same size.
  c Cars will not be necessary in either place.
  d Both cities are very futuristic.

4 What does the article suggest about Istanbul's ferry
system?
  a It would be difficult for the city to function without it.
  b The network is in need of modernization.
  c The largest passenger boats are the most comfortable.
  d It is similar to the system in New York City.

5 According to the article, what is the most remarkable
aspect of Hyperloop?
  a The technology is a kind of modern train.
  b Compared to other transportation, it will be more
  comfortable.
  c It will be an inexpensive way to get from place to
  place.
  d Passengers will be able to travel at very high speeds.

6 Which option would be a suitable alternative title for the
article?
  a How transportation can promote healthy living
  b Getting around without relying on cars
  c Technology is changing transportation
  d The Role of the Car in Modern Cities

Environmentally Friendly Transportation Solutions  🎧 59

1 Every year on September 22nd, Car Free Days are celebrated around the world. In participating cities, citizens and residents are encouraged to leave their cars at home and use alternative means of transportation to get to school or work. The goal of Car Free Days is to help people see what life in their cities would be like with fewer cars. Some cities even allow people to use public transportation for free throughout the day.

Car Free Days were first organized in the 1950s, notably in the Netherlands, Belgium, and New York City. In 1998, the French government instituted a national Car Free Day, leading the European Commission to fund the program throughout Europe. Within two years, the movement had spread to more than 1,000 cities. Currently, the world's largest Car Free Day takes place in Bogotá, Colombia.

2 It's difficult to imagine that a modern city could function entirely without cars, but there are proposals around the world to develop urban areas that will do just that. In 2012, the city of Chengdu, China, partnered with an American architectural firm and made plans to develop a 1.3 square kilometer area that will be entirely car free. The site has been given the name Chengdu Great City and will be a satellite* of the main Chengdu metropolitan area. Once complete, it will house 80,000 people. Residents will be able to walk everywhere within fifteen minutes along broad, tree-lined promenades and there will be no need for vehicles of any kind.

Similarly, the government of Abu Dhabi is in the process of constructing Masdar City, a futuristic urban space. When it is finished, the development will house 50,000 people and will provide employment for 60,000. Instead of cars, Masdar residents and visitors will get around by Personal Rapid Transit automobiles (PRTs). PRTs are small, driverless pods* that are powered by rechargeable batteries. Although Masdar is not yet complete, the PRT system is already operational and has been praised as an environmentally friendly transportation solution. It is hoped that in the future, other cities will follow Chengdu and Masdar and develop car-free zones of their own.

3 The city of Istanbul, Turkey, often attracts praise for its elaborate ferry network. Roughly 300,000 people commute to work by ferry on a daily basis. The city has almost 40 passenger boats in service, some of which can accommodate more than 2,000 people per journey. The importance of ferries in Istanbul is a consequence of the city's geography. The city's European and Asian sides are divided by the Bosphorus Strait.

Recently, cities such as London, Paris, and New York have been looking to expand their ferry networks as a way to cut down on car use.

4 Extraordinary technology is currently in development that will allow passengers to travel overland at a rate almost as fast as the speed of sound. This exciting new mode of transportation is called Hyperloop.

One way to think of Hyperloop is as a kind of futuristic train. The technology is a series of compartments that can be propelled through tubes either above or below ground. After they are set in motion, the pods levitate* above their tracks using magnetic suspension and zip to their destination at high speeds. Hyperloop will be both a comfortable and convenient way to travel. Moreover, fare prices will be economical. For these reasons, it is expected that the technology will reduce our dependency on conventional means of transportation such as cars, buses, trains and even planes. The site of the world's first Hyperloop has not yet been chosen, but possible locations have been identified in the United Arab Emirates, Europe, and the US.

satellite *a small city located next to a larger area*
pod *a small self-contained space*

levitate *to rise above the ground*

7C Sustainable Cities

GRAMMAR Nominalization

1 Which of these nouns are nominalizations? Complete the chart.

area	celebration	change	city
conservation	creation	decrease	division
encouragement	energy	health	improvement
party	pollution	quality	reduction
space	system		

Nominalizations	Non-nominalizations

2 Write nouns formed from the verbs and adjectives.

1 applicable → _____
2 argue → _____
3 careless → _____
4 contribute → _____
5 depart → _____
6 difficult → _____
7 discover → _____
8 independent → _____
9 inquire → _____
10 interfere → _____
11 invest → _____
12 predict → _____
13 solve → _____
14 urban → _____

3 Complete the second sentence so that it means the same as the first using these words. There are two words you don't need.

construct	construction	consumer	consumption
explanation	failure	imposition	inability
negligence	objection	similarity	

1 The committee objected to the revised proposal.
The committee raised an _____ to the revised proposal.

2 The wall collapsed because of negligent construction workers.
The wall collapsed because of _____ on the part of construction workers.

3 They could not explain the delays to the project.
They had no _____ for the delays to the project.

4 I was amazed by the fact that they were unable to explain their own proposal.
I was amazed by their _____ to explain their own proposal.

5 If they don't display the permit, a fine will be imposed.
_____ to display the permit will result in the _____ of a fine.

6 The two new designs are strikingly similar.
The _____ between the two new designs is striking.

7 It took ten years to build the new train station.
The _____ of the new train station took ten years.

8 People are using less electricity.
Electricity _____ has gone down.

4 Read and choose the correct options to complete the text.

The Buenos Aires Metrobus is a network of dedicated bus lanes and stations. Starting in 2011, the city government began **(1)** _____ of several major arteries to allow buses to have **(2)** _____ lanes. The first street **(3)** _____ was the 9 de Julio Avenue, which is often said to be the widest street in the world. It was **(4)** _____ transformation. Many city planners and **(5)** _____ objected to it because the project required **(6)** _____ 1,500 trees and destroying several green spaces. Other complaints pointed to the **(7)** _____: there was already a subway line running under the 9 de Julio Avenue. However, once the system was in **(8)** _____, the complaints vanished because the updated transportation system helped to **(9)** _____ travel times. It also helped to reduce traffic downtown. Buses that used to run on very narrow streets were diverted to the new dedicated bus lanes on the 9 de Julio Avenue. The reduction in noise and **(10)** _____ in narrow central streets is notable.

1 **a** redesigning   **c** redesigned
   b the redesign   **d** to redesign
2 **a** exclusive   **c** exclusivity
   b the exclusive   **d** the exclusivity
3 **a** the redesign of   **c** to be redesigned
   b to redesign   **d** design
4 **a** a controversy   **c** controversy
   b the controversy of   **d** a controversial

5 **a** the environment   **c** environment
  b involved with the   **d** environmentalists
    environment

6 **a** cutting down   **c** cutting down of
  b the cutting down   **d** cut down

7 **a** redundancy project   **c** project redundant
  b redundancy of the   **d** redundant of the project
    project

8 **a** operation   **c** the operation
  b starting to operate   **d** operator

9 **a** the reduction   **c** reduction
  b the reduction of   **d** reduce

10 **a** the air pollution   **c** air pollution
  b polluted   **d** pollution of

5 Complete the text with the noun forms of the words in parentheses.

Urban farming has seen a huge **(1)** _____ (increase) in **(2)** _____ (popular) in the last few decades. A program in Barcelona runs a network of urban farms, where ordinary citizens grow vegetables, flowers, and herbs using organic methods. What's special about this program is that **(3)** _____ (participate) is limited to people who are 65 or older.

Working on a farm allows these people to build strong **(4)** _____ (relate) and benefit from physical **(5)** _____ (active). The farms also provide opportunities for environmental **(6)** _____ (educate) through the **(7)** _____ (involve) of schoolchildren in farm programs. These programs also provide an opportunity for **(8)** _____ (interact) between children and the elderly. As with other urban farming **(9)** _____ (initiate), an added benefit is the **(10)** _____ (create) of additional green spaces in the city.

6 Complete the second sentence so that it means the same as the first sentence. Use the word in parentheses and between one and four other words.

1 When it comes to managing resources, we need a comprehensive approach.
When it comes to _____ (management), we need a comprehensive approach.

2 Everyone was shocked by the fact that he failed to report the water leaks in the tunnel.
Everyone was shocked by _____ (failure) to report the water leaks in the tunnel.

3 We concluded that the architectural plans for the project were inaccurate.
We _____ (reached) that the architectural plans for the project were inaccurate.

4 This clearly illustrates what can go wrong when environmental impact studies are not conducted.
This _____ (provides) what can go wrong when environmental impact studies are not conducted.

5 The city examined what the committee proposed.
The city examined _____ (committee's).

6 A lack of agreement resulted in the budget being rejected.
A lack of agreement resulted in _____ (of).

7 The project was delayed because of opposition from neighbors.
_____ (delays) were due to opposition from neighbors.

PRONUNCIATION Words with two stress patterns

7 Listen and underline the stressed syllable in the words in bold. Then practice saying the sentences. 🎧 **60**

1 There's been a significant **increase** in traffic congestion.
2 Public **transportation** can be a real nightmare sometimes.
3 Train cancellations **present** a particular problem for commuters.
4 The government is going to **increase** funding for public transportation.
5 I bought a bike as a **present** for myself so that I could ride to work.
6 How do they plan to **transport** the building materials?

7D What a Driverless World Could Look Like

TED TALKS

AUTHENTIC LISTENING SKILLS

1 Read the sentences from the TED Talk and make notes on what you think the speaker says next. Then listen to the extracts and check your ideas. 🎧 **61**

1 I cannot tell you how much I enjoy watching cities from the sky, from an airplane window.

2 Isn't it absurd that we created cars that can reach 130 miles per hour and we now drive them at the same speed as 19th-century horse carriages?

3 We've been stuck in an endless debate between creating a car-centric society or extensive mass-transit systems. And I think we should transcend this.

4 But what would happen when whole cities become driverless?

WATCH ▶

2 Choose the correct options to complete the sentences.

1 According to Kabbaj, New York and Hong Kong project *energy / calmness* when seen from above.

2 The approach of building new roads and enlarging existing ones works well for *fast-growing emerging cities / established urban centers*.

3 Airbus is working on flying *urban taxis / delivery vehicles*.

4 Eighty-five percent of cars have *children in the back seat / only one passenger*.

5 If a whole city were driverless, then we wouldn't need *traffic lights / cars*.

6 The current generation of driverless cars has to cope with *buses and taxis / human unpredictability*.

3 Answer the questions below.

1 How many hours did people in the US spend commuting in 2014? _____

2 How many Pyramids of Giza could the Egyptians have built in that time? _____

3 How many miles of blood vessels do we have in our bodies? _____

4 What percentage of urban traffic is caused by people looking for parking? _____

5 According to Kabbaj, how many drivers could fit into one London bus? _____

4 Complete the sentences with these words.

development	failure	improvement
interference	need	

1 According to Kabbaj, there's an urgent _____ to re-think our urban transportation system.

2 A more efficient transportation system would lead to an _____ in people's quality of life.

3 The _____ of new transportation options is already underway.

4 If there are only driverless vehicles on the roads, there will be less _____ from human error.

5 According to Kabbaj, _____ to re-think the way our cities work will only lead to more frustration.

VOCABULARY IN CONTEXT

5 Match the words in bold in the sentences (1–6) with the words or phrases (a–f).

1 Kabbaj had **a sudden realization** when he recognized the similarity between traffic and blood flow. _____

2 Realizing that 30% of traffic in cities is caused by people looking for parking **made him see things differently**. _____

3 Kabbaj encourages the audience to imagine driving when there are children in the car who are getting **bored and unable to keep still**. _____

4 Some modern cities **consider cars to be the most important thing**. _____

5 The concept that more automation could create a more organic system seems to **involve two opposite ideas**. _____

6 One of the **characteristics** of our circulatory system is its efficiency. _____

a was a real eye-opener	**d** restless
b attributes	**e** be a paradox
c are car-centric	**f** an "aha moment"

7E Opinion Poll

SPEAKING

1 Listen to the speakers 1–6 . Is the speaker asking for (A) or giving (G) information? 🎧 **62**

1 _____   4 _____
2 _____   5 _____
3 _____   6 _____

2 Match the two parts of the sentences. There is one ending that you don't need.

1 Would you mind answering _____
2 I wonder if I could _____
3 I've got a feeling _____
4 I don't know _____
5 As far as I know, the airport _____
6 I don't mind participating in the survey, _____

a but I have no idea about road conditions in that part of town.
b although, of course, I'm speaking generally.
c a few questions about your daily commute?
d is still being renovated.
e off the top of my head, but I could probably find out.
f ask you a couple of questions about the local bus system.
g that train fares are going to go up sometime soon.

3 Choose the correct options to complete the sentences and questions.

1 I'm carrying _____ a survey.
   a out   c over
   b on

2 Would you _____ answering a few questions?
   a bother   c care about
   b mind

3 Do you have _____ how to solve this problem?
   a the idea   c any idea
   b such an idea

4 I'm afraid I don't know _____.
   a offhand   c to hand
   b in hand

5 I'm not sure. Not _____ the top of my head, anyway.
   a on   c off
   b at

6 _____ I know, it's impossible.
   a As far as   c As much as
   b As well as

7 _____, more people prefer the train.
   a Generally talking   c Generally saying
   b Generally speaking

8 I don't have _____ what the answer is.
   a the clue   c clues
   b a clue

4 Complete the conversation. Then listen and check your answers. 🎧 **63**

A: I'm **(1)** _____ out a survey on taxi use in the city. Do you have time to answer a **(2)** _____ questions?

B: Sure, but **(3)** _____ speaking, I don't take taxis very often. I use my car.

A: Oh, I understand. Well, do you **(4)** _____ to know the cost of an average taxi fare?

B: Sorry, but I have no **(5)** _____. As I said, I don't really take taxis.

A: That's OK. The reason I'm interested is because a couple of months ago, the base fare went up by $2. I'd like to **(6)** _____ if you think that's a big increase.

B: I suppose it is… In fact, for people who take taxis a lot, I **(7)** _____ it's a lot of money.

A: **(8)** _____ I ask one more question?

B: Of course.

A: If taxis were less expensive, do you think you would use them more often?

B: I'd **(9)** _____ so. I'd use them once in a while, at least.

A: Thanks for your **(10)** _____.

B: No problem.

5 Read the questions below and write down a short answer to each one. Then listen to how other students answered and think about how you can improve your responses. 🎧 **64**

1 What is your opinion of public transportation in your area? How could it be improved?
2 Do you think cities should offer public transportation 24 hours a day? Why? Why not?
3 When traveling long distances, most people prefer flying rather than taking a bus or train. Why do you think that is?
4 Should children pay to use public transportation? Up to what age should they ride for free?

WRITING A report

6 Match the sentences (1–7) with the summaries (a–g).

1 Business owners downtown have expressed frustration with daily congestion issues. _____

2 It is suggested that a park-and-ride system be introduced in the area. _____

3 Overall, it would appear that carpooling is the preferred method of dealing with the issue. _____

4 This report has been written to provide information about the results of an investigation into traffic congestion in the downtown. _____

5 More than half of residents interviewed said that they encountered traffic jams on a regular basis. _____

6 With regard to charging congestion fees, the city council said it was an option worth investigating. _____

7 Local government officials, business owners, and residents were asked about their experiences with congestion and invited to propose solutions. _____

a using a quantity expression
b summarizing the questions asked
c expressing people's disapproval
d explaining the purpose
e making a recommendation
f explaining the findings
g summarizing the findings

7 Choose the best options to complete the report.

(1) _____ This report has been written to provide information on an investigation into community gardening. Community gardening is when an urban space is gardened by the community to grow fruit, vegetables, and other plants. An area of wasteland near Main Street is currently available for redevelopment.

(2) _____ The purpose of the survey was to establish support for the proposal. Residents from a number of neighborhoods and students from schools in the city participated in the survey. **(3)** _____ It was found that around three quarters of all those surveyed fully approved of the proposal. Most were enthusiastic about having a shared space in which to grow food inexpensively.

(4) _____ Several students also noted the environmental benefits.

(5) _____ While enthusiasm for a community garden was strongly expressed, some participants raised potential issues. There was concern about the cost of equipment and other expenses. A small minority predicted that the novelty of the project would soon wear off and the garden would not be maintained. However, this prospect was not widely accepted.

(6) _____

(7) _____ Overall, it appears that the program will be implemented with widespread support.

(8) _____

1 a Purpose of the report   **b** Community gardening
2 a We already know there's pollution in the area, plus lots of local homes don't have gardens, so it seems like a good idea to create a new community garden for people.
   b Given that pollution is an issue in the area, and many of the surrounding properties do not have gardens, the council has proposed a new community gardening program.
3 a New sports facilities   **b** General enthusiasm
4 a Just over half said they believed the project would bring people together and increase local pride.
   b Fifty-two percent of residents think the community garden will be a friendly place to hang out in.
5 a Concerns raised   **b** Too expensive
6 a And anyway, the council said they would supply most of the equipment needed, as well as helping with other costs.
   b Furthermore, the council made a commitment to provide gardening equipment and to subsidize other costs.
7 a Recommendations   **b** Some disadvantages
8 a What many people want is an area where young people can play.
   b It is proposed that the garden include a play area for young people.

8 Read the report again. Then choose the correct words or phrases to complete the summary.

The report is about a proposed community gardening program. It begins with **(1)** *an explanation / a criticism* of community gardening, **(2)** *how / where* the garden would be situated and what **(3)** *issues / benefits* it could bring. It also explains who **(4)** *participated in / designed* the survey. The second paragraph mainly discusses **(5)** *positive / negative* reactions to the proposal, while the third paragraph covers **(6)** *decisions made / possible problems*. The report finishes with a **(7)** *summary / survey* of the main views expressed as well as some **(8)** *issues / recommendations* regarding the scheme.

9 A national research group is carrying out an investigation on ways of improving public transportation options and services. Write a report about the situation in your town.

Review

1 Match the words to make phrases about journeys.

1	company	a	shuttle service
2	daily	b	the metro
3	during	c	rush hour
4	make	d	transportation
5	public	e	congestion
6	stuck	f	commute
7	take	g	in gridlock
8	traffic	h	a connection

2 What suffix is used to change these words to verbs? Complete the chart with the verb form.

broad	classification	collaboration	communication
electric	formula	hard	imitation
long	memory	minimum	operation
origin	priority	pure	simple
stable	strong	subsidy	weak

-ate	-en	-ify	-ize
	broaden		

3 Match the questions (1–6) with the answers (a–f). Then complete the answers with one word.

1 Have you brought some food for the party? _____
2 Have you ever been sailing? _____
3 Should we take a taxi to the airport tomorrow? _____
4 Would anyone like a raffle ticket? _____
5 Why did you wear that uniform? _____
6 All of this rain is going to flood the garden, isn't it? _____

a No, but I'd like _____.
b Because I was told _____.
c We should've _____, but we didn't.
d I'd like to buy _____.
e It appears _____.
f I'd really like _____, but it'll be very expensive.

4 Complete the text with these phrases.

An industrial scale test
Pollution created by people living in cities
the electricity produced
The harvesting of the algae
The installation of
With the application of his paint

(1) _____ can cause increasing ill-health. So, what's the solution? Two inventors have come up with some interesting answers.

Artist and designer Daan Roosegaarde has embraced biomimicry to make trees come alive. (2) _____, trees are transformed into lights! Taking inspiration from nature, Daan mixes DNA from marine bacteria and plants to create a beautiful, soft, jellyfish-like glow. (3) _____ still needs to be carried out, but if successful, our cities could soon be lit by trees.

In Hamburg, meanwhile, the walls of houses are being converted into power stations. (4) _____ panels filled with a bio-skin of algae is a novel way to reduce our carbon footprint. (5) _____ to create power could lead to a reduction in heating and lighting bills for residents and (6) _____ could even be fed back into the grid.

5 Are these sentences correct or incorrect? Correct those that are incorrect.

1 The council regretted the lack of investing in the city's infrastructure.

_____

2 The disrupt caused by the strikes was bad for the economy.

_____

3 The project wouldn't have been a success without her contribution.

_____

4 A number of local residents volunteered to look after the new conserving area.

_____

5 Government interference in the building work caused significant delays.

_____

6 Our departing was delayed because of a problem at the airport.

_____

8A A typical teenager?

VOCABULARY Teenage stereotypes

1 Review Are these adjectives positive or negative? Complete the chart.

annoyed	bored	confused	delighted
embarrassed	excited	grateful	impatient
lonely	nervous	pleased	relaxed
scared	stressed		

Positive	Negative

2 Review Complete the sentences with the adjectives from Activity 1.

1 Sam never worries about anything. She's
_____.

2 Javier's younger sister took his bike without asking again. He feels _____.

3 Huma has to give a presentation in front of 200 people this afternoon. She feels _____.

4 Yasuko isn't interested in the movie, she'd rather do something else. She's _____.

5 Amare doesn't understand the question. He's
_____.

6 Li Qiang can't wait to see his favorite band in concert next weekend. He's _____.

7 Mika never has anybody to eat lunch with. She feels
_____.

8 Branca has an exam tomorrow and three essays to write by Friday. She's _____.

3 Choose the correct options to complete the email.

Hi from Argentina!
Having a great time on the school trip to Iguzau Falls! Every day, we go on different walks to see incredible views of the falls. We have to stay on the paths though to
(1) _____.
Some of my classmates are feeding the animals we see along the trails, even though there are signs everywhere

telling people not to. I haven't though. You know me—I usually just prefer to **(2)** _____.
A group of my friends are taking a speedboat trip below the falls tomorrow, but I'm not sure whether to go with them. I may **(3)** _____ instead.
I've heard there's a helicopter ride over the falls and also guided eco-tours into the rainforest. I'll see what I'm in the **(4)** _____ for tomorrow morning!
Anyway, hope you're having a good vacation, too, Ravi!

–Alessio

1 a follow the crowd
  b avoid danger
  c weigh the pros and cons
  d take calculated risks

2 a obey the rules
  b follow the crowd
  c question what people say
  d give in to peer pressure

3 a follow the crowd
  b think of the consequences
  c take calculated risks
  d do my own thing

4 a mood
  b moody
  c good mood
  d attitude

4 Match the words to make phrases.

1	avoid	**a**	the rules
2	come	**b**	it safe
3	couldn't	**c**	of the consequences
4	do	**d**	the pros and cons
5	follow	**e**	me a thrill
6	give	**f**	the crowd
7	obey	**g**	care less
8	play	**h**	danger
9	question	**i**	what people say
10	take	**j**	my own thing
11	think	**k**	calculated risks
12	weigh	**l**	across

5 Cross out the word or phrase that does <u>not</u> belong.

1 *think of the consequences / be impulsive / weigh the pros and cons / take calculated risks*

2 *follow the crowd / be influenced by peers / question what people say / peer pressure*
3 *moody / cheerful / in a good mood / a positive attitude*
4 *play it safe / avoid danger / take risks / obey the rules*
5 *take risks / impulsive / lack self-control / avoid danger*

6 Correct the mistake in each sentence.

1 Gisela could care less what people think of her clothes.

_____

2 Ibrahim doesn't like to take risks so he decided to play that safe.

_____

3 Liam has always been an even-temper, friendly kind of guy.

_____

4 With practice and self-controlled, you can break any bad habit.

_____

5 She's been really stressed lately and, as a result, in a terrible moody.

_____

6 Theresa doesn't like getting into trouble so she always obeys the consequences.

_____

7 It's easy to follow your crowd, but far more difficult just to be yourself.

_____

7 Put the words in the correct order to make sentences.

1 and / consequences / doesn't / often / risks / She / takes / the / think of / .

_____

2 themselves / to / roller coasters / thrill / give / ride / People / a / .

_____

3 best / with / self-control / you / someone, / When / to practice / feel / it's / angry / .

_____

4 the / decisions / pros / Weigh / important / before / and / cons / making / .

_____

5 just / peer / own / Try / and / do / to resist / your / thing / pressure / .

_____

8 **Extension** Complete the text with these words and phrases.

benefit of the doubt	charming	hypercritical
image	intelligent	judge
judgemental	reputation	vulnerable

We're all **(1)** _____ at times; it's impossible not to form opinions about others, but we'd never want to be viewed as unfair or **(2)** _____. Generally, a person's **(3)** _____ is very important to them. People typically want to project a certain **(4)** _____ to others and, depending on the situation, they may want to come across as strong instead of **(5)** _____ or **(6)** _____ rather than unfriendly. And, of course, everyone would like to appear reasonably **(7)** _____! Whether we **(8)** _____ ourselves or others, we should give people the **(9)** _____—most of us are just trying to be ourselves.

9 **Extension** Match the synonyms.

1 gregarious   **a** judgemental
2 cool-headed   **b** self-sufficient
3 indifferent   **c** calm
4 prejudiced   **d** apathetic
5 hypercritical   **e** outgoing
6 guarded   **f** delightful
7 independent   **g** biased
8 charming   **h** careful

LISTENING

10 Listen to the conversation and choose the correct answers to the questions. 🎧 **65**

1 What does the young woman say to her friend that she's noticed lately?
 a his attitude
 b his skin problem
 c his bad behavior

2 How does the young man say he never used to feel?
 a indecisive
 b lonely
 c self-conscious

3 What does the young woman offer to give her friend?
 a a party
 b a skin treatment
 c something to help him sleep

4 What else does the young man complain about?
 a his friends
 b his moods
 c his parents

5 Why does the young man say he's having trouble falling asleep?
 a He has difficulty calming his thoughts.
 b He hears too much noise in the street.
 c He never feels tired at night.

6 What does the young woman think is the cause of her friend's problems?
 a illness
 b peer pressure
 c adolescence

7 How does the young woman describe her friend's problems?
 a temporary
 b unfortunate
 c inexplicable

8 How would you describe this friendship?
 a selfish
 b supportive
 c false

11 Listen to the talk and choose the correct answers to the questions. 🎧 **66**

1 How would you describe the overall tone of the talk?
 a very depressing and pessimistic
 b hopeful and totally unrealistic
 c serious, but hopeful

2 In addition to gender, what is the other major difference discussed by the speaker?
 a pre- and post-adolescence
 b being married and unmarried
 c elementary school and high school

12 Listen to the talk again. Match the words to make phrases. Then practice saying the phrases. 🎧 **66**

1 future	**a** pressure
2 demographic	**b** gaps
3 global	**c** statistics
4 articulate	**d** education
5 peer	**e** and wise
6 exactly	**f** careers
7 gender	**g** the same
8 high school	**h** averages

13 Listen again. Are the following sentences true (T) or false (F)? 🎧 **66**

1 Young boys see gender as an obstacle in their lives just as much as young girls do. _____

2 A nine-year-old child would not yet be considered an adolescent. _____

3 Juliana Meirelles says girls are calmer and more reliable than boys. _____

4 It sounds like Shimon Perel might like to play skipping games, but is embarrassed to. _____

5 UNICEF is an organization that is part of the United Nations. _____

6 Claudia Cappa says that gender gaps are reduced in high school education. _____

7 From the talk, it can be concluded that most children are opposed to bullying. _____

GRAMMAR Adverbials

14 Underline the adverbial in each sentence. Then match the sentences (1–7) with the descriptions of what the adverbial is expressing (a–g).

1 Frankly, I've never thought he was as funny as everyone says he is. _____
2 I'm definitely going to Spain next month. I just need to buy my tickets. _____
3 I'm very interested in joining the chess club. I'd like more information about it. _____
4 The vet handled the kitten carefully because it was so young. _____
5 I've always wanted to see the Great Wall of China. _____
6 Suddenly, the truck in front of us swerved into the other lane. _____
7 We'll probably go out to eat after we see the play. _____

a attitude
b degree
c frequency
d time
e manner
f a very high degree of certainty
g some certainty

15 Choose the correct options to complete the text.

I **(1)** *probably / always / really* go to a show in the West End every time I visit London. **(2)** *In fact / Definitely / Probably*, I've seen over twenty shows there. The performers are **(3)** *certainly / rarely / completely* some of the best in the world; nearly every critic says so. I'm **(4)** *definitely / constantly / politely* reading reviews of all the shows that are on and when a new one opens, I book my tickets **(5)** *frankly / suddenly / quickly* because they're likely to sell out. I like to get to the theater very early and wait **(6)** *fully / patiently / carefully* while enjoying the excitement of the West End. I'm **(7)** *definitely / always / almost* one of the West End's biggest fans!

16 Put the words in the correct order to make sentences.

1 whole / politely / The / family / me / spoke / very / to / .

_____

2 two / a / seldom / more / I / day / eat / than / meals / .

_____

3 My / definitely / bed / tired / constantly / I'm / that / the reason / uncomfortable / is / .

_____

17 Choose the correct options to complete the sentences.

1 _____, American Don Kellner has held the world record for the highest number of parachute jumps since 1991, when he made his 15,000th skydive.
   a Frankly   c Probably
   b Amazingly   d Occasionally
2 Now, with over 43,000 jumps, Kellner is _____ the most experienced skydiver in the world.
   a carefully   c really
   b fully   d certainly
3 Kellner is passionate about skydiving. _____, he married his wife Darlene in a ceremony while skydiving!
   a Frankly   c Certainly
   b In fact   d Then
4 Kellner _____ skydives together with Darlene and he _____ goes more than a couple of weeks without jumping.
   a occasionally, rarely   c occasionally, always
   b certainly, probably   d probably, always
5 Kellner and his partner own a skydiving company and _____ consider safety their number one priority when teaching others to skydive.
   a always   c have always
   b almost   d really
6 To skydive _____, it's important to plan each jump _____, just like Don Kellner has done for all his thousands of jumps.
   a patiently, fully   c safely, carefully
   b carefully, frankly   d fully, safely

18 Put the adverbial in parentheses in the correct position in each sentence in the text.

1 I would never want to try rock climbing. (frankly)
2 The sport seems tiring and dirty, and it's dangerous. (certainly)
3 I wouldn't want to go rock climbing even if I was sure that the climb would go safely. (probably)
4 My parents both have a fear of heights and I have had one, too. (always)
5 A couple of my friends love to rock climb, and they tell me that it's peaceful and great exercise. (very)
6 But I wouldn't feel comfortable or safe. (definitely)
7 I know I'd never be able to relax. (in fact)

8B Teenage Superheroes

VOCABULARY BUILDING Binomial expressions

1 Complete the sentences with these binomial expressions. There are two you don't need.

facts and figures	here and there	law and order
name and address	odds and ends	safe and sound
trials and tribulations	wear and tear	

1 We didn't walk anywhere in particular. We just wandered
_____.

2 It goes without saying that
_____ is a vital part of society.

3 Let me start this presentation by giving you some
_____.

4 There's nothing important in that drawer, just a few
_____.

5 Don't forget to include your
_____ on the form.

6 I love our sofa, but it's beginning to show signs of
_____.

READING

2 Read the article and complete the chart. Write no more than two words and/or numbers for each answer.

Name	Country	Invention	Age (at time of invention)	Cost of technology
Jack Andraka	USA	**(1)** _____ screening test	15	$0.03 per test
Marita Cheng	Australia	a special program for **(2)** _____ to get involved in science	19	–
Thato Kgatlhanye	**(3)** _____	backpacks with solar panels and reflective strips	18	$20 per bag

3 Read the article and match the questions (a–c) with the sections (1–3). You may use a number more than once.

Which teenager
a was able to solve multiple problems at once? _____
b is doing work that will have an effect on medicine? _____
c is changing life in a rural community? _____

4 Read the statements. Are the sentences true (T), false (F), or is the information not given (NG)?

1 Jack Andraka had difficulty finding a laboratory that was interested in working with him. _____
2 Jack Andraka's invention led to a reduction in costs. _____
3 As a child, Marita Cheng imagined developing technology that would help people like her mother. _____
4 The article suggests that Marita Cheng's project is likely to have a long-term impact on education. _____
5 Thato Kgatlhanye's project has expanded from her home community to several other countries. _____
6 None of the teenagers described had support from businesses. _____
7 All of the teenagers described are trying to use their education and experiences to help others. _____

The Amazing Inventions of Three Teenage Heroes 🎧 67

1 Jack Andraka was only fifteen years old when he developed a groundbreaking way to detect pancreatic cancer. Two years earlier, a close family friend had died from the disease, an experience that motivated Jack to research the illness. Jack was alarmed to learn that the survival rate for that type of cancer was less than 2%. This was mainly due to the fact that the screening test* was expensive and highly inaccurate. Jack thought there had to be a better way.

After intense research, Jack realized that a protein called mesothelin multiplies in the blood in the early stages of the disease. With the help of a professor at Johns Hopkins University, Jack developed a small paper sensor* that could identify the protein and therefore determine when cancer was present. Whereas the previously used technique cost $800, Jack's test cost just three cents.

2 Marita Cheng was interested in engineering from childhood. She believed that science and math were powerful tools that could make the world a better place. Her mother worked as a cleaner in a hotel, and one of Marita's ideas was to build a robot that could help do household chores. In Marita's mind, there would be no limits to what she could invent once she became an engineer. Consequently, after high school, she decided to study mechatronics* and computer science at the University of Melbourne.

In Marita's class of 50 students, only five were women. Marita was very surprised by this until she realized that in Australia as a whole, fewer than 10% of engineers were women. Marita didn't think that made sense. How could society be sure it was developing the best technology if the skills of half of the population weren't represented? To solve this problem, Marita decided to run a series of workshops in local schools. Marita thought that if girls were introduced to science and technology in a fun way, when they grew up, they would be more likely to study engineering. The project, Robogals, was a success. Within a year, more than 2,000 girls had participated in the program. Since then, Robogals has expanded to more than ten countries.

3 In the South African community where Thato Kgatlhanye grew up, it was common for children to carry their books to school in plastic bags. Many children had to walk long distances from rural villages and the bags were very uncomfortable. When Thato was eighteen years old, she had the idea to start an innovative company that would change this situation. As a result of her creativity, the company simultaneously solved two other problems.

Thato's idea was to weave* plastic bags into a textile and sew the material into sturdy backpacks. Fitted with two straps, the bags would be comfortable to carry. Had she stopped there, Thato would already have succeeded in making a difference to many children. However, she also equipped the bags with solar technology. Special panels charge up as students walk to and from school, and can then serve as lights in homes without electricity. Furthermore, Thato fitted the bags with reflective strips. As many children walk to school along busy roads, traffic accidents can be a problem. The strips increase visibility and make children's journeys to school much safer. Since 2013, Thato's company has produced more than 10,000 backpacks.

screening test *a test used to check whether someone has a disease*
sensor *a device used to show whether something is present*

mechatronics *a subject that combines electronics and mechanical engineering*
weave *to make something by twisting long objects together*

8C A Good Night's Sleep

GRAMMAR Expressing habitual actions and states

1 Choose the option which means the same as the first sentence.

1 When I was a child, I went to the playground with my friend next door every afternoon.
   a When I was a child, I used to go to the playground with my friend next door every afternoon.
   b When I was a child, I was used to going to the playground with my friend next door every afternoon.

2 My parents keep telling me to go to bed earlier.
   a My parents would always tell me to go to bed earlier.
   b My parents are always telling me to go to bed earlier.

3 When I was a small child, I would always spend summer afternoons playing in my room when my parents thought I was sleeping.
   a When I was a small child, my parents had a tendency to sleep, but I preferred to stay in my room playing.
   b When I was a small child, I used to spend summer afternoons playing in my room when I was supposed to be sleeping.

4 Most people tend to sleep less during the summer.
   a People are used to sleeping less during the summer.
   b People usually sleep less during the summer.

5 My dad is always telling me to stop looking at my phone.
   a My dad will keep telling me to stop looking at my phone.
   b My dad is used to telling me to stop looking at my phone.

2 Complete the sentences and questions with these words and phrases. There is one that you don't need.

'm not used to used to (x2)	tend will	use to would

1 When I was a child, I _____ be very shy.
2 My parents _____ keep telling me to stop texting my friends and it really annoys me!
3 I _____ getting up so early.
4 I never take naps because I _____ not to feel sleepy in the afternoon.
5 Did you _____ listen to music in bed?
6 I _____ sleep with a teddy bear.

3 Read and underline the verb constructions that express a habitual action or state in the past.

"Everybody saw the ocean as a big blue tank of water, but for me there was something more going on and I wanted to know what it was. My parents used to buy second-hand *National Geographic* magazines from this little shop down the road. I'd flip through them and see these beautiful images. I used to think, wow, one day that could be me. I wanted to be that explorer and discover what no one else had discovered." – Asha de Vos, marine biologist.

"My Uncle Tom was fortunate enough to have a career with the FBI, which took him across the world. Upon coming home, he would always share tales of his travels. We would sit down and he would take out a globe and spin it and ask me to put my finger gently on it until it stopped somewhere. He would then quiz me about the place and, if I wasn't familiar with it, he would tell me everything he knew. Through this he showed me the vastness and great diversity of the world, but, at the same time, its accessibility, if you wanted to explore it." – Donald Slater, archeologist.

"My parents left El Salvador to escape the civil war and give the family an opportunity at an education and a fighting chance at a stable living. My parents would always say that there are a lot of things that people can take from you, but an education is something no one can take. So my upbringing was my most powerful motivator." – Steve Ramirez, neurobiologist.

4 Choose the correct options to complete the sentences.

1 I didn't *use to / used to* like soccer.
2 My grandfather never *use to / used to* sleep more than four hours.
3 Did she *use to / used to* do ballet when she was a child?
4 I *never used to / didn't used to* stay up past midnight.
5 Teenagers *use to / have a tendency to* stay up chatting with their friends on social media.
6 My grandmother *would / used to* have a very annoying alarm clock.
7 Did you *use to / get used to* sleep in on Sundays?

5 Read the text and choose the correct options.

How many times have you been told that you should sleep for at least eight hours? Well, that may not be the best advice. Despite research suggesting that an eight-hour sleep is unnatural, people still **(1)** _____ to believe that it's what we should get. According to research, however, up until the late 17th century, people **(2)** _____ have a split sleep pattern. They **(3)** _____ sleep for about four hours, then be awake for an hour or two and then sleep another four hours. The first sleep **(4)** _____ begin a couple hours after dusk. During the waking period that followed, people **(5)** _____ be quite active: they **(6)** _____ read, pray, do chores, and even visit neighbors. People **(7)** _____ think that insomnia was a problem.

Written references to the first and second sleep date as far back as Homer's Odyssey. How did something that **(8)** _____ the norm become such an anomaly? Historians believe it was connected with the industrial revolution and streetlights. People started working longer hours and the night—which **(9)** _____ a time when you couldn't do much but stay at home—suddenly became "fashionable" as streetlights promoted nightlife. Electricity in the home also made the day longer. The first sleep, which **(10)** _____ a couple hours after dusk and last for four hours, started later and later, and ended in the early hours of the morning. At that point, the second sleep fell out of fashion.

Scientists do wonder if the single chunk of sleep that **(11)** _____ is actually good for us. So next time you wake up in the middle of the night, relax. It may be what your body is designed to do.

1	**a** tend	**b** use	**c** will
2	**a** will	**b** used to	**c** were used to
3	**a** tend to	**b** were used to	**c** would
4	**a** will	**b** would	**c** has a tendency to
5	**a** used to	**b** tend	**c** will
6	**a** were used to	**b** would	**c** kept
7	**a** weren't used to	**b** wouldn't	**c** didn't use to
8	**a** would be	**b** was used to being	**c** used to be
9	**a** used to be	**b** would	**c** use to be
10	**a** used to start	**b** was used to starting	**c** use to start
11	**a** we used to get	**b** we are now used to	**c** we now get used to

6 Complete the second sentence so that it means the same as the first sentence. Use the word in parentheses and between one and four other words.

1 Parents are usually concerned about screen time.
Parents _____ about screen time. (tend)

2 When my brother was a child, he would always sing in his sleep.
When my brother was a child, he _____ in his sleep. (used)

3 Teenagers tend to sleep longer than younger children.
Teenagers _____ sleep longer than younger children. (tendency)

4 I'm accustomed to having a nap after lunch every day.
_____ a nap after lunch every day. (used)

5 Some people don't fall asleep easily after watching TV.
_____ fall asleep easily after watching TV. (tend)

6 When I was younger, I always used to stay up to watch a movie on Friday nights.
When I was younger, _____ to watch a movie on Friday nights. (would)

8D The Mysterious Workings of the Adolescent Brain

TEDTALKS

AUTHENTIC LISTENING SKILLS

1 Read the description of the terms relating to brain science. Then listen to Part 1 of the TED Talk. Did this information help you to understand the talk? 🎧 **68**

> **MRI**, or Magnetic Resonance Imaging, is a technique used to create images of the body's internal organs, such as the brain.
>
> The **prefrontal cortex** is an outer layer covering the front parts of the brain.

WATCH ▶

2 Are the sentences true (T) or false (F)?

1 An MRI allows scientists to take a video of the brain while a person is doing a task. _____

2 Blakemore has discovered that brain development is complete in early childhood. _____

3 The prefrontal cortex is the only region of the brain that does not change during adolescence. _____

4 The photo of Michael Owen shows that everyone has a completely different emotional response to a given situation. _____

5 Blakemore's lab conducts experiments with both adolescents and adults. _____

6 The experiment with moving objects on shelves shows that adolescents are no different from adults. _____

7 Teenagers sometimes have difficulty seeing other people's points of view. _____

8 Adolescence is an idea that we have only recently developed in modern society. _____

3 Complete the quotations from the TED Talk with these adverbs.

dramatically	instinctively	mainly	radically
really	widely		

1 "Fifteen years ago, it was _____ assumed that the vast majority of brain development takes place in the first few years of life."

2 "… _____ due to advances in brain imaging technology such as magnetic resonance imaging, or MRI, neuroscientists have started to look inside the living human brain of all ages, …"

3 "… we now have a really rich and detailed picture of how the living human brain develops, and this picture has _____ changed the way we think about human brain development…"

4 "One of the brain regions that changes most _____ during adolescence is called prefrontal cortex."

5 "This introduces a _____ interesting condition whereby there's a kind of conflict between your perspective and the director's perspective."

6 "You're going to _____ go for the white truck, because that's the top truck from your perspective, …"

VOCABULARY IN CONTEXT

4 Match the words in bold in the sentences (1–6) with the words or phrases (a–f).

1 Our understanding of the way that the human brain functions has **radically** improved in recent years. _____

2 The brain **undergoes** changes throughout our lives, not only during childhood. _____

3 Blakemore showed how people reacted **within a split second of** an event, without time for thinking consciously. _____

4 **Believe it or not**, normal, healthy, intelligent adults make errors about 50 percent of the time. _____

5 An adolescent is more **prone to taking** risks than an adult. _____

6 Some people get **a kick** from taking risks. _____

a enjoyment
b this is surprising
c in a big and important way
d likely to take
e immediately after
f experiences

8E Looking on the Bright Side

SPEAKING

1 Listen to the statements (1–4) and match them with the descriptions (a–e). There is one description that you don't need. 🎧 69

Statement 1 _____   Statement 3 _____
Statement 2 _____   Statement 4 _____

a someone who feels better after speaking to a friend
b someone who is showing understanding
c a person who wants to help, but isn't able to
d a person who has made an offer to help
e someone who is offering encouragement

2 Complete the conversation with these words and phrases. There are two that you don't need.

as bad as you imagine	frustrating	irritated
look on the bright side	that would help	to lend a hand
to let you down	understanding	what a pain

A: Kerry told me she'd help me organize a surprise party for Caroline, but so far she hasn't done anything.
B: (1) _____.
A: I know.
B: When is Caroline's birthday?
A: It's next Tuesday… the 30th.
B: (2) _____. You still have more than a week!
A: Yeah, I guess you're right. But I'm pretty stressed.
B: I'm more than happy (3) _____, if (4) _____.
A: Thanks. I'd appreciate that. Maybe you could help me call some of her friends.
B: Sure. Just give me their numbers. And try not to be angry with Kerry. I know it's
(5) _____, but I'm sure she didn't mean (6) _____.
A: You're right. Thanks for being so
(7) _____.

3 Read each sentence and write a response. Then listen and compare your answers with some sample answers. 🎧 70

1 I dropped my phone in the sink and now it doesn't seem to be working.
Showing understanding: _____

2 I'm worried about the test tomorrow. I don't feel prepared enough.
Offering help: _____

3 I don't think my presentation went very well. At the end, the audience looked a bit confused.
Offering encouragement: _____

4 We were stuck in traffic for an hour this morning.
Showing understanding: _____

5 It's supposed to rain tomorrow and we were planning to go to the beach.
Offering encouragement: _____

4 Read the following questions and make notes about how you would answer them. Listen to the speaking exam where other students have answered the questions. Then add to your notes to improve your answers. 🎧 71

1 What are your hobbies and interests?
How did you get involved in them?
In the future, what other activities would you like to be involved in?

2 Describe your daily routine.
Has your routine always been the same?
What's the most difficult aspect of your routine?

3 Where do you live?
Do you like living there?
How has the place where you live influenced you?

PRONUNCIATION Intonation to show understanding

5 Listen to the sentences. Do they end with a falling tone (F) or a rising tone (R)? 🎧 72

1 You must have been so frustrated. _____
2 Is there anything I can do to help? _____
3 It might not be as bad as you imagine. _____
4 I'm not surprised you felt let down. _____
5 Would you like me to say something to him? _____
6 That's totally understandable. _____

WRITING An essay comparing advantages and disadvantages

6 Complete the instructions on writing an essay with *should* or *shouldn't*.

1 You _____ read the question at least twice.
2 You _____ analyze the question.
3 You _____ ignore instruction words (e.g. explain) and topic words (e.g. advice).
4 You _____ begin writing without planning.
5 You _____ decide what you must include and what you can include if you want.
6 You _____ decide what style of writing is appropriate.
7 You _____ check any other instructions.
8 Your essay _____ follow a structure.
9 The essay _____ present more advantages than disadvantages.
10 You _____ exceed the word count.

7 Complete the essay with these words and phrases.

benefit	drawback	First of all,
Furthermore,	I believe	main
On the other hand,	pros and cons	Secondly,
various factors		

In some parts of the world, including Austria, Argentina, and Brazil, sixteen-year-olds can vote in elections. However, in the vast majority of countries worldwide, the legal voting age is eighteen or older. This essay will consider whether sixteen or eighteen is the ideal voting age. Both have several **(1)** _____.

(2) _____ the right to vote at sixteen has many merits. Young people are the future, so they should have a say in shaping the future.
(3) _____ today's sixteen-year-olds have grown up with the internet and are more informed than teenagers of previous generations. The
(4) _____ of involving younger people politically is that they become more invested. However, a **(5)** _____ is that sixteen-year-olds may not have the maturity required for making important decisions. **(6)** _____ some are young enough to be easily influenced and manipulated.

The **(7)** _____ advantage to an older voting age is that eighteen is widely recognized as the age of independence and adulthood. Moreover, eighteen-year-olds have more life experience. They generally know who they are and are less likely to be exploited.

(8) _____ the difference between the age of sixteen and eighteen is very slight. Additionally, in some countries, there are as many sixteen-year-olds in employment as eighteen-year-olds, putting them on an equal footing.

Whether sixteen or eighteen is a better voting age depends on **(9)** _____. My own view is a compromise. **(10)** _____ that optional voting should begin at sixteen and mandatory at eighteen, giving sixteen-year-olds the option of participating in elections and eighteen-year-olds the responsibility of always casting a vote.

8 Read the essay again and match the two parts of the sentences. There are four endings you don't need.

1 In some countries, sixteen-year-olds _____
2 In most countries, the voting age _____
3 The internet has provided sixteen-year-olds _____
4 Involving younger people makes them _____
5 It's a disadvantage that sixteen-year-olds _____
6 Generally, eighteen-year olds are considered _____
7 It would be harder to manipulate _____
8 The writer feels that sixteen-year-olds should have _____

a more invested in politics.
b eighteen-year-olds.
c sixteen-year-olds.
d may not be mature enough.
e with more knowledge.
f an optional vote.
g is eighteen.
h to be independent adults.
i can already vote.
j with a disadvantage.
k is sixteen.
l a mandatory vote.

9 You're going to write an essay comparing advantages and disadvantages. Read the questions and write your essay.

What are the advantages and disadvantages of these options when finishing high school? Which do you think is the best?
• Going straight to college
• Taking a year to work or travel before starting college

Explain why, using specific reasons and examples to support your answer.

Review

1 Match the two parts of the sentences.

1 I worry about what other people think of me, _____
2 I never give in _____
3 Maggie doesn't mind taking risks, _____
4 Don't just follow the crowd _____
5 I'm just weighing the pros and cons, _____
6 Doing something risky _____
7 Think of the consequences _____

a and then I'll make a decision.
b but my sister couldn't care less.
c always gives me a thrill.
d but Jo prefers to play it safe.
e before you make a final decision.
f and do what everyone else does.
g to peer pressure.

2 Complete the binomial expressions.

1 bed and _____
2 brothers and _____
3 facts and _____
4 first and _____
5 ladies and _____
6 law and _____
7 loud and _____
8 odds and _____
9 safe and _____
10 short and _____
11 thunder and _____
12 trials and _____
13 ups and _____
14 wear and _____

3 Correct the mistake in each sentence.

1 I hadn't certainly estimated how long it would take to write the essay.

_____

2 My mother tells me always that I need to think before I speak.

_____

3 We wouldn't really want to go without a reservation because the restaurant is the most definitely popular in town.

_____

4 We always aren't in agreement, but we manage to compromise on most issues.

_____

5 They won't probably make it to the wedding because of their busy work schedules.

_____

6 The class has completed the unit on politics and government almost.

_____

7 Patiently Mr. Richardson has been waiting for several hours.

_____

4 Choose the correct options to complete the sentences.

1 My mom *will* / *would* often wake us up really early on Sundays. I hate it when she does that!
2 I didn't *use to* / *used to* like classical music.
3 Alex *never used to* / *didn't used to* be so talkative.
4 When we were children, we *tend to* / *used to* stay up late on Saturdays.
5 Grandma *was used to* / *would* always tell us stories about her uncle's farm.
6 My sister *is always telling me* / *is used to always telling me* to turn off my tablet at night.

5 Choose the two sentences that have the same meaning.

1 a When I was a child, I would spend most weekends with my grandparents.
   b When I was a child, I was used to spending most weekends with my grandparents.
   c I used to spend most weekends with my grandparents when I was a child.
2 a People tend to check social media as soon as they wake up.
   b People have a tendency to check social media as soon as they wake up.
   c People are getting used to checking social media as soon as they wake up.
3 a My little brother sometimes woke me up when he had a bad dream.
   b My little brother kept waking me up when he had a bad dream.
   c My little brother would always wake me up when he had a bad dream.
4 a I used to like watching horror movies in bed.
   b I would like to watch horror movies in bed.
   c I often watched horror movies in bed.

9 A Healthy Life

9A How to Stay Well

VOCABULARY Health and fitness

1 Review Complete the sentences with these words and phrases.

captained	compete	gold medal
great attitude	great technique	scored
smashed	world championships	world records

1 Heptathlete Jessica Ennis-Hill won a
_____ at the 2012 Olympics.

2 He _____ the US cycling team for
two seasons.

3 She has a really _____—she never gives
up, even if she's losing.

4 Having _____, whether it's footwork or
handling a racket, is essential for success in sports.

5 Amazingly, they _____ seven goals
in the second half!

6 Athletes that _____ at the
highest level internationally may take part in the
_____.

7 Jamaican sprinter Usain Bolt _____ three
_____ at the Beijing Olympics.

2 Review Choose the correct words to complete the
sentences.

1 Jian-Yang plays basketball for the school team. He's a
forward / backward / front.

2 Have you been watching Liliana play? She just scored a
great *game / record / goal*.

3 He's a talented swimmer who has *held / won / set* more
than 50 medals during his career.

4 She was one of the most productive members of the
hockey team last *season / period / calendar*.

5 Tennis players need to be very *aware / energetic /
passionate* to make it through a long match.

6 Jack is playing brilliantly. He's the real *shine / sun / star* of
the team this year.

3 Choose the correct options to complete the text.

Studies show that a poor diet and lack of exercise can lead
to a variety of problems. Eating foods that lack nutrients and
contain a lot of refined sugar will have a
(1) _____ on your body.

Avoid eating too much meat, but ensure that your diet
includes foods that are rich in **(2)** _____, like
fish, dairy products, and eggs.

A **(3)** _____ diet, filled with vegetables,
fruits, and wholegrain foods, will give you energy and keep
your body running as well as possible.

Consider eating fruit or some naturally sweet vegetables to
satisfy a sweet craving. Choosing to eat refined sugar
(4) _____ is a wise decision for your health.

A diet of mainly wholefoods and water, along with exercise
and sleep, will help relieve stress and will benefit your
overall **(5)** _____.

1	**a** moderation effect	**4**	**a** as much as possible
	b stressful effect		**b** nutrients
	c detrimental effect		**c** in moderation
2	**a** carbohydrates	**5**	**a** sedentary lifestyle
	b protein		**b** well-being
	c wholefoods		**c** nutrients
3	**a** nutritious		
	b nutrient		
	c nutrition		

4 Match the two parts of the sentences.

1 Protein is found in _____

2 Carbohydrates are found in _____

3 Wholefoods include _____

4 Eating wholefoods will have _____

5 Living a sedentary lifestyle will have _____

6 Eating refined sugars _____

a a beneficial effect on your body.

b in moderation is a healthy decision.

c lean meat, seafood, beans, soy, and eggs.

d fruit, vegetables, nuts, and wholegrains.

e a detrimental effect on your body.

f sugar, bread, potatoes, and pasta.

5 Complete the sentences with these words and phrases. There are two that you don't need.

beneficial	detrimental	enhance
intake	nutrients	obesity
refined sugars	sedentary lifestyle	well-being
wholefoods		

1 Be careful about your salt _____; too much salt can cause high blood pressure.

2 A _____ coupled with a poor diet can lead to _____.

3 When possible, choose to eat _____ instead of _____.

4 Eating processed food and too many carbohydrates can have a _____ effect on your body.

5 _____ your diet by trying new foods or preparing foods you like in new ways.

6 If you eat balanced meals, you'll ensure you get the proper amount of _____ to power your body.

6 Put the words in the correct order to make sentences.

1 The way / prepared / is / absorbs / the body / affect / the amount / nutrients / of / can / food / .

_____

2 moderation / best / sugars / in / refined / to eat / It's / .

_____

3 needs / it / nutritious wholefoods / body / your / A diet / offers / the energy / of / .

_____

4 stress, / relieve / get / regularly / help / To / exercise / .

_____

5 to put / choose / you / affects / well-being / its / your / body / What / in / .

_____

7 **Extension** Choose the correct options to complete the text.

The demands of modern life can be stressful for people of all ages. Many of us look for ways to **(1)** *reduce / enhance* the stress in our busy lives. Eating a balanced diet of foods that **(2)** *serve / nourish* your body, drinking plenty of water, and getting the proper amount of sleep each night, are three important ways to keep your stress levels under control. Getting **(3)** *energy / exercise* consistently helps reduce stress and can be **(4)** *invigorating / well-balanced* when you're feeling mentally or physically tired. Practicing **(5)** *mindfulness / forgetfulness* through meditation, yoga, and other techniques also helps to manage stress. Yoga **(6)** *supports / postures* can help to relieve tension in the body. Whatever method of stress relief you choose, it will surely contribute to your overall **(7)** *wellness / being*.

8 **Extension** Complete the sentences with these words.

cholesterol	minerals	organic
output	renew	supplements
vigor	vitamins	

1 People often search for healthy ways to increase their productivity or _____.

2 Some people take dietary _____ to ensure their body receives all the _____ and _____ it needs to perform at its best.

3 Other people choose to buy and eat only _____ fruit and vegetables.

4 It's important to eat plenty of vegetables and avoid fatty foods that are high in _____.

5 Taking a break from technology from time to time can help _____ your _____.

LISTENING

9 Listen to the conversation and choose the correct answers to the questions. 🎧 **73**

1 Why is Mrs. Jacobs there?
  a The doctor wants to talk about her test results.
  b She needs to collect some medication.
  c The doctor wants her to be involved in her husband's care.
  d Her husband needs her help to get around.

2 What two health issues is Mike's doctor discussing today?
  a excess weight and blood pressure
  b lack of exercise and unhealthy diet
  c blood pressure and cholesterol
  d high cholesterol and fatty foods

3 Why doesn't the doctor want to prescribe any medication?
  a He still thinks there are alternatives.
  b He knows that it won't help.
  c Mike already takes a lot of tablets.
  d Mrs. Jacobs is opposed to the idea.

4 What does the doctor want Mike to eat less of?
  a salt and olive oil
  b saturated fats and salt
  c all meats and oils
  d salt and potatoes

5 What else does the doctor want Mike to do?
  a drink less coffee
  b consider retiring
  c reduce his stress levels
  d do more exercise

6 When should Mike make an appointment to see the doctor again?
  a after the test results
  b as soon as possible
  c in three months
  d when he's feeling better

10 Listen to a talk about the elderly in China. What do you think is the speaker's main message? 🎧 **74**

a Don't oversleep, and exercise in moderation.
b Stay active, both mentally and physically.
c Go to outdoor parks as often as you can.
d Practice martial arts to stay fit and healthy.

11 Listen again. Match the words to make phrases. Then practice saying the phrases. 🎧 **74**

1 senior	**a** benefits
2 meditative martial	**b** mortality
3 perceived health	**c** art
4 stress	**d** to longevity
5 socioeconomic	**e** management
6 risk of	**f** citizens
7 average life	**g** expectancy
8 contributing factors	**h** status

12 Listen again and complete the sentences. Then practice saying the sentences. 🎧 **74**

1 Millions of Chinese senior citizens gather in parks to _____.

2 Some 30,000 outdoor recreation areas _____ as part of a nationwide fitness program.

3 T'ai chi is a meditative martial art of _____ exercises.

4 T'ai chi has become _____ because of its perceived health benefits and stress management.

5 Researchers _____ people's basic health, socioeconomic status, family support, and other factors.

6 The study found that regular exercisers, aged 80 and older, _____ of mortality by 20 percent.

7 In 2015, China had an _____ of 76.1 years.

8 It's hard to say exactly what the main _____ to longevity are.

GRAMMAR Relative clauses with prepositions

13 Match the two parts of the sentences.

1 Have you found a good study group _____
2 He will be going to a new school, _____
3 There's a wonderful new English teacher, _____
4 I have a notebook _____
5 There are many students in the school _____
6 There are many after-school clubs to join, _____
7 It's your test and exam scores _____
8 I went to see my English teachers, _____

a the most popular of which is probably gymnastics.
b that I could go to?
c at which he will have to wear a uniform.
d whose classes you should definitely go to.
e for whom math does not come easily.
f which I write in every day.
g that not studying has an effect on.
h both of whom said I have a lot of potential.

14 Choose the correct options to complete the sentences.

1 Who was the woman _____ you were talking?
   a with whom   c to who
   b whom with   d whom

2 You need to understand that it is your relationships _____ a lack of trust will have an impact.
   a on which   c what
   b with which   d on what

3 He has made a lot of new friends in class, all _____ live near one another.
   a with whom   c whom
   b that   d of whom

4 It's her best friend that she needs to apologize most _____ .
   a with   c to
   b on   d who

5 He plays on several sports teams, a number _____ have games on Saturdays.
   a of them   c which
   b of which   d who

6 It's your health _____ a poor diet has a detrimental effect _____ .
   a with, on   c with, for
   b that, with   d that, on

15 Rewrite the sentences as one sentence using a relative clause and a preposition.

1 Have you met Yoon, the new student? Pablo was talking to her. (informal)
   Have you met Yoon, the new student who Pablo was talking to?

2 My neighbor has a massive new dog. I'm quite afraid of it. (informal)
   _____
   _____

3 The professor visited several large colleges. None of them made him feel comfortable. (formal)
   _____
   _____

4 You should always eat regular meals. The most important meal is possibly breakfast. (formal)
   _____
   _____

5 Around ten o'clock, my mother has a cup of coffee. She adds low-fat milk to it. (informal)
   _____
   _____

6 The school has hired some new teachers. A number of the new teachers are under 30. (formal)
   _____
   _____

7 There's a new movie about the first space flight. I'm definitely interested in it. (informal)
   _____
   _____

9B The Role of the Mind in Achieving Well-being

VOCABULARY BUILDING Adjective suffixes
-able and *-ible*

1 Complete the sentences with these words. There are two words you don't need.

accessible	achievable	disposable
edible	inflatable	legible
memorable	preventable	rechargeable
washable		

1 I tried to read the label on the bottle, but it was no longer _____.

2 They're installing a new door to make the building _____ to disabled people.

3 Finding a cure for malaria is a goal that is _____ within our lifetime.

4 Doctors are working hard to protect the population against _____ diseases.

5 It's extremely dirty—you should wear _____ gloves when you clean it.

6 I only use _____ batteries because I think the other ones are wasteful.

7 Is your uniform _____ or does it have to be dry-cleaned?

8 The berries of that plant are _____—they taste really delicious.

READING

2 Read the statements. Are the sentences true (T), false (F), or is the information not given (NG)?

1 The Roman poet Juvenal thought that mind and body were completely separate things. _____

2 Davidson had been interested in meditation since he was a child. _____

3 Brain activity was measured using a combination of CT scans and ultrasounds. _____

4 The level of gamma waves in meditators' minds was a critical part of Davidson's study. _____

5 Research has shown that neural activity in the left prefrontal cortex reflects sadness. _____

6 Davidson proved that regular meditation changes the way your brain behaves. _____

7 Buddhists tend to be physically healthy because they meditate regularly. _____

3 Read and choose the correct options.

1 The quotation from Juvenal in paragraph 1 is closest in meaning to which of the following?
  a If people are unhappy, they should think carefully about their feelings.
  b The mind-body connection is an undeniable fact of existence.
  c Knowledge has a negative effect on human existence.

2 Which of the following statements about Richard Davidson is <u>not</u> mentioned in the article?
  a He was a Buddhist for many years before he decided to become a researcher.
  b He taught at the University of Wisconsin-Madison, where he studied people's emotions.
  c He researched meditative states among people who practiced Buddhism.

3 Davidson's experiments showed that
  a researchers should focus on the euphoria that people experience.
  b meditating has a measurable impact on the mind.
  c inner peace is only achievable through quiet breathing.

4 The "tangible manifestation" in paragraph 2 refers to
  a increased happiness.
  b breathing rates.
  c physical changes.

5 According to the article, the immune system is regulated in part by
  a the right prefrontal cortex.
  b the anterior insula.
  c resonance imaging in the brain.

6 What is implied about Angelina Jolie, Halle Berry, and Oprah Winfrey?
  a They were dissatisfied with their lives before they tried meditation.
  b They have founded important charitable organizations that help children.
  c They are well-known celebrities who have benefited from meditation.

7 The word *advocates* in paragraph 5 is closest in meaning to
  a participants.   **c** meditators.
  b supporters.

8 The advice that "we should all learn from the wisdom of the past" implies that
  a it's surprising that meditation has genuine benefits.
  b the Romans were remarkable scientists and researchers.
  c ancient thinkers knew more than we might imagine.

The Role of the Mind in Achieving Well-being 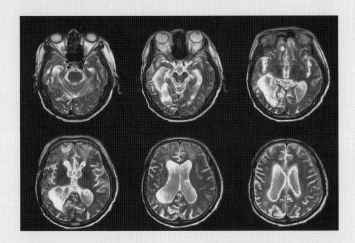 🎧 75

1 The mind-body connection has long been a key part of our understanding of health and happiness. Thousands of years ago, the Roman poet Juvenal summed up the relationship in the well-known Latin phrase, *Mens sana in corpore sano*. This sentence is best translated as, "a healthy mind in a healthy body." The idea of a link between physical and psychological well-being is easy to accept. After all, most people know from experience that when they're in a good mood, they also feel better physically. Similarly, when people feel down, they often feel physically unwell. However, for many years there was no concrete evidence to support this widely accepted idea.

2 In the 1990s, neuroscientist Richard Davidson decided to look for proof of the connection between physical health and mental well-being. Davidson had recently begun teaching at the University of Wisconsin-Madison and had founded a laboratory dedicated to the study of emotions. He had the idea of examining the minds of people who meditated regularly. The simple technique of sitting comfortably for several minutes, eyes closed and attention directed on breathing, was said to produce feelings of intense love and compassion, even euphoria*. Davidson thought it was likely that these powerful feelings would have a tangible manifestation. If he could identify physical changes that took place when people meditated, he would have strong evidence that physical and mental well-being were related.

3 For the study, Davidson and his colleagues recruited long-term practitioners of Buddhism. Meditation is an important part of the Buddhist faith and is believed to be a way to achieve inner peace. The people that Davidson worked with were very experienced meditators and had spent an average of 34,000 hours in mental training. Davidson asked them to alternate between a meditative state and a neutral state while he measured activity in the brain using magnetic resonance imaging*. The results of the study were fascinating. Davidson was able to measure a very high level of gamma waves in the participants' brains when they meditated. Gamma waves are a type of neural activity* related to concentration and focus. Brain scans of people who did not meditate regularly did not show this activity.

4 Davidson subsequently carried out further experiments and made other interesting discoveries. He was able to prove that in addition to having higher levels of gamma waves, people who meditate show more activity in an area of the brain called the anterior insula, which has a role in regulating the immune system. This aspect of Davidson's research suggested that meditation could help people maintain better overall health. Meanwhile, he also identified increased activity in the left prefrontal cortex, an area of the brain understood to be associated with happiness. As such, he was able to confirm that the feelings of contentment the meditators described had a physical basis. Although many questions remain, Davidson's studies have confirmed that meditation has a powerful and measurable effect on the body.

5 Partly due to Davidson's research, meditation is experiencing renewed popularity. Celebrities, such as Angelina Jolie, Halle Berry, and Oprah Winfrey, have taken up the practice. Meanwhile, director David Lynch has founded a charitable organization that aims to reduce stress by promoting meditation in schools, at health centers and among veterans*. These public figures, as well as participants in Lynch's programs, speak about the experience of meditation in ways that are completely consistent with the feelings that the meditators in Davidson's study described. Indeed, the feelings of happiness and peace that they experienced are in keeping with what advocates of the practice have been saying for thousands of years. Perhaps we should all learn from the wisdom of the past. Ancient practices could have other health benefits that are waiting to be uncovered by modern science.

euphoria *a feeling of great happiness*
magnetic resonance imaging (MRI) *a technique used to create images of the body's internal organs, such as the brain*

neural activity *activity in the cells that send and receive messages in the brain*
veteran *a person who has fought in a war*

9C Prevention as Cure

GRAMMAR Articles

1 Match the words in bold in the sentences (1–7) with the descriptions of the use of the article (a–e). The descriptions can be used more than once.

1 My favorite instrument is **the piano**. _____
2 **The doctor** told me to stay at home until the swelling goes down. _____
3 **Health** is **people's** primary concern. _____
4 **A crew cut** is a very short hairstyle for men. _____
5 **The blue whale** is an endangered species. _____
6 **The causes of many types of cancer** are still unclear. _____
7 A lot of **the health problems that we face** are due to lifestyle. _____

a introducing a singular countable noun that is specified or known
b referring to a single object that represents the whole group or class of the object, or a species
c referring to an example of something
d with plural nouns, referring to the group in general, and with uncountable nouns, referring to a concept in general
e with plural nouns or uncountable nouns made specific by a relative clause or prepositional phrase

2 Choose the correct options to complete the sentences.

1 _____ back hurts a lot.
  a My   **b** The   **c** A
2 _____ elderly require more personalized healthcare.
  a –   **b** The   **c** An
3 You should go to the doctor every year for _____ check-up.
  a a   **b** the   **c** –
4 I have _____ very bad cold.
  a –   **b** the   **c** a
5 The vaccine only protects you against certain strains of _____ disease.
  a a   **b** –   **c** the
6 It's harder to fight off _____ illnesses when you're stressed and tired.
  a –   **b** the   **c** an

3 Complete the sentences with these words or no word (–).

a	an	his	my	the
your	–			

1 He hurt _____ back last week.
2 Nurses sometimes wear _____ uniform.
3 He is _____ honest doctor.
4 If you try to read in the dark, you'll strain _____ eyes.
5 Most people in this country have _____ health insurance.
6 _____ very young and elderly are the most at risk.
7 She doesn't believe in _____ alternative medicine.
8 You should see _____ specialist your brother was recommending.
9 I broke _____ left hip last year.
10 _____ antibiotic does not fight infections caused by viruses.

4 Complete the text with *a/an, the,* or the zero article (–).

Activity trackers are **(1)** _____ very popular way to keep track of **(2)** _____ physical activity and **(3)** _____ calorie consumption. But are they accurate and reliable? A recent study conducted by **(4)** _____ researchers at Stanford University looked at seven of **(5)** _____ most popular trackers and focused on two measurements: **(6)** _____ heart rate and how many calories were burned. **(7)** _____ 60 volunteers who took part in **(8)** _____ study included 31 women and 29 men.

For heart rate, researchers compared
(9) _____ trackers to
(10) _____ findings from an EKG or electrocardiogram. It turns out most of them were pretty accurate and reliable, with **(11)** _____ error margin of just five percent in six out of
(12) _____ seven trackers analyzed.

To measure calories burned, researchers compared
(13) _____ trackers' findings to those of
(14) _____ instrument that measures oxygen and carbon dioxide in a person's breath.
(15) _____ trackers' calorie measurements, it turns out, were incredibly inaccurate.
(16) _____ degree of inaccuracy ranged from 27 percent for **(17)** _____ most accurate tracker, to 93 percent for
(18) _____ most inaccurate one.

Researchers concluded that **(19)** _____ people should not base their food intake on how many calories **(20)** _____ activity tracker says they're burning.

5 Put the words in the correct order to make sentences.

1 home-cooked / best / a / the / is / medicine / meal / .

_____

_____

2 elderly / get / the / often / more / colds / .

_____

_____

3 daily injection / a / for / diabetes / his / has / he / .

_____

_____

4 endangered / the / an / animal / is / species / no / panda / longer / .

_____

_____

5 his / for / my / really / brother / a / cat / wants / birthday / .

_____

_____

6 Read the two sentences and decide if they are the same (S) or different (D).

1 A vaccine is a preparation used to provide immunity against diseases.
Vaccines are preparations used to provide immunity against diseases. _____

2 Most children's immune systems can fight off diseases.
The immune system of most children can fight off the disease. _____

3 I see a specialist at a local clinic.
I see the specialist at the local clinic. _____

4 Elderly people are more prone to infections.
The elderly are more prone to infections. _____

5 Too much time in front of a computer can strain the eyes.
Too much time in front of the computer can strain the eyes. _____

6 The researchers are working on a new vaccine.
Researchers are working on the new vaccine. _____

7 Choose the correct options to complete the text.

Dr. Ludwig is **(1)** _____ obesity expert and professor of nutrition at Harvard University. He wrote **(2)** _____ book entitled *Always Hungry*.
(3) _____ main message of the book is that what causes obesity is not **(4)** _____ excess of calories, but **(5)** _____ excess of **(6)** _____ sugar and **(7)** _____ refined or processed carbohydrates. Dr. Ludwig believes that **(8)** _____ low fat, high carbohydrate diet people have been eating for **(9)** _____ last four decades is making us unhealthy. In his book, he explains why he recommends **(10)** _____ high fat diet without processed carbohydrates. Of course, he also recommends **(11)** _____ active lifestyle with **(12)** _____ regular exercise.

	a	**b**	**c**	**d**
1	a	an	–	the
2	a	an	–	the
3	A	An	–	The
4	a	an	–	the
5	a	an	–	the
6	a	an	–	the
7	a	an	–	the
8	a	an	–	the
9	a	an	–	the
10	a	an	–	the
11	a	an	–	the
12	a	an	–	the

9D My Simple Invention, Designed to Keep My Grandfather Safe

TEDTALKS

AUTHENTIC LISTENING SKILLS

1 Read and complete Part 2 of the TED Talk. Then listen and check your answers. 🎧 **76**

My desire **(1)** _____ create a sensor-based technology perhaps stemmed from my lifelong love **(2)** _____ sensors and technology. When I was six years old, **(3)** _____ elderly family friend fell down in the bathroom and suffered severe injuries. I became concerned about my own grandparents **(4)** _____ decided to invent a smart bathroom system. Motion sensors would be installed inside the tiles **(5)** _____ bathroom floors to detect the falls of elderly patients whenever they fell down in **(6)** _____ bathroom. Since I was only six years old at the time and I **(7)** _____ graduated from kindergarten yet, I didn't **(8)** _____ the necessary resources **(9)** _____ tools to translate my idea into reality, but nonetheless, my **(10)** _____ experience really implanted in me a firm desire to use sensors **(11)** _____ help the elderly people. I really believe that sensors **(12)** _____ improve the quality of life of the elderly.

WATCH ▶

2 Choose the correct options to complete the sentences.

1 Every 67 seconds, someone in the United States is diagnosed with *cancer / Alzheimer's*.
2 Shinozuka's grandfather suddenly *got lost / fell over* when they were walking in the park.
3 His grandfather's *eating / wandering* at night caused the family significant stress.
4 Shinozuka's initial invention was a *pair of socks / pillow* with a sensor.
5 Shinozuka had to create a sensor, design a circuit and *code a smartphone app / find a manufacturer*.
6 Using Bluetooth low-energy technology, he avoided the need for *charging cables / heavy, bulky batteries*.

7 Shinozuka successfully created *two prototypes / an initial prototype* of his wearable sensor.
8 He is testing his invention at several *hospitals / residential care facilities* in California.

3 Choose the correct options to complete the sentences.

1 Alzheimer's is a growing problem *of / for* which many people are unaware.
2 Sensors are a technology which Shinozuka has always been interested *to / in*.
3 Shinozuka's grandfather was the person *for which / for whom* the original invention was developed.
4 Shinozuka is developing a mat which *patients will step on / on patients will step* when they get out of bed.
5 Carers are among the people *for whom / for that* this invention will relieve stress.
6 Coding was one of the topics that Shinozuka had to learn more *about / about that*.
7 The correlations between nighttime wandering and daytime activities are a topic *which / about which* researchers would like to understand more.
8 Shinozuka hopes that there are many people *of whom / for whom* his invention will mean a significant improvement in their quality of life.

VOCABULARY IN CONTEXT

4 Match the words in bold in the sentences (1–6) with the phrases (a–f).

1 Shinozuka and his family **had direct personal experience of** the difficulties of dealing with Alzheimer's. _____
2 Shinozuka and other family members had to constantly **watch his grandfather and check he was OK**. _____
3 After extensive research and testing, Shinozuka realized that he would need to change his **initial** ideas about materials. _____
4 Shinozuka's desire to come up with a sensor-based solution **was caused by** his lifelong interest in technology. _____
5 Since he wasn't familiar with all of the techniques needed to build his product, Shinozuka looked for video **lessons with instructions** to help him. _____
6 It is hoped that data collected from Shinozuka's inventions will help establish **links** between patients' daily habits and their nighttime wandering. _____

a keep an eye on his grandfather
b tutorials
c experienced firsthand
d stemmed from
e correlations
f preliminary

9E Stronger Together

WRITING A proposal

1 Complete the text with these words. There are two words you don't need.

bullet points	clarity	examples
findings	formal	informal
introduction	repetition	report
style	sub-headings	title

When writing a proposal, choose a relevant
(1) _____ to reflect the topic and use
(2) _____ for each section. In your
(3) _____, briefly state what the proposal
includes: the research, the **(4)** _____, and
your recommendations. Unlike in a(n)
(5) _____, the recommendations section is
typically longer. Use **(6)** _____ to list your
recommendations. To avoid **(7)** _____,
use a variety of expressions to make your recommendations.
Throughout the proposal, use **(8)** _____
language and an impersonal **(9)** _____.
Support your main points with concrete
(10) _____ (use *for instance*, *such as*, *like*,
etc.). Finish by stating the benefits of implementing the
recommendations in your proposal.

2 Choose the best options to complete the proposal.

Introduction

The proposal is based on an invitation to students by our
teacher, Ms. Brown, to submit ideas for this year's school trip.
It **(1)** *has / outlines* details regarding the schedule and
budget, and suggests an ideal location. It **(2)** *concludes /
ends* by making recommendations on how students might get
the maximum benefit from this trip.

Schedule and budget

(3) *Based on / Having* feedback from previous school trips, early
April is the preferred period for travel. It is far enough ahead
of exam time for students to feel they can relax and enjoy
themselves. As with other years, a generous budget has been
contributed from the school fund. Rather than students paying
their own money to increase the budget for the trip, it has been
(4) *said / suggested* that a series of fundraising events be run by
senior students.

Recommendations

It is suggested that Scotland be the destination for this year's
school trip. There are **(5)** *lots of / several* ways in which students
could benefit from this choice.

- **(6)** *Number one / First and foremost*, it is recommended
  as an inexpensive alternative to London or any major city
  where costs would be significantly higher.
- Secondly, it is clear that Scotland **(7)** *gives / would provide*
  students with a welcome opportunity to practice their
  English.
- Finally, the school **(8)** *could consider organizing / should
  organize* this as a camping trip in the beautiful Scottish
  countryside, which would keep costs down. In addition,
  plans could be made for various day trips, for example,
  into the nearby cities of Edinburgh and Glasgow.

Conclusion

(9) *If you use / By implementing* this recommendation, our senior
student group could have both an affordable and a memorable
school trip. It would enable them to experience two aspects of
life in Scotland: city and countryside. If this **(10)** *great idea /
suggestion* is implemented, students would not only enjoy
a range of outdoor activities in the Scottish Highlands, they
would also discover the history and culture the cities have to
offer.

3 Write at least 250 words on the topic below. Give reasons
for your answer and include any relevant examples from
your knowledge or experience.

Nowadays, worry is something that causes problems for
many students.

What are the most serious problems associated with
student worries and what solutions can you suggest?

SPEAKING

4 Listen to the proposals and choose the best response to each statement. 🎧 **77**

1 a It's a good idea in principle, but I want to know what kind of classes you're going to offer.
  b You need to bear in mind that a lot of fitness centers already offer those classes.

2 a Yes, but the problem is how? People just have too much work.
  b It's worth remembering that most people are already very stressed.

3 a It's a good idea in principle, but aren't most people already aware of how important sleep is?
  b Do you think you could summarize your recommendations in a simpler way?

4 a Yes, but the problem is, people don't eat enough fresh fruit and vegetables.
  b I think it's a great idea. I wonder if it'd be feasible to offer a salad bar.

5 a Yes, but the problem is, these days people need their computers to do just about everything.
  b Yes, but you need to bear in mind that people should cut down screen time.

5 Listen to the proposals and complete the responses. 🎧 **78**

1 _____, but school trips can be so difficult to organize.

2 _____ a lot of people are on vacation at this time of year.

3 _____ to provide a bike trail.

4 _____ the hall might not be available every week.

6 Read part of a lecture about yoga and make notes about how you would answer the question that follows. Then listen to how another student answered the question. 🎧 **79**

Yoga has become extremely popular in recent years and, these days, you can find yoga studios just about everywhere. What many people don't realize is that the practice is thousands of years old. It was practiced in ancient India as early as the 5th century BC, and some scholars believe it may have existed for much longer. Yoga was introduced to the west in the 19th century when a Bengali physician called N.C. Paul published a famous book about the practice, and it grew in popularity in the 1980s. In 2016, yoga was awarded world heritage status by UNESCO.

Yoga has numerous health benefits. It has long been known that the practice is an effective way to increase flexibility and muscle strength. It also gives people more energy, improves athletic performance, and boosts immunity. How incredible to think that stretching and breathing exercises can protect us from disease! Yoga's physical benefits are, of course, in addition to the emotional rewards. Yoga helps people to relax, focus, and even to feel happier. It is sometimes recommended as a treatment for depression.

The scientific community has become increasingly interested in researching the relationship between yoga and well-being. Recent studies have demonstrated that yoga can help people fight asthma, arthritis, and anxiety. Some doctors even believe that yoga can play a role in overcoming cancer. In years to come, additional benefits of yoga are sure to be discovered.

Question: Explain what the professor suggests about the future of yoga.

PRONUNCIATION Intonation in responses

7 Listen and underline the words that are stressed in the sentences. Then practice saying the sentences. 🎧 **80**

1 It's a good idea in principle, but it's hard to stop drinking coffee.
2 I really like the idea of reducing my sugar intake.
3 It's worth remembering that not everyone has access to nutritious food.
4 That sounds like an excellent way of losing weight!
5 Growing our own vegetables is a great idea!
6 Yes, but the problem is, refined sugar is in so many of our foods.
7 You need to bear in mind that organic food is often more expensive.
8 Laughter yoga is a fantastic way to relieve stress.

Review

1 Complete the words in the sentences.

1 Too much r _ _ _ _ _ d   s _ _ _ r can have a
d _ _ _ _ _ _ _ _ _ l   e _ _ _ _ t on the body.
2 Eating mainly w _ _ _ _ _ _ _ _ s will have a
b _ _ _ _ _ _ _ _ l   e _ _ _ _ t on the body.
3 Living a s _ _ _ _ _ _ _ y   l _ _ _ _ _ _ _ e can lead
to o _ _ _ _ _ y.
4 Exercise is a great way to r _ _ _ _ _ e   s _ _ _ _ s.
5 If your body doesn't receive enough n _ _ _ _ _ _ _ s,
you may feel sluggish or tired.

2 Complete the adjectives with *-able* or *-ible*. Then add a
related verb.

Adjective	Verb
access	
afford	
dispos	
aud	—
enjoy	
feas	—
memor	—
recycl	
renew	
leg	—
vis	—

3 Are these sentences correct or incorrect? Correct those
that are incorrect.

1 Apollo 11 was the first space mission in who human
beings landed on the moon.

_____

2 The crew of Apollo 11 consisted of three men, all of
whom were experienced astronauts.

_____

3 There were many calculations of that had to be made
before Apollo 11 could launch in July 1969.

_____

4 The three astronauts made several transmissions to
Earth as they traveled to the moon, two of whom were
televised.

_____

5 The astronauts spent over 21 hours on the moon, after
which they returned safely to Earth.

_____

4 Choose the correct options to complete the sentences.

1 I hurt *the* / *my* shoulder climbing – / *the* at the gym.
2 More attention should be paid to *the* / – health of
the / – school-age children.
3 My favorite school subject is *the* / – history.
4 I have *a* / *an* unusual problem.
5 I heard it on – / *the* radio.
6 She works for *a* / *the* non-profit organization that helps
the / – disabled.
7 *Koalas* / *The koalas* are found only in Australia.
8 He is *the* / *a* doctor at *a* / *an* hospital in Boston.

5 Complete the text with *a/an*, *the*, or the zero article (–).

Here's the truth about some common beliefs regarding
colds and flu!

"I didn't wear **(1)** _____ coat and I caught
(2) _____ cold."

(3) _____ coat will keep you warm and
protect you from hypothermia, but it won't keep colds
away. Colds are caused by **(4)** _____
viruses. It is true that it's more common to get
(5) _____ colds in winter, but
that's because viruses can survive better in
(6) _____ colder weather.

"Just take some vitamin C."

It turns out that **(7)** _____ vitamin C won't
prevent or help a cold. This long-held belief has been
proved false in **(8)** _____ recent studies.
However, vitamin C is pretty harmless and
(9) _____ body will get rid of what
it doesn't need.

A Healthy Life **109**

10 Ideas

10A Expressing Ideas

VOCABULARY Making your point

1 Review Match the words and phrases (1–7) with their definitions (a–g).

1 sort it out _____
2 be offended _____
3 hint _____
4 conscious _____
5 complimentary _____
6 awkward _____
7 discourage _____

a embarrassing and difficult to deal with
b to feel upset about something someone said or did
c to do what is necessary to deal with a disagreement
d to say what you think or feel in an indirect way
e aware of something
f to try to persuade someone not to do something
g expressing admiration for someone or something

2 Review Complete the sentences with these words and phrases. There are two that you don't need.

awkward	be offended	compliment
complimentary	discourage	discrimination
misunderstanding	stereotype	stereotypical
work it out		

1 _____ of any type is not tolerated at this school.
2 It was a/an _____ British day in September: cloudy, wet, and windy.
3 Please don't _____. It was just a _____.
4 There was a/an _____ silence and then everybody laughed.
5 People seem to like the book. Dozens of the reviews are very _____.
6 His negative comments failed to _____ her from pursuing her dream.
7 I told them to stop arguing and just _____.

3 Choose the correct options to complete the teacher's comments.

In general, your presentation was very good. You spoke loudly and clearly, and you **(1)** _____ with the audience throughout. However, once or twice you seemed to **(2)** _____. Always glance at your notes to remind yourself what you're going to say next.

Additionally, you made too many **(3)** _____. Consider folding your hands in front of you while speaking. The content of your speech was very informative, however, be sure to explain technical **(4)** _____ in your presentation. Your audience may not be familiar with all the terms you use. You could also try varying your intonation. It can be a very good way to **(5)** _____ your listeners' attention.

1 a made eye contact   c stuck to the point
  b lost your train of thought d misinterpreted
2 a use facial expressions   c stick to the point
  b get your point across   d lose your train of thought
3 a gestures   c analogies
  b facial expressions   d comparisons
4 a points of view   c analogies
  b jargon   d comparisons
5 a misinterpret   c engage
  b lose   d convey

4 Choose the correct options to complete the text.

When I give a presentation, I use several techniques. I tell myself to keep it brief. It's important to be clear and **(1)** *concise / advise*, but at the same time, I try to be accurate and use **(2)** *blank / precise* words as necessary. I always try to **(3)** *rephrase my answer / stick to the point* so that the audience don't get bored and I **(4)** *engage / convey* their **(5)** *attention / gestures* throughout the talk. I often include **(6)** *analogies / jargon* to explain more complex ideas and I sometimes use **(7)** *hand / facial* expressions to help **(8)** *elaborate on my point / get my point across*. During the talk, if I lose my train of thought and **(9)** *my mind goes blank / I don't make eye contact*, I remind myself to take a deep breath and consult my notes.

5 Complete the sentences with these expressions.

back up her argument with facts	convey his ideas more concisely
define technical jargon	elaborate on the point
make eye contact	rephrase the answer more precisely

1 Ayesha looked down at the floor the whole time she was speaking. She should _____ with the audience.

2 Mikhail didn't give enough information about the first thing he talked about. He should _____.

3 When Kuan-yin gave her response, no one understood what she meant. She should _____.

4 Faisal's speech was much too long. He should

_____.

5 When Pilar made her argument, she didn't give any specific details or examples. She should

_____.

6 Marion didn't adequately explain what some of the scientific terms meant. She should _____.

6 Put the words in the correct order to make sentences.

1 by / practicing / expressions / speech / in / Control / mirror / and gestures / your / facial / the / your / .

_____

2 notes / train / Use / of / lose / thought / you / that / so / don't / your / .

_____

3 asking / audience / questions / by / them / your / Engage / .

_____

4 blank / if / mind / Don't / your / goes / panic / .

_____

5 point / in order to / concisely / to / message / the / convey / your / Stick / .

_____

7 **Extension** Complete the sentences with the correct form of these verbs.

attract	draw	give	hold	pay	turn

1 It's now time to _____ our attention to a completely different topic.

2 These safety instructions are very important so please _____ me your full attention.

3 We knocked on the window to _____ his attention.

4 The presentation was pretty boring and completely failed to _____ my attention.

5 I can't remember exactly what he said because I wasn't really _____ attention.

6 The campaign is designed to _____ people's attention to the environmental impact of the proposals.

8 **Extension** Which part of the face do these words connected with facial expressions describe? Complete the chart.

blink	blush	flare	flushed
grin	narrow	pale	pout
widen	wrinkle		

Eyes	Nose	Mouth	Skin

LISTENING

9 Listen and choose the correct answers to complete the sentences. 🎧 **81**

1 Sheila knows how _____ Kevin is about his presentation today.
- **a** panicked
- **b** unsure
- **c** anxious
- **d** unprepared

2 Sheila thinks that people will love Kevin's proposal if he can get his _____ across.
- **a** main points
- **b** opposing view
- **c** different ideas
- **d** specific details

3 Sheila tells Kevin that people can lose track when he _____.
- **a** uses gestures
- **b** moves around
- **c** stares at the wall
- **d** speaks too quickly

4 Sheila tells Kevin that he might want to _____ his main points.
- **a** touch on
- **b** repeat
- **c** anticipate
- **d** approach

5 Sheila tells Kevin to _____ questions from the audience.
- **a** avoid
- **b** be prepared for
- **c** worry about
- **d** explain

6 Sheila and Kevin had a discussion about all of this _____.
- **a** today
- **b** last week
- **c** many times
- **d** yesterday

10 Listen and match the words to make phrases. Then practice saying the phrases. 🎧 **82**

1 digital		**a** and white
2 reflect		**b** photo
3 closer		**c** of questions
4 learned		**d** the reader
5 informing		**e** experts
6 their mission		**f** together
7 forensic		**g** age
8 an altered		**h** its lesson
9 black		**i** to ensure
10 the complexities		**j** the reality

11 Listen again. Are the sentences true (T) or false (F)? 🎧 **82**

1 People generally don't care whether photos are real. _____

2 The original photo of the camel train was vertical. _____

3 The magazine changed its photographic policy after the cover incident. _____

4 In the past, photo alteration wasn't such a big problem because it was less sophisticated. _____

5 It's much easier today to see that a photograph isn't real. _____

6 Forensic analysis guarantees that altered photos will never be accepted. _____

7 Photographic pixel information is a strong indication of whether a photo is real. _____

8 Overprocessing does not always mean that a photo will be rejected. _____

PRONUNCIATION   Question intonation

> Remember that the intonation of a question can depend on whether the speaker is asking for confirmation, information, or agreement, or expressing surprise.

12 Listen to the questions. Does each one end with a rising (R) or falling tone (F)? Then practice saying the questions. 🎧 **83**

1 He's going to college in the fall, isn't he? _____

2 Her idea was concise and to the point, wasn't it? _____

3 Are they going to give the presentation together? _____

4 You lost your train of thought, didn't you? _____

5 You're not really considering that, are you? _____

6 Wait, he's going to do what? _____

GRAMMAR Advanced question types

13 Complete the tag questions.

1 She's a wonderful doctor, _____?

2 You haven't finished your exam yet, _____?

3 Let's go to dinner after the play, _____?

4 Someone told you the meeting started at ten, _____?

5 We didn't see him again after he left the cafe, _____?

6 My brother is a great football player, _____?

7 She hasn't told him about the wedding yet, _____?

8 I'm getting much better at English, _____?

14 Rewrite the questions to make indirect or negative questions.

1 Does the school offer advanced language classes? (indirect)

Do you know if *the school offers advanced language classes*?

2 What tool would I need to fix this broken pipe? (indirect)
Can you tell me _____?

3 Did you realize you were going to miss the bus? (negative)
_____ going to miss the bus?

4 Do I usually see you at the station coffee shop? (negative)
_____ at the station coffee shop?

5 Did he audition for the lead role in the play? (indirect)
Could you tell me if _____?

6 Have I explained the grammar clearly enough? (indirect)
I'd like to know if _____.

15 Put the words in the correct order to make questions.

1 Can / why / late / the lesson / you / tell / me / he / was / for / ?

_____

2 said / what / to / the / Sorry, / you / teacher / ?

_____

3 realize / difficult / biology / you / Didn't / was / advanced / ?

_____

4 essay / tell / Could / you / me / if / next week / due / the / is / ?

_____

5 try / Let's / shall / tickets, / we / to / get / ?

_____

6 at me / Why / the teacher / staring / keeps / think / do / you / ?

_____

16 Complete the interview. Write one or two words in each space.

Interviewer: Thanks for taking the time to talk to me today. I'd **(1)** _____ know more about your career as a photojournalist for several major newspapers.

Photojournalist: Of course. I'm happy to be here.

I: Could you tell me how you **(2)** _____ in this profession?

P: I got my start through a friend who worked at a newspaper. He'd seen my photographs and thought I'd be good at taking interesting photographs quickly.

I: Can you tell me what things or subjects **(3)** _____?

P: Well, I photograph lots of things of interest to the public. I started working locally, taking photographs of events in the city. Then I started working in other countries, mainly those experiencing political problems.

I: You've been to some pretty dangerous places, **(4)** _____?

P: Yes, I suppose I have, but it's been worth it. I feel like I'm making a difference.

I: Several of your colleagues told me you're the most committed photojournalist they've ever worked with.

P: Excuse me, they **(5)** _____?

I: They said you're a very committed photographer.

P: Well, I appreciate that. I love my work and I think I can help people with my photos.

I: Finally, why do **(6)** _____ you've been so successful?

P: I think I have a sensitivity to how people are feeling. My photographs show more than what's happening; they show the human side of each event I photograph.

10B A New Way to See the Word

VOCABULARY BUILDING Adjectives ending in *-ful* and *-less*

1 Complete the sentences with these words. There are two words you don't need.

doubtless	fearful	fearless	forgetful
fruitful	meaningless	regretful	tasteful

1 When giving a talk, be careful not to use _____ phrases.

2 You'll _____ feel pretty nervous when you stand up to speak, but try to relax.

3 Choose something _____ to wear—a presenter's appearance is important.

4 John needs a detailed set of notes because he's _____.

5 I'm _____ that my mind will go blank when someone asks a question.

6 The discussion was really _____; we've now got some great ideas for the presentation.

READING

2 Read the article and choose the correct options.

1 According to the article, Hans Rosling is primarily famous for
  a discovering the cause of konzo.
  b his work with the Cuban government.
  c his speeches about public health.
  d his time at the Karolinska Institute.

2 What did Rosling believe about statistics?
  a More money should be devoted to their collection.
  b They should be presented in a way that makes them easier to understand.
  c Numbers are difficult to explain to people.
  d College students should be required to study them.

3 What was similar about Rosling's experiences in Africa and Cuba?
  a He used data to determine the cause of illnesses.
  b In the communities he studied, the diseases had the same cause.
  c Rosling spoke about both trips in his TED lectures.
  d He studied both the diseases he discovered using Trendalyzer software.

4 What did Rosling realize when he started teaching at the Karolinska Institute?
  a Swedish university students were very knowledgeable about public health.
  b Many people were interested in helping him with his research.
  c The university disagreed with his conclusions about konzo.
  d A lot of students lacked information about global health problems.

5 Which description best explains what Trendalyzer is?
  a Trendalyzer is a tool that governments use to understand health issues.
  b Trendalyzer is software that helps people present data more clearly.
  c Trendalyzer is a program that helps researchers analyze their data.
  d Trendalyzer is the name of the organization founded by Rosling.

3 Read the article again and answer the questions. Write no more than four words and/or a number for each answer.

1 What is the main symptom of konzo?
  _____

2 What does bitter cassava contain?
  _____

3 In Pinar del Rio, what was causing blurry vision and numbness? _____

4 In Trendalyzer, what are different countries represented by? _____

5 In paragraph 5, what adjective does the writer use to describe Rosling's research?
  _____

4 Read the statements. Do they reflect the writer's claims (Y), not reflect the writer's claims (N), or is the information not given (NG)?

1 The writer suggests that Rosling had a big impact on the way numerical presentations are conveyed. _____

2 The text implies that Rosling's time in Cuba was more important than his experiences in Africa. _____

3 The writer suggests that members of Rosling's family are making important contributions to his work, particularly in the field of education. _____

4 The writer believes that Trendalyzer is a very easy program to use. _____

A New Way to See the World 🎧 84

1 Few people have a more compelling* presentation style than Swedish academic Hans Rosling. An accomplished statistician, doctor, and public health expert, in the second half of his career Rosling became internationally famous as a dynamic public speaker. Rosling's genius was to realize that many people don't understand basic facts about the world. Rosling decided that the solution was to present statistical information through innovative graphics, bringing numerical data to life in a way that everyone could understand. The project was extremely successful. Rosling's first speech, a TED Talk, has been viewed more than 11 million times. His other lectures have also received global attention.

2 Rosling's belief in the importance of data came from experiences he had early in his career as a doctor. He spent two decades working as a medical officer and researcher in rural Africa. He lived and worked in Mozambique, the Democratic Republic of the Congo, and Tanzania. At the time, many people were suffering from a mysterious illness called *konzo*, which caused paralysis*. Rosling studied a population of 500,000 in an effort to understand what was causing the disease. When he analyzed this information, Rosling realized that the problem came from diet. The communities where the disease was worst all ate a lot of bitter cassava*, which contains a toxin*. When the plant is soaked in water, the toxin disappears, but due to water shortages people had been skipping this step, with terrible consequences.

3 Rosling used similar methods in Pinar del Rio, Cuba, to determine what was causing a different illness. About 40,000 people were suffering from blurry vision* and numbness* in their legs, and the government didn't know why. After studying the communities that were most affected, Rosling realized that the cause was a lack of protein. At the time, there were limits on the amount of meat people could have. There was not enough meat for everyone, so many adults had been giving their portions to children, pregnant women, and the elderly. Rosling met with government leaders and showed them the numbers. He explained that unless people began to consume more protein, the disease would continue to spread.

4 Rosling came to the conclusion that data needed to play a bigger role in the fight against poverty and disease. This belief was strengthened when he began teaching at the Karolinska Institute, a prestigious university in Stockholm. His students were hardworking and intelligent, but there were large gaps in their knowledge of global health and poverty. Data had helped Rosling to solve two medical crises. How were his students going to do the same if they didn't know the facts? Rosling asked his son to help him. Together they built a program called Trendalyzer, which turns numbers into shapes and colors that fly across a computer screen. In the program, countries are represented by bubbles of different sizes. The bubbles move horizontally to show how countries change over time and grow or shrink as populations get bigger and smaller. Even people with no knowledge of statistics can understand complex ideas when they are expressed in this highly visual way.

5 Trendalyzer made Rosling famous. After using the software in his first TED Talk, he acquired a large following. Over the next few years, he went on to make many more speeches and convinced people that presentations about statistical topics could be enjoyable, even exciting. Rosling died of pancreatic cancer in February 2017, leaving a great legacy in the form of his valuable research and presentation style. His most significant achievement was helping people to see the world through facts, not preconceptions*. Today, Rosling's son and daughter-in-law continue his work by publishing free teaching material based on his methods. They have also made Trendalyzer freely available so that everyone can take advantage of this powerful tool.

compelling *very interesting and keeping your attention*
paralysis *loss of the ability to move*
bitter cassava *a starchy vegetable common in tropical countries*
toxin *a poisonous substance that causes illness*

blurry vision *not being able to see clearly*
numbness *not being able to feel*
preconception *an opinion formed before you have information about something*

10C Ideas Worth Spreading

GRAMMAR Subordinate and participle clauses

1 Choose the correct options to complete the sentences.

1 _____, the phone started to ring.
   a As I was walking into the house
   b Walking into the house
   c When walked into the house

2 _____ by a dog, the child ran back inside.
   a Chased   **c** Having chased
   b Chasing

3 _____ the building, please take off your shoes.
   a Before entered   **c** Before entering
   b Once entered

4 _____ time to ask his parents, he made the decision on his own.
   a Didn't have   **c** Haven't had
   b Not having

5 _____ by what he heard from other people, he didn't accept the job.
   a Discouraging   **c** Discouraged
   b Been discouraged

6 _____ the course, she was able to progress to the next level.
   a Once having completed   **c** Completed
   b Once completed

2 Read the two sentences and decide if they are the same (S) or different (D).

1 As he walked down the path, John stumbled and fell.
   Walking down the path, John stumbled and fell. _____

2 Having worked as a teacher, he knew what to do when his own son was struggling at school.
   Working as a teacher, he knew what to do when his own son was struggling at school. _____

3 Not wanting to have any debt, he never had a credit card.
   He never had a credit card because he didn't want to have any debt. _____

4 When listening to that song, I thought of my grandparents.
   Having listened to that song, I thought of my grandparents. _____

5 Having won the prize, I wanted to tell the whole world.
   When I won the prize, I wanted to tell the whole world. _____

3 Read the text and underline the participle clauses.

Margaret Ann Bulkley was born in Cork, Ireland, in 1789. After attending medical school disguised as a man, she was one of the first known doctors to successfully deliver a baby by caesarean section.

Having been abandoned by her father, Bulkley reached out to her uncle in London, James Barry, who helped her and her mother and sister to relocate there. Her uncle introduced her to physician Edward Fryer and Francisco Miranda, a Venezuelan general. The two gentlemen became her mentors.

Shortly after introducing Bulkley to Miranda and Fryer, her uncle died. Miranda and Fryer continued to support Bulkley's education, eventually encouraging her to attend medical school. Determined to become a doctor, Bulkley agreed to pose as a man, since at the time only men could attend medical school. In honor of her uncle, she used the pseudonym James Barry. The original idea was for Bulkley to relocate to Venezuela after medical school to be a doctor there, but Miranda's death put an end to that plan. Having lost the opportunity to practice medicine in Venezuela, Bulkley decided to work in England… as a man!

After graduating from medical school, Bulkley (now Barry) joined the British army and eventually moved to South Africa. While practicing medicine in Cape Town, Barry performed a successful caesarean section on July 26, 1826.

After leaving South Africa in 1828, Barry lived in Malta and Canada, where she continued to practice medicine. Having returned to London in 1859 after developing bronchitis, she was discharged from the army. After her death in 1865, the news became public that Barry was indeed a woman. The British army sealed all records pertaining to Barry, denying all news reports about her work and career. Records were finally released in 1950.

4 Rewrite the sentences using a subordinate clause instead of a participle clause.

1 Having finished dinner, I sat down to watch TV.
After *I finished dinner, I sat down to watch TV*.

2 The morning being so hot, we decided to swim in the river.
As _____
_____ .

3 Having nothing left to say, he left and slammed the door.
Since _____
_____ .

4 I lost my phone walking home from work.
While _____
_____ .

5 Not having eaten all day, I was desperate for my mom's chicken soup.
Since _____
_____ .

6 Taken care of properly, these boots will last several years.
If _____
_____ .

5 Read each sentence and choose the correct meaning of the participle clause.

1 Waiting for the train, I noticed a strange man on the platform.
a reason   **c** time
b result   **d** condition

2 Used carefully, this product will last years!
a reason   **c** time
b result   **d** condition

3 The car alarm went off suddenly, scaring the crowd that had gathered.
a reason   **c** time
b result   **d** condition

4 Having nothing left to say, she hung up.
a reason   **c** time
b result   **d** condition

5 Knowing some Arabic, I had no problem understanding directions.
a reason   **c** time
b result   **d** condition

6 Walking down the street, I found two abandoned kittens.
a reason   **c** time
b result   **d** condition

7 The weather being so nice, we decided to go to the beach.
a reason   **c** time
b result   **d** condition

8 Washed in hot water, that sweater will certainly shrink.
a reason   **c** time
b result   **d** condition

9 Having stayed up all night, I just couldn't concentrate in class the next day.
a reason   **c** time
b result   **d** condition

10 The fire spread rapidly through the row of houses, leaving fifty people homeless.
a reason   **c** time
b result   **d** condition

6 Complete the second sentence so that it means the same as the first. Use the word in parentheses and between one and four other words.

1 Having slept badly, she was completely exhausted the next morning.
_____ , she was completely exhausted the next morning. (since)

2 Not being able to attend school, he taught himself how to build houses.
He taught himself how to build houses
_____ to attend school. (because)

3 After she completed all the training, she went to work in Botswana.
_____ , she went to work in Botswana. (having)

4 He jumped into the river because he didn't realize it was dangerous.
_____ , he jumped into the river. (not)

5 Once she saw how many people didn't have access to clean water, she decided to do something to help.
_____ how many people didn't have access to clean water, she decided to do something to help. (having)

10D TED's Secret to Great Public Speaking

TEDTALKS

WATCH ▶

1 Watch Part 1 of the TED Talk without sound and check (✓) the non-verbal cues* Chris Anderson uses.

1 nodding his head _____
2 shaking his head _____
3 raising his eyebrows _____
4 widening his eyes _____
5 narrowing his eyes _____
6 looking up _____
7 looking down _____
8 raising a finger _____
9 gesturing with both hands _____
10 pointing to other visuals _____
11 leaning backward _____
12 leaning forward _____

2 Watch Part 1 again and match the gestures Chris Anderson uses (1–4) with the particular words he says (a–d).

1 gesturing with both hands
2 raising his eyebrows
3 pointing to other visuals
4 raising a finger

a "… a personal secret."
b "… an inspiring call to action."
c "But there is one thing…"
d "… listening to many hundreds of amazing TED speakers,…"

3 Are the statements are true (T) or false (F)?

1 The key to a great TED Talk is to share a childhood story. _____
2 After hearing hundreds of great TED Talks, Anderson has concluded that they don't have anything in common. _____
3 When a speaker talks, the brain patterns representing his or her key idea are repeated in the audience's brains. _____
4 According to Anderson, your personal worldview is the collection of ideas you have and the connections between those ideas. _____
5 Anderson says that the reason ideas really matter is because they make us feel motivated in the morning. _____
6 Metaphors can help the audience understand complex and unfamiliar ideas. _____

* The Student Book covers collaborative listening in this unit. Since independent practice of this topic is difficult, activities on non-verbal cues as seen in the TED Talk are presented as an alternative.

4 Watch Part 3 of the TED Talk and complete the chart below. Write no more than three words for each answer.

Guidelines for giving an effective TED Talk
1 Limit your talk to just one (1) _____ :   • give context   • share (2) _____   • make it vivid
2 Give your listeners a (3) _____ :   • stir your audience's (4) _____   • use questions   • reveal a disconnection in someone's (5) _____
3 Build your idea out of concepts that your audience (6) _____ :   • use their language   • use metaphors
4 Make your idea (7) _____ :   • Ask yourself: "Who does this idea (8) _____ ?"

VOCABULARY IN CONTEXT

5 Match the words in bold in the sentences (1–6) with the words or phrases (a–f).

1 When listening to the talk, the audience's minds begin to **work in the same way as** the speaker's. _____
2 It's **astonishing** how quickly an audience begins to think like the speaker when he or she delivers a powerful message. _____
3 Sometimes it's difficult to see structure in the apparent **state of disorganization** of our thoughts. _____
4 According to Anderson, there are a few key characteristics that **combine to form** a good TED Talk. _____
5 When speakers are very nervous, they worry that the audience will **understand the thoughts and feelings they are trying to hide**. _____
6 An effective story-teller can **link several ideas into** a complex pattern that still communicates a strong message. _____

a make up
b see right through them
c startling
d sync with
e tangle
f weave together

10E Changing Perspectives

SPEAKING

1 Complete the sentences with these words and phrases. There are two that you don't need.

and because	any questions	can see
does that mean	more than	now
put your hands up	share	talk to you
that's it	the interesting thing	your attention

1 I'm going to _____ about organic food.

2 I want to _____ some interesting data.

3 _____ if you're familiar with this debate.

4 _____, what should be done?

5 As you _____, it's a complex issue.

6 _____ is, there's no concrete definition.

7 But _____ that, it means we need to think carefully.

8 So, what _____ in practice?

9 Are there _____?

10 Thank you for _____.

2 Listen to the statements (1–5) and match them with the descriptions (a–f). There is one description you don't need. 🎧 **85**

Statement 1 _____

Statement 2 _____

Statement 3 _____

Statement 4 _____

Statement 5 _____

a an audience member who is asking a question

b a speaker who is finishing a presentation

c a speaker who is highlighting an interesting point

d a speaker who is inviting the audience to ask questions

e a speaker who is explaining the topic of a presentation

f a speaker who is asking the audience to share what they know

3 Read and complete the extract from a presentation. Use one word in each gap. Then listen and check your answers. 🎧 **86**

This morning, I'm here to **(1)** _____ to you about social networks. Put your **(2)** _____ up if you're a member of a social network. That's **(3)** _____ I was expecting—just about everybody! In today's world, people frequently discuss the impact that social networks have on our lives and relationships.

For **(4)** _____, you've probably had the experience of being out with a group of friends and **(5)** _____ has been on their phones. That's clearly a problem—**(6)** _____ that's not what I'm going to **(7)** _____ on. Instead, I'm going to **(8)** _____ about the ways that social networks affect our brains.

(9) _____ research has shown that when you sign in to a social network, a compound called dopamine is released in your brain. Dopamine is the same substance that's released when you accomplish a goal, do exercise, or fall in love. That's **(10)** _____, right?

4 Imagine that you need to do a presentation. What's the best way to get your ideas across? There are two suggestions below. Add some more ideas.

Tell a joke.

Ask the audience questions.

5 Now listen to two students having a conversation about this topic. The students are taking a speaking exam. Which ideas do they mention? 🎧 **87**

PRONUNCIATION Intonation of signpost expressions

6 Listen to the sentences. Pay attention to the signpost expressions in bold. Does each expression end with a falling tone (F) or a rising tone (R)? 🎧 **88**

1 **To expand a little on that**, I would like to share an idea. _____

2 **To summarize**, we can say that the response was surprising. _____

3 **Turning now to** the results, we can see where most people agree. _____

4 **To illustrate that**, let's look at some statistics. _____

5 **To go back to** our story, we found all the participants we needed. _____

6 **To elaborate on that**, I can tell you what the most difficult part was. _____

WRITING A review

7 Match the two parts of the sentences.

1 The title of your review should be _____
2 At the beginning, provide general background information, like _____
3 Come up with a strong first sentence to _____
4 When you describe the content of the event, mention _____
5 Talk about the audience and describe _____
6 Support your points _____
7 Use a range of expressive adjectives such as _____
8 In your evaluation of the event, say _____
9 At the end of the review, state whether _____
10 Your review doesn't have to be only _____

a their reaction and the atmosphere.
b how it had an impact on you personally.
c positive or negative; it can be both.
d the venue, the date, etc.
e who was performing and what they did.
f with examples.
g relevant and short.
h you would recommend the event to others.
i *thrilling, disappointing, unforgettable.*
j immediately engage the reader's attention.

8 Match the parts of the review of a play (1–10) with the descriptions (a–j).

(1) Jewelry Box, last night's play at the Northwest Theater, was very special indeed. Don't be deceived by the plain title; this production will astonish you. **(2)** The fact that it was written by a virtually unknown playwright is part of the surprise. The fact that she is only 24 years old is the other part. Sophie Jin is a name to remember. Her script shows a talent for observation that is far beyond her years.

(3) With a cast of only three, **(4)** the play takes us on a journey through one year in the lead character's life, during which he experiences rejection, lost love, and a deepening sense of loneliness. In anyone else's hands, these serious and universal themes would make for a boring two hours at the theater, but not here. Jin balances the narrative with humor and a clever dose of humanity. **(5)** It has to be said that the direction by Manny Martinez did a superb job of bringing out the very best in the three actors. **(6)** These actors, I might add, are all new to the business and they were absolutely fantastic.

(7) For me, the dialog was as rich for what it said as it was for all the things that it didn't say. This is a play that leads you to a point where you speculate about events and relate them to your own life. **(8)** I was captivated from the first scene and I wasn't ashamed to display a whole range of emotions along with my fellow audience members. We laughed, we cried, and, at the end, the applause was almost deafening as the cast took countless curtain calls. I came away feeling I'd been part of an unforgettable performance. **(9)** Running for three nights only, hurry, I urge you, **(10)** and get tickets for this excellent piece of theater.

a information about the cast's experience _____
b when the play can be seen _____
c information about the director _____
d how the reviewer and audience reacted _____
e the name of the play and where it can be seen _____
f the broad themes of the play _____
g whether the reviewer recommends the play _____
h the number of actors in the play _____
i what the reviewer especially liked _____
j information about the playwright _____

9 Read the notice from an entertainment website. Write your review.

MOVIE REVIEWS WANTED!

How often have you found yourself with a little free time and all you want to do is watch a great movie? We've all been there… the problem is deciding what to watch, isn't it?! That's why, here at Movie Central, we've decided to create a collection of positive, negative, and mixed reviews to help our members choose the next movie they'll watch. Please send a review to the email address below. It can be the last movie you saw, your favorite movie of all time, or even the one you never want to see again!

Review

1 Complete the words to make phrases about making your point.

1 _ _ _ _ eye contact
2 your mind goes _ _ _ _ _ _
3 _ _ _ _ _ _ _ _ _ _ on your point
4 _ _ _ _ _ to the point
5 _ _ _ _ your _ _ _ _ _ of thought
6 _ _ _ _ _ _ your audience
7 _ _ _ _ _ _ expressions
8 _ _ _ _ up your argument

2 Complete the sentences with these adjectives.

doubtful	fearless	hopeful	pointless
tasteful	thankful	thoughtless	wasteful

1 He'll never agree—it's _____ arguing with him.
2 The decor in the restaurant was simple, but _____.
3 The forecast is for rain, so it's _____ whether the event can go ahead tomorrow.
4 The situation is improving, so we're _____ that there'll be a successful outcome.
5 I'm sorry, I shouldn't have said that, it was really _____ of me.
6 We're so _____ to my parents for everything they've done to help us.
7 You're going to throw all that food away? I think that's rather _____.
8 A team of _____ firefighters rescued several families from the blaze.

3 Change the question or statement into the question form given in parentheses.

1 Do you know how much you weigh? (negative question)
_____
2 I'd like to know how much exercise you do each day. (direct question)
_____
3 What did the doctor say? (echo question)
_____
4 Did the nurse check your blood pressure? (negative question)
_____
5 I don't know where the doctor's office is. (echo question)
_____
6 Do you know if she's still in hospital? (direct question)
_____

7 I think we need to eat more healthily. (tag question)
_____
8 Can you tell me what you'd recommend eating? (direct question)
_____

4 Match the two parts of the sentences.

1 Walking through the park, _____
2 After falling twice off my desk, _____
3 Having lied to my friend, _____
4 Once proved safe in clinical trials, _____
5 Having been lied to by my friend, _____
6 Having proved the medicine was safe for animals, _____

a my new phone fell out of my pocket and the screen broke!
b I was very disappointed.
c the vaccine started being administered.
d I bumped into an old friend.
e I felt very embarrassed.
f he convinced a lab to start manufacturing it.

5 Choose the correct options to complete the sentences.

1 _____ by the news, he collapsed onto a chair.
  a Overwhelming
  b Overwhelmed
  c Being overwhelming
2 They decided to expand quickly, _____ their products in an additional twenty countries.
  a launched
  b launching
  c when they launched
3 _____ a scientist, I can tell you this experiment is poorly designed.
  a Been
  b When being
  c Being
4 _____ by the press, he proceeded to remove the website.
  a After discrediting
  b After being discredited
  c Discrediting
5 Brought up in London, _____.
  a she later moved to Moscow with her family
  b her parents relocated the family to Moscow
  c having moved to Moscow with her family

UNIT 6

Review

attend school (phr)	/əˈtɛnd skul/
class size (phr)	/klæs saɪz/
develop skills (phr)	/dɪˈvɛləp skɪlz/
do homework (phr)	/du ˈhoʊmˌwɜrk/
elementary school (n)	/ˌɛləˈmɛntri skul/
get bad grades (phr)	/gɛt bæd greɪdz/
get good grades (phr)	/gɛt gʊd greɪdz/
get an education (phr)	/gɛt ən ˌɛdʒəˈkeɪʃən/
high school (n)	/haɪ skul/
online learning (phr)	/ˈɔnˌlaɪn ˈlɜrnɪŋ/
take exams (phr)	/teɪk ɪgˈzæmz/

Unit Vocabulary

accessories (n)	/əkˈsɛsəriz/
approach to (phr)	/əˈproʊtʃ tu/
assumption (n)	/əˈsʌmpʃən/
be given a warning (phr)	/bi ˌgɪvən ə ˈwɔrnɪŋ/
be punctual (phr)	/ˌbi ˈpʌŋktʃuəl/
bully (v)	/ˈbʊli/
bullying (n)	/ˈbʊliɪŋ/
challenge to (phr)	/ˈtʃæləndʒ tu/
change in (phr)	/ˈtʃeɪndʒ ɪn/
clash (n)	/klæʃ/
clear up (v)	/ˌklɪr ˈʌp/
comparison between (phr)	/kəmˈpærɪsənbɪˌtwin/
comprehensive (adj)	/ˌkɑmprɪˈhɛnsɪv/
conclude (v)	/kənˈklud/
conflict between (phr)	/ˈkɑnflɪkt bɪˌtwin/
counterpart (n)	/ˈkaʊntərˌpɑrt/
damage to (phr)	/ˈdæmɪdʒ tu/
decrease in (phr)	/ˈdikris ɪn/
detention (n)	/dɪˈtɛnʃən/
disruptive (adj)	/dɪsˈrʌptɪv/
distinct (adj)	/dɪˈstɪŋkt/
drastic (adj)	/ˈdræstɪk/
enforce (v)	/ɪnˈfɔrs/
gap between (phr)	/ˈgæp bɪˌtwin/
give a punishment (phr)	/ˈgɪv ə ˈpʌnɪʃmənt/
improvement in (phr)	/ɪmˈpruvmənt ɪn/
inappropriate (adj)	/ˌɪnəˈproʊpriət/
influence on (phr)	/ˈɪnfluəns ɔn/
innovative (adj)	/ˈɪnəˌveɪtɪv/
insight (n)	/ˈɪnsaɪt/
literacy (n)	/ˈlɪtərəsi/
misbehave (v)	/ˌmɪsbɪˈheɪv/
misbehavior (n)	/ˌmɪsbɪˈheɪvjər/
need for (phr)	/ˈnid fɔr/
norm (n)	/nɔrm/
offensive (adj)	/əˈfɛnsɪv/
peer (n)	/pɪr/
principle (n)	/ˈprɪnsəpəl/
punishment for (phr)	/ˈpʌnɪʃmənt fɔr/
radically (adv)	/ˈrædɪkli/
regime (n)	/reɪˈʒim/
respect for (phr)	/rɪˈspɛkt fɔr/
responsibility for (phr)	/rɪˌspɑnsəˈbɪləti fɔr/
restorative approach (n)	/rɪˌstɔrətɪv əˈproʊtʃ/
show disrespect (phr)	/ˌʃoʊ ˌdɪsrɪˈspɛkt/
skip class (phr)	/ˈskɪp ˈklæs/
suspend (v)	/səˈspɛnd/
take away privileges (phr)	/ˌteɪk əˈweɪ ˈprɪvəlɪdʒɪz/
talent for (phr)	/ˈtælənt fɔr/
threat to (phr)	/ˈθrɛt tu/
thrive (v)	/θraɪv/
unthinkable (adj)	/ʌnˈθɪŋkəbəl/
vandalism (n)	/ˈvændəˌlɪzəm/
what is on their minds (phr)	/ˌwɑt ɪz ˌɔn ðɛər ˈmaɪndz/
workplace (n)	/ˈwɜrkˌpleɪs/

Extension

distraction (n)	/dɪˈstrækʃən/
extra credit (phr)	/ˈɛkstrə ˈkrɛdət/
focus (v)	/ˈfoʊkəs/
improve (v)	/ɪmˈpruv/
overachieve (v)	/ˌoʊvərəˈtʃiv/
pace yourself (phr)	/peɪs jərˈsɛlf/
procrastinate (v)	/prəˈkræstəˌneɪt/
study habits (phr)	/ˈstʌdi ˈhæbəts/
take notes (phr)	/teɪk noʊts/
think positively (phr)	/θɪŋk ˈpɑzətɪvli/

Vocabulary Building

advice on (phr)	/ədˈvaɪs ɔn/
attitude to (phr)	/ˈætɪˌtud tu/
ban on (phr)	/ˈbæn ɔn/
clash between (phr)	/ˈklæʃ bɪˌtwin/
difference between (phr)	/ˈdɪfrəns bɪˌtwin/
focus on (phr)	/ˈfoʊkəs ɔn/
impact on (phr)	/ˈɪmpækt ɔn/
increase in (phr)	/ˈɪnkris ɪn/
rise in (phr)	/ˈraɪz ɪn/

Vocabulary in Context

clear up any misconceptions (phr)	/klɪr ʌp ˈɛni ˌmɪskənˈsɛpʃənz/
fast forward (v)	/ˌfæst ˈfɔrwərd/
five consecutive years (phr)	/ˌfaɪv kənˈsɛkjətɪv ˌjɪrz/
have a very long way to go (phr)	/ˌhæv ə ˈvɛri lɔŋ ˌweɪ tə ˌgoʊ/
set the tone (phr)	/ˌsɛt ðə ˈtoʊn/

UNIT 7

Review

catch (v)	/kætʃ/
destination (n)	/ˌdɛstəˈneɪʃən/
excursion (n)	/ɪkˈskɜrʒən/
expedition (n)	/ˌɛkspəˈdɪʃən/
flight (n)	/flaɪt/
go for a ride (phr)	/goʊ fɔr ə raɪd/
get lost (phr)	/gɛt lɔst/
get off (phr v)	/gɛt ɔf/
get on (phr v)	/gɛt ɑn/
get to (phr v)	/gɛt tu/
take a route (phr v)	/teɪk ə rut/
taxi (n)	/ˈtæksi/
miss (v)	/mɪs/
ride (n/v)	/raɪd/
route (n)	/rut/
voyage (n)	/ˈvɔɪədʒ/

Unit Vocabulary

breakdown (n)	/ˈbreɪkˌdaʊn/
carpool (v)	/ˈkɑrˌpul/
communicate (v)	/kəˈmjunɪkeɪt/
commute (n/v)	/kəˈmjut/
commuter (n)	/kəˈmjutər/
commuting (n)	/kəˈmjutɪŋ/
component (n)	/kəmˈpoʊnənt/
congested (adj)	/kənˈdʒɛstɪd/
congestion (n)	/kənˈdʒɛstʃən/
connection (n)	/kəˈnɛkʃən/
consumption (n)	/kənˈsʌmpʃən/
crossing (n)	/ˈkrɔsɪŋ/
drop someone off (phr v)	/ˌdrɔp sʌmwʌn ˈɔf/
electrify (v)	/ɪˈlɛktrɪfaɪ/
fumes (n)	/fjumz/
gridlock (n)	/ˈgrɪdˌlɑk/
happen to (phr v)	/ˈhæpən ˌtu/
imitate (v)	/ˈɪmɪteɪt/
imitation (n)	/ˌɪmɪˈteɪʃən/
infrastructure (n)	/ˈɪnfrəˌstrʌktʃər/
innovate (v)	/ˈɪnoʊveɪt/
innovation (n)	/ˌɪnoʊˈveɪʃən/
journey (n)	/ˈdʒɜrni/
lengthen (v)	/ˈlɛŋθən/
memorize (v)	/ˈmɛməraɪz/
obstacle (n)	/ˈɑbstəkəl/
originate (v)	/əˈrɪdʒəneɪt/
overview (n)	/ˈoʊvərˌvju/
purely (adv)	/ˈpjʊrli/
purify (v)	/ˈpjʊrɪfaɪ/
radical (adj)	/ˈrædɪkəl/
rate (v)	/reɪt/
regulate (v)	/ˈrɛgjəˌleɪt/
replicate (v)	/ˈrɛplɪkeɪt/
restrict (v)	/rɪˈstrɪkt/
resume (v)	/rɪˈzum/
rush hour (n)	/ˈrʌʃ ˌaʊər/
shaped (adj)	/ʃeɪpt/
shuttle service (n)	/ˈʃʌtəl ˌsɜrvɪs/
smog (n)	/smɑg/
stabilize (v)	/ˈsteɪbəlaɪz/
stuck (adj)	/stʌk/
subway (n)	/ˈsʌbˌweɪ/
transportation (n)	/ˌtrænspɔrˈteɪʃən/
underlying (adj)	/ˌʌndərˈlaɪɪŋ/
unify (v)	/ˈjunɪfaɪ/
urbanize (v)	/ˈɜrbənaɪz/
vehicle (n)	/ˈviɪkəl/
walker (n)	/ˈwɔkər/

Extension

carbon footprint (n)	/ˈkɑrbən ˈfʊtˌprɪnt/
cycle (n/v)	/ˈsaɪkəl/
exceed (v)	/ɪkˈsid/
high-occupancy vehicle (n)	/haɪ-ˈɑkjəpənsi ˈvihɪkəl/
lane (n)	/leɪn/
self-driving car (n)	/sɛlf-ˈdraɪvɪŋ kɑr/
share a car (phr)	/ʃɛr ə kɑr/
shuttle (n/v)	/ˈʃʌtəl/
speed limit (n)	/spid ˈlɪmət/
obey (v)	/oʊˈbeɪ/
pick up (phr v)	/pɪk ʌp/
pollution (n)	/pəˈluʃən/

Vocabulary Building

collaborate (v)	/kəˈlæbəreɪt/
formulate (v)	/ˈfɔrmjəˌleɪt/
justify (v)	/ˈdʒʌstɪfaɪ/
maximize (v)	/ˈmæksɪmaɪz/
prioritize (v)	/praɪˈɔrɪtaɪz/
simplify (v)	/ˈsɪmplɪfaɪ/
strengthen (v)	/ˈstrɛŋθən/
subsidize (v)	/ˈsʌbsɪdaɪz/
utilize (v)	/ˈjutɪlaɪz/

Vocabulary in Context

aha moment (phr)	/ˈɑhɑ ˌmoʊmənt/
attributes (n)	/ˈætrɪˌbjuts/
car-centric (adj)	/ˌkɑr ˈsɛntrɪk/
eye-opener (n)	/ˈaɪ ˌoʊpənər/
paradox (n)	/ˈpærədɑks/
restless (adj)	/ˈrɛstləs/

UNIT 8

Review

annoyed (adj)	/əˈnɔɪd/
confused (adj)	/kənˈfjuzd/
delighted (adj)	/dɪˈlaɪtəd/
embarrassed (adj)	/ɪmˈbɛrəst/
excited (adj)	/ɪkˈsaɪtəd/
grateful (adj)	/ˈɡreɪtfəl/
lonely (adj)	/ˈloʊnli/
pleased (adj)	/plizd/
relaxed (adj)	/rɪˈlækst/
scared (adj)	/skɛrd/
stressed (adj)	/strɛst/

Unit Vocabulary

adolescent (n)	/ˌædəˈlɛsənt/
assignment (n)	/əˈsaɪnmənt/
brutal (adj)	/ˈbrutəl/
cheerful (adj)	/ˈtʃɪrfəl/
come across (phr v)	/ˌkʌm əˈkrɑs/
conservative (adj)	/kənˈsɜrvətɪv/
consistently (adv)	/kənˈsɪstəntli/
couldn't care less (phr)	/ˌkʊdənt kɛr ˈlɛs/
distinctive (adj)	/dɪˈstɪŋktɪv/
do my own thing (phr)	/ˌdu maɪ ˌoʊn ˈθɪŋ/
drawback (n)	/ˈdrɔˌbæk/
dual (adj)	/ˈdul/
engage in (phr v)	/ɪnˈɡeɪdʒ ˌɪn/
even-tempered (adj)	/ˌivən ˈtɛmpərd/
fish and chips (n)	/ˌfɪʃ ænd ˈtʃɪps/
follow the crowd (phr)	/ˈfɑloʊ ðə ˈkraʊd/
foremost (adj)	/ˈfɔrˌmoʊst/
generalization (n)	/ˌdʒɛnərəlaɪˈzeɪʃən/
give me a thrill (phr)	/ˌɡɪv mi ə ˈθrɪl/
humility (n)	/hjuˈmɪləti/
impulsive (adj)	/ɪmˈpʌlsɪv/
influenced by peers (phr)	/ˌɪnfluənst baɪˈpɪrz/
insecurities (n)	/ˌɪnsəˈkjʊrɪtiz/
moody (adj)	/ˈmudi/
nonetheless (adv)	/ˌnʌnðəˈlɛs/
outweigh (v)	/ˈaʊˌtweɪ/
overwhelming (adj)	/ˌoʊvərˈwɛlmɪŋ/
peer pressure (n)	/ˈpɪr ˌprɛʃər/
perspective (n)	/pərˈspɛktɪv/
phenomenon (n)	/fəˈnɑməˌnɑn/
play it safe (phr)	/ˌpleɪ ɪt ˈseɪf/
rebellious (adj)	/rɪˈbɛljəs/
reconcile (v)	/ˈrɛkənˌsaɪl/
self-conscious (adj)	/ˌsɛlf ˈkɑnʃəs/
self-controlled (adj)	/ˌsɛlf kənˈtroʊld/
stereotype (n)	/ˈstɛrioʊˌtaɪp/
thunder and lightning (n)	/ˌθʌndər ænd ˈlaɪtnɪŋ/
torn between (phr)	/ˈtɔrn bɪˌtwin/
transition (n)	/trænˈzɪʃən/
weigh the pros and cons (phr)	/weɪ ðə ˌproʊz ænd ˈkɑnz/
worthy (adj)	/ˈwɜrði/

Extension

benefit of the doubt (phr)	/ˈbɛnəfɪt ʌv ðə daʊt/
charming (adj)	/ˈtʃɑrmɪŋ/
hypercritical (adj)	/ˌhaɪpərˈkrɪtɪkəl/
image (n)	/ˈɪmədʒ/
intelligent (adj)	/ɪnˈtɛlədʒənt/
judge (v)	/dʒʌdʒ/
judgmental (adj)	/dʒədʒˈmɛntəl/
reputation (n)	/ˌrɛpjəˈteɪʃən/

Vocabulary Building

bed and breakfast (n)	/ˌbɛd ænd ˈbrɛkfəst/
black and white (adj)	/ˌblæk ænd ˈwaɪt/
brothers and sisters (n)	/ˌbrʌðərz ænd ˈsɪstərz/
facts and figures (phr)	/ˌfækts ən ˈfɪɡərz/
first and foremost (phr)	/ˌfɜrst ænd ˈfɔrˌmoʊst/
here and there (phr)	/ˌhɪr ænd ˈðɛr/
husbands and wives (n)	/ˌhʌzbəndz ænd ˈwaɪvz/
law and order (n)	/ˌlɔ ænd ˈɔrdər/
loud and clear (phr)	/ˌlaʊd ænd ˈklɪr/
men and women (n)	/ˌmɛn ænd ˈwɪmɪn/
name and address (n)	/ˌneɪm ænd əˈdrɛs/
odds and ends (n)	/ˌɑdz ænd ˈɛndz/
peace and quiet (phr)	/ˌpis ænd ˈkwaɪət/
safe and sound (adj)	/ˌseɪf ænd ˈsaʊnd/
short and sweet (phr)	/ˌʃɔrt ænd ˈswit/
trials and tribulations (phr)	/ˌtraɪəlz ænd ˌtrɪbjuˈleɪʃənz/
undergo (v)	/ˌʌndərˈɡoʊ/
ups and downs (phr)	/ˌʌps ænd ˈdaʊnz/
wear and tear (n)	/ˌwɛər ænd ˈtɛər/

Vocabulary in Context

believe it or not (phr)	/bɪˈliv ɪt ɔr ˌnɑt/
kick (n)	/kɪk/
prone to (adj)	/ˈproʊn ˌtu/
within a split second of (phr)	/wɪðˌɪn ə ˌsplɪt ˈsɛkənd əv/

UNIT 9

Review

attitude (n)	/ˈætəˌtud/
captain (v)	/ˈkæptən/
compete (v)	/kəmˈpit/
energetic (adj)	/ˌɛnərˈdʒɛtɪk/
forward (n)	/ˈfɔrwərd/
goal (n)	/ɡoʊl/
gold medal (n)	/ɡoʊld ˈmɛdəl/
passionate (adj)	/ˈpæʃənət/
season (n)	/ˈsizən/
set (v)	/sɛt/
score (n/v)	/skɔr/
smash (v)	/smæʃ/
star (n)	/stɑr/
technique (n)	/tɛkˈnik/
win (v)	/wɪn/
world championship (n)	/wɜrld ˈtʃæmpiənˌʃɪp/
world record (n)	/wɜrld ˈrɛkərd/

Unit Vocabulary

account for (phr v)	/əˈkaʊnt ˌfɔr/
address (v)	/əˈdrɛs/
affordable (adj)	/əˈfɔrdəbəl/
alert (adj)	/əˈlɜrt/
assign (v)	/əˈsaɪn/

audible (adj)	/ˈɔdəbəl/
beneficial (adj)	/ˌbɛnɪˈfɪʃəl/
carbohydrate (n)	/ˌkɑrboʊˈhaɪˌdreɪt/
chronic (adj)	/ˈkrɑnɪk/
commonly (adv)	/ˈkɑmənli/
curable (adj)	/ˈkjʊrəbəl/
detrimental (adj)	/ˌdɛtrɪˈmɛntəl/
drink plenty of water (phr)	/ˌdrɪŋk ˈplɛnti əv ˈwɔtər/
eat naturally (phr)	/ˌit ˈnætʃərəli/
enhance (v)	/ɛnˈhæns/
enjoyable (adj)	/ɛnˈdʒɔɪəbəl/
feasible (adj)	/ˈfizəbəl/
get enough sleep (phr)	/ɡɛt ɪˌnʌf ˈslip/
have a balanced diet (phr)	/hæv ə ˌbælənst ˈdaɪət/
horrible (adj)	/ˈhɑrəbəl/
in moderation (phr)	/ˌɪn ˌmɑdəˈreɪʃən/
intake (n)	/ˈɪnteɪk/
isolation (n)	/ˌaɪsəˈleɪʃən/
label (v)	/ˈleɪbəl/
lifelong (adj)	/ˈlaɪfˌlɔŋ/
loneliness (n)	/ˈloʊnlinəs/
longevity (n)	/lɑnˈdʒɛvəti/
machine-washable (adj)	/məˌʃin ˈwɑʃəbəl/
moderate (adj)	/ˈmɑdərət/
moderation (n)	/ˌmɑdəˈreɪʃən/
nap (n)	/næp/
nutrient (n)	/ˈnutriənt/
nutritious (adj)	/nuˈtrɪʃəs/
obese (adj)	/oʊˈbis/
obesity (n)	/oʊˈbisəti/
occasional (adj)	/əˈkeɪʒənəl/
outlet (n)	/ˈaʊtˌlɛt/
plausible (adj)	/ˈplɔzəbəl/
practice the art of appreciation (phr)	/ˌpræktɪs ðə ˌɑrt əv əˌpriʃiˈeɪʃən/
protein (n)	/ˈproutin/
recyclable (adj)	/riˈsaɪkləbəl/
reduce (v)	/rɪˌdus/
refillable (adj)	/riˈfɪləbəl/
refined sugar (n)	/rɪˌfaɪnd ˈʃʊɡər/
refundable (adj)	/rɪˈfʌndəbəl/
relax (v)	/rɪlæks/
relieve stress (phr)	/rɪˌliv ˈstrɛs/
renewable (adj)	/rɪˈnuəbəl/
specifically (adv)	/spəˈsɪfɪkli/
stamina (n)	/ˈstæmɪnə/
stay active (phr)	/steɪ ˈæktɪv/
unaffected (adj)	/ˌʌnəˈfɛktɪd/
unprocessed foods (phr)	/ˌən prɑˌsɛst fudz/
visible (adj)	/ˈvɪzəbəl/
well-being (n)	/ˌwɛl ˈbiɪŋ/

Extension

cholesterol (n)	/kəˈlɛstəˌrɔl/
energy (n)	/ˈɛnərdʒi/
invigorating (adj)	/ɪnˈvɪɡəˌreɪtɪŋ/
mindfulness (adj)	/ˈmaɪndfəlnəs/
mineral (n)	/ˈmɪnərəl/
nourish (v)	/ˈnɜrɪʃ/
organic (adj)	/ɔrˈɡænɪk/
output (n)	/ˈaʊtˌpʊt/
posture (n)	/ˈpɑstʃər/
renew (v)	/rɪˈnu/
supplements (n)	/ˈsʌpləmənts/
support (v)	/səˈpɔrt/
vigor (n)	/ˈvɪɡər/
vitamin (n)	/ˈvaɪtəmən/
well-balanced (adj)	/wɛl-ˈbælənst/
wellness (n)	/ˈwɛlnəs/

Vocabulary Building

achievable (adj)	/ə'tʃivəbəl/
disposable (adj)	/dɪ'spoʊzəbəl/
edible (adj)	/'ɛdɪbəl/
inflatable (adj)	/ɪn'fleɪtəbəl/
legible (adj)	/'lɛdʒəbəl/
memorable (adj)	/'mɛmərəbəl/
preventable (adj)	/prɪ'vɛntəbəl/
rechargeable (adj)	/ri'tʃɑrdʒəbəl/
washable (adj)	/'wɑʃəbəl/

Vocabulary in Context

correlation (n)	/ˌkɔrə'leɪʃən/
experience firsthand (phr)	/ɪk'spɪriəns ˌfɜrst'hænd/
keep an eye on (phr)	/ˌkip æn 'aɪ ɔn/
preliminary (adj)	/pri'lɪmɪnəri/
stem from (phr v)	/'stɛm ˌfrəm/
tutorial (n)	/tu'tɔriəl/

UNIT 10

Review

awkward (adj)	/'ɑkwərd/
complimentary (adj)	/ˌkɑmplə'mɛntəri/
conscious (adj)	/'kɑnʃəs/
discourage (v)	/dɪ'skɜrɪdʒ/
discrimination (n)	/dɪˌskrɪmə'neɪʃən/
hint (n/v)	/hɪnt/
misunderstanding (n)	/ˌmɪsəndər'stændɪŋ/
offended (adj)	/ə'fɛndəd/
stereotypical (adj)	/ˌstɛrioʊ'tɪpɪkəl/

Unit Vocabulary

analogy (n)	/ə'nælədʒi/
analytical (adj)	/ˌænə'lɪtɪkəl/
back up (phr v)	/ˌbæk 'ʌp/
backing (adj)	/'bækɪŋ/
bundle (n)	/'bʌndəl/
circuit (n)	/'sɜrkɪt/
concisely (adv)	/kən'saɪsli/
contrast (v)	/kən'træst/
convey (v)	/kən'veɪ/
cookies (n)	/'kʊkiz/
doubtless (adj)	/'daʊtləs/
elaborate on (phr v)	/ɪ'læbəˌreɪt ɔn/
empathy (n)	/'ɛmpəθi/
engage (v)	/ɪn'geɪdʒ/
eventful (adj)	/ɪ'vɛntfəl/
exclaim (v)	/ɪk'skleɪm/
exquisite (adj)	/ɪk'skwɪzɪt/
facial expression (n)	/ˌfeɪʃəl ɪk'sprɛʃən/
forget one's point (phr)	/fərˌgɛt wʌnz 'pɔɪnt/
fruitless (adj)	/'frutləs/
gesture (n)	/'dʒɛstʃər/
get across (phr v)	/ˌgɛt ə'krɑs/
giggle (v)	/'gɪgəl/
glimpse (n)	/glɪmps/
heartless (adj)	/'hɑrtləs/
homeless (adj)	/'hoʊmləs/
hopeful (adj)	/'hoʊpfəl/
hopeless (adj)	/'hoʊpləs/
infectious (adj)	/ɪn'fɛkʃəs/
jargon (n)	/'dʒɑrgən/
jobless (adj)	/'dʒɑbləs/
lengthy (adj)	/'lɛŋθi/
lose my train of thought (phr)	/ˌluz maɪ ˌtreɪn əv 'θɔt/
make eye contact (phr)	/ˌmeɪk 'aɪ kɑntækt/

meaningful (adj)	/'minɪŋfəl/
metaphor (n)	/'mɛtəfɔr/
mind goes blank (phr)	/ˌmaɪnd goʊz 'blæŋk/
misinterpret (v)	/ˌmɪsɪn'tɜrprɪt/
neatly (adv)	/nitli/
nostalgia (n)	/nɔ'stældʒə/
novelty (n)	/'nɑvəlti/
partially (adv)	/'pɑrʃəli/
pointless (adj)	/'pɔɪntləs/
powerful (adj)	/'paʊərfəl/
powerless (adj)	/'paʊərləs/
precise (adj)	/prɪ'saɪs/
raging (adj)	/'reɪdʒɪŋ/
rational (adj)	/'ræʃənəl/
rephrase (v)	/ˌri'freɪz/
republic (n)	/rɪ'pʌblɪk/
run around (phr v)	/ˌrʌn ə'raʊnd/
scramble (n)	/'skræmbəl/
sheer (adj)	/ʃɪr/
skillful (adj)	/'skɪlfəl/
snap (v)	/snæp/
stick to the point (phr)	/ˌstɪk tu ðə 'pɔɪnt/
summarize (v)	/'sʌməraɪz/
surge (v)	/sɜrdʒ/
tactful (adj)	/'tæktfəl/
tactless (adj)	/'tæktləs/
tasteless (adj)	/'teɪstləs/
tender (adj)	/'tɛndər/
thankful (adj)	/'θæŋkfəl/
thoughtful (adj)	/'θɔtfəl/
thoughtless (adj)	/'θɔtləs/
unrest (n)	/ʌn'rɛst/
wasteful (adj)	/'weɪstfəl/
worthless (adj)	/'wɜrθləs/

Extension

attract attention (phr)	/ə'trækt ə'tɛnʃən/
blink (v)	/blɪŋk/
blush (v)	/blʌʃ/
draw attention to (phr)	/drɔ ə'tɛnʃən tu/
flare (v)	/flɛr/
flushed (adj)	/flʌʃt/
give attention to (phr)	/gɪv ə'tɛnʃən tu/
grin (n/v)	/grɪn/
hold attention (phr)	/hoʊld ə'tɛnʃən/
narrow (adj)	/'nɛroʊ/
pale (adj)	/peɪl/
pay attention (phr)	/peɪ ə'tɛnʃən/
pout (n)(v)	/paʊt/
turn attention to (phr)	/tɜrn ə'tɛnʃən tu/
widen (v)	/'waɪdən/
wrinkle (n/v)	/'rɪŋkəl/

Vocabulary Building

doubtful (adj)	/'daʊtfəl/
fearful (adj)	/'fɪrfəl/
fearless (adj)	/'fɪrləs/
forgetful (adj)	/fər'gɛtfəl/
fruitful (adj)	/'frutfəl/
meaningless (adj)	/'minɪŋləs/
regretful (adj)	/rɪ'grɛtfəl/
tasteful (adj)	/'teɪstfəl/

Vocabulary in Context

make up (phr v)	/ˌmeɪk 'ʌp/
see right through (phr verb)	/ˌsi ˌraɪt 'θru/
startling (adj)	/'stɑrtəlɪŋ/
sync with (phr verb)	/'sɪŋk ˌwɪð/
tangle (n)	/'tæŋgəl/
weave together (phr v)	/ˌwiv tə'gɛðər/